Dynamics of Memory and Identity in Contemporary Europe

Dynamics of Memory and Identity in Contemporary Europe

Eric Langenbacher, Bill Niven, and Ruth Wittlinger

berghahn
NEW YORK · OXFORD
www.berghahnbooks.com

Published in 2012 by

Berghahn Books

www.berghahnbooks.com

© 2012, 2015 Eric Langenbacher, Bill Niven, and Ruth Wittlinger
First paperback edition published in 2015.

All rights reserved. Except for the quotation of short passages
for the purposes of criticism and review, no part of this book
may be reproduced in any form or by any means, electronic or
mechanical, including photocopying, recording, or any information
storage and retrieval system now known or to be invented,
without written permission of the publisher.

Library of Congress Cataloging-in-Publication Data

Dynamics of memory and identity in contemporary Europe / edited by
Eric Langenbacher, Bill Niven, and Ruth Wittlinger.
   p. cm.
   Includes bibliographical references and index.
   ISBN 978-0-85745-577-2 (hardback : alk. paper) – ISBN 978-1-78238-917-0
(paperback : alk. paper) – ISBN 978-0-85745-581-9 (ebook)
   1. Europe–History–Philosophy. 2. Collective memory–Europe.
3. Group identity–Europe. I. Langenbacher, Eric. II. Niven, William
John, 1956– III. Wittlinger, Ruth, 1961–
   D1055.D95 2012
   940.01–dc23

2012001678

British Library Cataloguing in Publication Data

A catalogue record for this book is available from the British Library

Printed on acid-free paper

ISBN: 978-0-85745-577-2 hardback
ISBN: 978-1-78238-917-0 paperback
ISBN: 978-0-85745-581-9 ebook

Contents

• • • • • • • • • • • • • • • •

Introduction
Dynamics of Memory and Identity in Contemporary Europe 1
Eric Langenbacher, Bill Niven, and Ruth Wittlinger

Chapter 1
Dynamics of Generational Memory: Understanding the East and
   West Divide 14
Harald Wydra

Chapter 2
Time-out for National Heroes? Gender as an Analytical Category
   in the Study of Memory Cultures 39
Helle Bjerg and Claudia Lenz

Chapter 3
The Memory-Market Dictum: Gauging the Inherent Bias in
   Different Data Sources Common in Collective Memory Studies 55
Mark A. Wolfgram

Chapter 4
Remembering World War II in Europe: Structures of Remembrance 69
Christian Gudehus

Chapter 5
Ach(tung) Europa: German Writers and the Establishment of
   a Cultural Memory of Europe 88
Hans-Joachim Hahn

Chapter 6
Critiquing the Stranger, Inventing Europe: Integration and
   the Fascist Legacy 102
Mark Wagstaff

Contents

Chapter 7
The Thread That Binds Together: Lidice, Oradour, Putten, and
    the Memory of World War II   120
Madelon de Keizer

Chapter 8
Memory of World War II in France: National and
    Transnational Dynamics   136
Henning Meyer

Chapter 9
The Field of the Blackbirds and the Battle for Europe   149
Anna Di Lellio

Chapter 10
Transformation of Memory in Croatia: Removing Yugoslav
    Anti-Fascism   166
Ljiljana Radonic

Chapter 11
German Victimhood Discourse in Comparative Perspective   180
Bill Niven

Chapter 12
Shaking Off the Past? The New Germany in the New Europe   195
Ruth Wittlinger

Conclusion
A Plea for an "Intergovernmental" European Memory   209
Eric Langenbacher

Notes on Contributors   222
Bibliography   226
Index   237

Introduction

Dynamics of Memory and Identity in Contemporary Europe

Eric Langenbacher, Bill Niven, and Ruth Wittlinger

In many ways, "Europe" has been an unqualified success story since 1945. The postwar period witnessed an unprecedented level of economic and political integration accompanied by a relatively long period of peace and stability. The European project has not only ensured Western European reconstruction and cooperation in the aftermath of World War II but–through a number of waves of enlargement–it has also overcome the continent's division in the aftermath of the fall of communism. The Europeanization of national polities, economies, and societies is quite far advanced, and the world's largest internal market–in spite of some serious challenges recently– is largely hailed as a success.

Increasing convergence in many policy areas, however, has not been accompanied by the emergence of "a European citizen" or a common European identity. Quite to the contrary, considerable expansion over the last twenty years–from twelve member states before the Berlin Wall fell to twenty-seven today (and more to come)–has left the Union more diverse than ever. In addition to the political cultural consequences of expansion, many national societies have become increasingly Euroskeptic in the aftermath of a number of "deepening" initiatives since the 1990s, especially the failed constitutional initiative and then the Lisbon Treaty, which arose out of the former effort.

A number of reasons can be put forward to account for the lack of a European identity. First, there is a multitude of different definitions as well as visions of Europe. There is no agreement among the current EU member states (or other European countries) as to what Europe is or what it should be. Is it just the world's biggest internal market that happens to consist of democratic nation-states which are, by and large, based on similar values or is it—as Benedict Anderson has termed it in the case of the nation-state—an "imagined community?" Is it a community based on a common Christian heritage, even though most European populations are thoroughly secularized and diversifying with the inclusion of many Muslim compatriots? If it is a (mere) geographical entity where are its borders?

Whereas the raison d'être of continued European integration was firmly grounded in the destructive experience of World War II and the need for a strong sense of European community in the face of the Soviet threat, over five decades later it is much more difficult to provide a convincing rationale for further integration or maybe even only the status quo. In his speech to Chatham House in October 2006, the President of the European Commission José Manuel Barroso acknowledged this when he pointed out that "sixty years of peace has meant that the image of Europe as a bastion against war is losing its resonance." In his view, the European Union needed: "new foundations. A new core purpose. One which looks forward, recognizes new realities, that draws inspiration from but does not depend upon the achievements of the past." Barroso suggested that this "new core purpose" of the European Union should be meeting the challenges facing Europe today, i.e., climate change, growing competition from China and India, global pandemics, mass migration, international terrorism, demographic change, and energy security.[1] Similarly, Jürgen Habermas has pointed out that at the beginning, "Europe" was a response to problems within the continent, whereas it is now directed at meeting the challenges brought to the region from the outside.[2] Thus, efforts to define a common European present, let alone determine a unifying vision of a common future, are extremely fraught at present. Moreover, efforts to construct a common past face serious challenges, as the logo adopted for the fiftieth anniversary celebrations of the signing of the Treaties of Rome in 2007 illustrated. In view of the fact that only six of the current members were part of the original set-up at the time, "Together Since 1957" was not very convincing or resonant.

Considering the relevance of the past in any construction of identity, the dynamics of memory in the new Europe are crucial to an understanding of the relationship between its people. Rather than contributing to a common European identity based on a shared past, references often relate to national pasts and frequently illustrate and underline previous division rather than present unity. In late 2009, Czech President Vaclav Klaus initially refused to sign the Lisbon Treaty because of fears that the attached European Charter of Human Rights might facilitate additional legal action from Sudeten Germans aimed at compensation or restitution for what they lost after their expulsion in the mid and late-1940s. After officials in

Berlin and Brussels agreed to an explicit exemption, Klaus backed down.[3] Then, in spring 2010, as the state finances of Greece deteriorated and German Chancellor Angela Merkel was very reluctant to agree to a bailout of the heavily indebted country, Deputy Prime Minister Theodoros Pangalos, opined that "Germany had no right to reproach Greece for anything after it devastated the country under the Nazi occupation, which left 300,000 dead. 'They took away the gold that was in the Bank of Greece, and they never gave it back. They shouldn't complain so much about stealing and not being very specific about economic dealings.'"[4] At the same time, in Spain, a case against high-profile judge Baltasar Garzón–who indicted Augusto Pinochet and several Bush Administration officials among others–proceeded, alleging that the judge "abused power" by pushing forward with investigations regarding Spanish Civil War and Franco era crimes, despite amnesty laws that had been promulgated during the transition to democracy in the late 1970s.[5] Perhaps most tragically, the plane crash in April 2010 that killed Polish President Lech Kaczynski and many other members of the Polish political elite occurred as these politicians were travelling to Belarus to commemorate the seventieth anniversary of the infamous Katyn massacre when the Soviets killed over 20,000 Polish officers. This happened in the context of unprecedented openness on the part of the Russian government led by Vladimir Putin. Although these gestures did not constitute an official apology (nor have Russian officials deemed the incident a war crime), they have started to address the bitter memories that have long strained Polish-Russian relations.[6]

Looking back over the decades since the end of the Cold War, every European country has witnessed frequent eruptions of collective memory–memories based on events from the bloody twentieth century. Far from being consigned to the "dustbins of history," these historical legacies are still very much alive in the present. Collective memories are helping to construct or deconstruct collective identities and the hegemonic values that constitute political cultures. As a consequence, memories are affecting school curricula, generational identities, domestic politics, and especially foreign policies and countries' international relations.[7] The strained relations between Germany and Poland, Estonia and Russia, Ukraine and Russia, Hungary and Slovakia, or Greece and Turkey (at least in Cyprus) in the twenty-first century would be impossible to understand without a deep grasp of earlier collective memories and their impact. And, of course, the memory of the Holocaust still looms large in all corners of the continent.

Given the clear importance of collective memory in Europe today, there is need for scholarship that explores its formation, forms, and pro-

Introduction

cesses from a truly trans-European perspective. This volume, which brings together scholars from across Europe and North America, performs this purpose. It does so not just through empirical case studies, but also by examining innovative conceptual and theoretical frameworks that underpin the evolution of collective memory in contemporary Europe.

Three additional motivations animate this project. First, there has been a global increase in the attention paid by world leaders, international institutions, scholars, and practitioners to the concerns of collective memory. These actors have engaged in countless debates and have initiated policies that speak to the concerns and influences of collective memory. However, many of these policies and theories have not yet received sustained and adequate attention in the academy—despite the countless countries where memory and related concerns such as working through a traumatic past and bringing perpetrators of human rights abuses to justice have come to the fore. Beyond Europe, contemporary examples include Argentina (which in April 2010 convicted a former junta leader for human rights abuses),[8] Chile, Colombia, Guatemala, Rwanda, South Africa, China, Japan, and South Korea. Although memory has always been a major feature of human interaction, these preoccupations intensified after the end of the Cold War with questions of transitional justice, human rights, and international law highlighted as never before. Clearly, collective memory is important globally and deserves sustained and in-depth study.

Second, despite a proliferation of studies on memory (and in related fields such as transitional justice) that have advanced concepts and theory,[9] the field of collective memory is still developing. Much of the most innovative work has been done in other languages, especially in French and German,[10] and thus is not well known among English speaking audiences. Moreover, the field of memory studies was founded and is still dominated by scholars of the humanities, especially in the disciplines of history, literature, and cultural studies. Although much theorizing has been done by sociologists (Maurice Halbwachs, Barry Schwartz, Jeffrey Olick), most social and especially political scientists have been slow to recognize the importance of memory and are only slowly advancing major theoretical works in the area. Theories and case studies about collective memory would thus benefit from an infusion of social scientific theories, methods, and epistemologies. Our volume intends to address these lacunae by providing conceptually and theoretically innovative contributions inspired by state-of-the-art literature from an interdisciplinary and social scientific perspective.

Third, the collapse of the Iron Curtain, the renationalization of Eastern Europe, and the subsequent eastward expansion of the European Union have all impacted the way the past is remembered in today's Eastern Europe. At the same time, memory in Western Europe has changed significantly in recent years, as the passing of totalitarian theory, the Europeanization/globalization of Holocaust memory, and an ever-increasing sense of the need to stage a more "self-critical" memory have led to a change of emphasis in memorialization and commemoration. Furthermore, the last decades have witnessed the renaissance of political communities below that of the modern nation-state (e.g., Scotland, Catalonia, Flanders, Bavaria) and a corresponding need for appropriate collective identity and memory constructs. With the construction of European-wide political and economic institutions, many actors and commentators felt that a European-level memory regime similarly needed to be constructed—one that transcended the confines of the traditional, Westphalian nation-state.

Thus, collective memory in all parts and all levels of Europe is in a state of flux. The contributions in this book examine the extent to which memory in today's European nations has been shaped by recent European developments such as the end of the Cold War, democratization, generational change, the widening of European alliances, and the tensions between resurgent national consciousness (arguably exacerbated by the opening of borders) and the spread of a "European" identity.

The Contributions to this Book

The volume begins with several theoretical and conceptual chapters that discuss aspects which are often neglected in memory studies: the generational background of memory in Europe, gender as an analytical category in the study of memory cultures, and the potential bias of data sources widely used in collective memory studies. Harald Wydra's "Dynamics of Generational Memory: Understanding the East and West Divide" explores the importance of a cohort-based approach highlighting generational conflict to an understanding of collective memory change in the two still distinctive halves of Europe. Wydra proposes that the conflict between generations forms the experiential background of leaders and their respective societies and argues that it is this generational background to different European memories that actively shapes different temporalities, symbols, and meanings in the new Europe. This background is the matrix where perceptions of time, symbols, and the intergenerational fabric of memory are created. Moreover, this is not simply some bygone past or legacy, rather, it consists of a dynamic process where biological finitude (in the deaths of individuals) and the rise of new generations–especially "decisive" or "strategic" generations–is the precondition for the search for meaning. Such a search is an active endeavor where some events, values, and aspirations may be forgotten but the importance of others may increase. Wydra traces these dynamics through analyses of several cases including Spain, Italy, Poland, Russia, and Germany, paying particular attention to the impact of various "ruptures" on cohort formation and collective memory construction. Being an integral part of a broader European cultural memory, the experiential background of Eastern Europe will remain a challenge for Europe's democratic future, but it is also essential to shift the center of gravity eastwards to confront this region's historical legacies.

Approaching the study of memory from a gender perspective in "Time-out for National Heroes? Gender as an Analytical Category in the Study of Memory Cultures," Helle Bjerg and Claudia Lenz explore the complexities of gender and family dynamics in the collective remembering of World War II. They argue that gender plays an important role in structuring the "national basic narratives" that have emerged in Western European countries occupied by Germany between 1940 and 1945. According to Bjerg and Lenz, such gendered narratives in family memory and the culture of memory connected to them offered very different possibilities of identification and authorization for men and women in the postwar era. Based on the theoretical assumption that knowledge about the past is both regulated and reproduced by power relations, they investigate which kind of topics and stories are told by and expected from men and women so that they gain authority as speakers. The empirical analysis underpinning their model is based on an examination of the transition of historical consciousness and the formation of cultures of memory of World War II in Danish and Norwegian families through three generations.

Mark A. Wolfgram's chapter entitled "The Memory-Market Dictum: Gauging the Inherent Bias in Different Data Sources Common in Collective Memory Studies" provides the third contribution to this volume which is largely interested in conceptual considerations. Wolfgram asks collective memory scholars to reflect critically on the different biases that inherently exist in the data with which they work. In his view, scholars working in the field of culture, symbols, identity, and memory often assume the a priori importance of their subject matter. After an intellectual justification of the importance of a culturalist approach to the study of politics that also encompasses a focus on collective memory studies and a brief methodological critique of many existing studies, Wolfgram provides what in his view is a more promising way forward. He argues in favor of the utility of the memory-market dictum, which highlights supply and demand issues, consumption of mediatized products, the role of capital, and the construction of collective memories as inherently social processes and not mere social objects. Wolfgram substantiates his argument through an empirical analysis of several television and film productions in postwar Germany, which–together with the theoretical discussion–in his view demonstrates a way forward to capture identity and collective memory formation at the European level.

The next contribution, "Remembering World War II in Europe–Structures of Remembrance" by Christian Gudehus, starts with the observation that every time Europe or European remembrance is spoken about, there is an underlying assumption that there is something like Europe, that European countries somehow belong together, and that references to the past, at least in their manifestations as history, are somehow significant if not of central importance. According to Gudehus, this approach is inherently normative, since it affirms Europe as a sphere which is re-created time and again in communicative acts pertaining to economic, cultural, geographical, and political issues with the result that such discourses determine not only which history, which countries, and which people are included but also those which are excluded. Rejecting such a normative approach, Gudehus asserts that his discussion does not construct a particular image of Europe and is not meant to contribute to the success of the European project. Removing his analysis as far as possible from any contemporary political discussion, he analyzes the various narrative modes that constitute structures of remembrance in the way World War II is remembered in a number of different European countries, including Germany, Austria, and Poland, and which, in his view, reside between national remembrance and meta-narrativity.

Most of our contributions are based on the assumption that–as scholars of collective memory will no doubt readily acknowledge–discussions and notions of the "new Europe" are incomplete without references to and acknowledgements of the "old Europe." This particularly applies to the following two contributions. Hans-Joachim Hahn's title is a combination of Thomas Mann's famous essay "Achtung Europa" and Hans-Magnus Enzensberger's travelogue *Ach Europa*. After some introductory remarks regarding the concept of cultural memory, Hahn draws on a number of outstanding German writers and philosophers who have contributed to the European idea in the twentieth century. His chapter thus considers the extent to which memory can shape the political culture of a society, thereby contributing towards the establishment of particular values. Hahn's contribution draws on a wide range of materials, such as essays and speeches by Hermann Hesse, Hugo von Hofmannsthal, José Ortega y Gasset, and Aristide Briand; but central to his discussion are the contributions by the Mann family (Thomas, Heinrich, and Klaus) as well as Count Richard Coudenhove-Kalergi and his *Pan Europa* movement. While some basic elements of Coudenhove-Kalergi's pan-European vision survived the war and became manifest in the early treaties of the European Community, supported by Winston Churchill's famous speech in 1946, the onslaught of the Cold War changed the intellectual climate, at least as far as Germany was concerned. In his view, most German writers did not wish to be used as tools in the Cold War rhetoric and—as interviews with Heinrich Böll and Günter Grass illustrate—felt uneasy within Western capitalist society which was driven by industrial expansion at all cost. Hahn's chapter ends with a discussion of Hans-Magnus Enzensberger's much more Euroskeptic position which is opposed to any form of a homogenizing superstructure and Peter Schneider's contribution, which, he argues, seems to strike a balance between Enzensberger's Euro-phobia and the modernist search for a European identity during the 1920s.

Mark Wagstaff in "Critiquing the Stranger, Inventing Europe: Integration and the Fascist Legacy" suggests that attempts to fashion a European social identity reflect the imperatives of nineteenth-century nation-building whilst attempting to supplant those imperatives through encouragement of new supranational identities and forms. The chapter argues that identities are products of memory and that substitution of external identities actively damages the techniques of memory that shape individual identity as part of the formation of national cohesion. Wagstaff begins by theorizing how individual identity is shaped and how it relies on memory, especially in societies where there is coherence of individuals with their economically productive role. The social identities produced from familial relationships are noted in context of how this organization of similarity and difference creates fault lines between a community of belonging and others. Drawing on the historical background preceding the end of World War II, the chapter sketches the history of the European Union from its early iteration as an attempt to ensure the conditions for fascism could not be repeated in Europe to a more activist body promoting pan-European interests and identity. Wagstaff's analysis also touches on the differential pressure that upheaval in global financial markets placed on European national economies in the currency union, the Eurozone. The necessity of bailing out several Eurozone members such as Greece and Ireland—action perceived as essential to maintain the integrity of the single currency—sparked an amount of popular debate which, according to Wagstaff, in its caricature of some nations as hard-working and others as feckless, allowed a superficial yet instructive glimpse of enduring biases beneath the mantle of union.

The volume then turns to specific case studies of memory and identity in postwar Europe. First, is Madelon de Keizer with "The Thread That Binds Together: Lidice, Oradour, Putten , and the Memory of World War II." In this comparative study of the postwar memory culture in Lidice (in what is now the Czech Republic), Oradour (in France), and Putten (in the Netherlands), de Keizer posits that the local memories of German war crimes in these places are deeply interconnected with a shared national and European memory of war and destruction. According to de Keizer, three phases after 1945 can be discerned in these representations. In the first or "national" phase (1945–1989), the memories of the consequences of the Nazi reprisals in Putten and Oradour were employed for their utility in forging a homogeneous national remembrance dialogue, while Lidice was called on for the specific Cold War remembrance policies of the eastern bloc. De Keizer suggests that a new phase of "Europeanization" of the memory of World War II began after 1989. From then on, all three places were integrated into a broad European culture of memory intended to prop up the goal of a united Europe. It was the events of 9/11, de Keizer argues, that have given the process of remembrance a new impetus to both the global and the local. In this last phase, de Keizer proposes that local identity formation in the context of globalization provides room for cultural diversity as well as the expression of European values.

Continuing with the French case, Hennig Meyer in "Memory of World War II in France: National and Transnational Dynamics" discusses the evolution of French memory culture by focusing on three memorial places: the Centre National Jean Moulin of Bordeaux founded in 1967 devoted to the memory of French resistance and German persecution; the Mémorial pour la Paix in Caen which was established in 1988; and the Centre de la memoire d'Oradour-sur-Glane inaugurated in 1999 which commemorates the German massacre of French civilians just before the end of the war. Meyer argues that each of these three memorial sites represents a different focus of French World War II memory: resistance in Bordeaux, liberation in Caen, and sacrifice or victimization in Oradour. Meyer's key aim is to show that there is a strong interdependence between the socio-historical context of a museum's creation and its representational content. With the help of these three examples, Meyer demonstrates that in different places and at different times memories can show tendencies towards a transnational memory. He points out that the centre in Bordeaux was created to disseminate the Gaullist idea of unity based on the experience of resistance which was strictly national and did not cater for a transnational context. In contrast to this, important changes in memory culture have resulted in Caen adopting universal peace as its key message, which clearly indicates a global rather than national agenda. Similarly, according to Meyer, Oradour goes well beyond the national and into the transnational context because of the experience it shares with many other sites regarding the crimes committed during the German occupation,.

Anna Di Lellio turns to Eastern Europe in "The Field of the Blackbirds and the Battle for Europe" arguing that historical memory is highly performative at the field of the blackbirds, a rolling Kosovo flatland six kilometers to the northwest of the capital Prishtina. At this site, in June 1389, a coalition of regional forces led by the Serbian Prince Lazar Hrebeljanović faced the Ottoman army of Sultan Murat. Both leaders were killed in a battle that apparently ended with no decisive victory on the day but led to the submission of the local nobility shortly thereafter. The Ottomans then ruled over the Balkans until the twentieth century. Monuments marking the battlefield are placed a few kilometers apart: a memorial to the fallen Christian heroes in the locality known as Gazimestan, north of the *turbe* (mausoleum) of the Sultan's standard-bearer, and the Sultan's *turbe* at Mazgit. According to Di Lellio , they are archeological and political signifiers of opposing camps, physical symbols of discourses and practices that "memory entrepreneurs" have adopted to plot national stories. Most notable and best known among them is the Serbian narrative of the battle, constructed as a unique tale of Christian martyrdom granting Serbia historical rights over Kosovo. Less obvious, plotlines built on the memorialization of the battle and its mythical protagonists are also relevant to Albanian and Turkish national discourses. In this chapter, Di Lellio shows how in the contemporary political context the old battlefield has become a highly resonant political symbol of a European identity for all.

The former Yugoslavia is also the focus of Ljiljana Radonic's "Transformation of Memory in Croatia: Removing Yugoslav Anti-Fascism." According to her, the nation-building process in Croatia has been characterized by the literal and symbolic delimitation from the old federal state of Yugoslavia and the search for national identity played a greater role than in newly formed, post-socialist countries which did not secede. After a short overview of the way World War II was confronted in Yugoslavia, Radonic's chapter examines the transformation in policy of approaching the past during three different historical stages: the first following the collapse of Yugoslavia in 1990/91 and President Franjo Tuđman's rise to power; second after Tudman's death and the regime-change in 2000; and third, after Tudman's "Croatian Democratic Union" regained power in 2003 under its new leader, Ivo Sanader. Radonic analyzes not only the new content of the hegemonic historical narrative, the participating and the silenced protagonists, but also the manner in which this hegemonic historical narrative was asserted; thus whether this occurred democratically or in a repressive manner. She also raises the question of how the Croatian case and its victim narrative fits into the thesis of the globalization or the Europeanization of the Holocaust and how Croatia adapted to this European standard of dealing with World War II.

Next, Bill Niven provides a discussion of the ever-influential German case in "German Victimhood Discourse in Comparative Perspective." He notes that analyses of German victimhood discourse have tended to focus on national questions such as whether or not the subject of German wartime suffering was long "taboo" in Germany, whether generational changes impacted on its reception, or whether domestic political changes have brought about a greater empathy for German victimhood. By contrast, this chapter seeks to contextualize the reinvigoration of interest in German historical suffering within wider European trends. While Niven looks at the continuing impact of Western European influences, he argues that many aspects of the German case today are only truly explicable through an analysis of memory trends in post-communist Eastern European countries. Like Poland, Czechoslovakia, and other Eastern European states, one half of Germany, namely the German Democratic Republic, was liberated from the grip of socialism in the late 1980s. Like former citizens of these other Eastern European Soviet satellite states, too, it was only natural that many eastern Germans would come to remember themselves as victims of the Soviet order. The "Germans as victims" culture is to a degree mirrored by a "Poles as victims" culture, for instance, with both Poles and Germans sharing a common history of Soviet domination. It remains to be seen how, or indeed if, the resulting tensions between a view of Germans as perpetrators and one acknowledging their historical suffering can be resolved.

Ruth Wittlinger's contribution "Shaking Off the Past? The New Germany in the New Europe" ends the volume with a discussion of the way collective memory of World War II and the Holocaust determined the Bonn Republic's European policy and how this has changed in the two decades since unification. Due to the presence of the past, Wittlinger argues, West Germany developed into a model European which was keenly committed to multilateralism, reluctant to express its national interest openly and explicitly, and disinclined to show any leadership. Germany's model Europeanism started to crumble in the final years of the Kohl chancellorship and an emphasis on costs and benefits intensified under Gerhard Schröder's chancellorship from 1998 onwards. According to Wittlinger, based on a much more assertive identification with the German nation than had previously been possible, Schröder showed no reluctance to express Germany's national interest openly and suggested that his generation's attitude towards Europe was a matter of choice, rather than necessity determined by the German past. Under Angela Merkel, Germany has also lost its traditional reluctance to show leadership in Europe. Wittlinger concludes that the memory of World War II and the Holocaust has lost its predictable grip not only on Germany's European policy but on the European project as a whole.

The contributions assembled here show, above all, that the European continent is at a crossroads–the long period of institutional foundation (including the projection of evolving institutions onto newly democratizing countries) now needs to be consolidated. In the economy, this means that the design flaws of the Euro need to be rectified. In the realm of political culture, a supportive European identity and culture need to be "imagined" to provide functional support–a new solidarity that will undergird common sacrifices. In the realm of memory, the continent is currently in a phase where a cultural memory, constructed for the long term, needs to emerge, not the least because the generations that witnessed the historical events on which many of the collective memories are based, are rapidly passing away. If anything else, this volume reveals the myriad strands of collective memory in Europe today at a crucial moment in which the European project is consolidating and institutionalizing itself for the long term.

Notes

1. José Manuel Barroso, "Seeing Through the Hallucinations: Britain and Europe in the 21st Century" Hugo Young Lecture, 16 October 2006, available at http://ldeg.org/pages/barrosospeech.html; accessed 14 September 2011.
2. Jürgen Habermas, "Europa: Vision und Votum," *Blätter für deutsche und internationale Politik* 52, no.5 (2007): 517–520, 517.
3. Edward Cody, "Europe's future, tangled by its past," *The Washington Post*, 23 October, 2009.
4. See http://www.telegraph.co.uk/finance/financetopics/financialcrisis/7309861/Greekrescue-in-danger-as-deputy-prime-minister-attacks-Nazi-Germany.html; accessed 12 September 2011.

Introduction

5. See http://www.nytimes.com/2010/03/26/world/europe/26spain.html; accessed 14 September 2011.
6. Michael Schwirtz, "Putin Marks Soviet Massacre of Polish Officers," *New York Times,* 7 April, 2010.
7. See Eric Langenbacher and Yossi Shain, eds., *Power and the Past: Collective Memory and International Relations* (Washington, 2010).
8. Charles Newberry and Alexei Barrionuevo, "25 Years for Leader of Argentine Dictatorship," *New York Times,* 20 April 2010.
9. Eviatar Zerubavel, *Time Maps: Collective Memory and the Social Shape of the Past* (Chicago, 2003); James Wertsch, *Voices of Collective Remembering* (Cambridge, 2002); David Art, *The Politics of the Nazi Past in Germany and Austria* (Cambridge, 2006); Wulf Kansteiner, *In Pursuit of German Memory: History, Television, and Politics after Auschwitz* (Athens, 2006); Jan-Werner Müller, ed., *Memory and Power in Post-war Europe: Studies in the Presence of the Past* (Cambridge, 2002); Jeffrey Olick, *States of Memory: Continuities, Conflicts, and Transformations in National Retrospection* (Durham, 2003); Richard Ned Lebow, Wulf Kansteiner, and Claudio Fogu, eds., *The Politics of Memory in Postwar Europe* (Durham, 2006); Małgorzata Pakier and Bo Stråth, eds., *A European Memory? Contested Histories and Politics of Remembrance* (New York, 2010).
10. Harald Welzer, Sabine Moller, Karoline Tschuggnall, *Opa war kein Nazi: Nationalsozialismus und Holocaust im Familiengedächtnis* (Frankfurt/Main, 2002); Aleida Assmann, *Der lange Schatten der Vergangenheit: Erinnerungskultur und Geschichtspolitik* (Munich, 2006); Edgar Wolfrum, *Geschichtspolitik in der Bundesrepublik Deutschland: der Weg zur bundesrepublikanischen Erinnerung 1948–1990* (Darmstadt, 1999).

Chapter 1

Dynamics of Generational Memory
Understanding the East and West Divide

●●●●●●●●●●●●●●●

Harald Wydra

States have always constructed civic identity by means of unremitting defenses against the memory of their violent origins. If "blessed acts of oblivion" are crucial to ensure collective identities, the political transformations of the last two decades arguably present Europe with a challenge. Across a complex array of repressed memories, denial, victim syndromes, and atonement, Western European societies, such as Germany and France, have come to adhere to the "foundational" memory of the end of Nazism and the singularity of the *Shoah*.[1] Genocide recognition, official apologies, and the rehabilitation of victims are all arguably a central feature for the reconstitution of democratic identity in Europe. With the end of communism, the singularity of this foundational European memory was relativized. Comparisons between the two totalitarian systems became more systematic and plausible. Western Europe has developed a culture of memorials, museums, and centers of commemoration focused on the centrality of the *Shoah*.[2] The new members who joined the European Union in 2004, however, claim the need for the acknowledgment of differences in historical legacies. At the beginning of the twenty-first century, European memory is characterized by a deep geopolitical asymmetry. A memorandum, drafted by prominent historians from Eastern Europe, argued that the new Europe has brought new historical experience, grievances, and complaints, so far ignored in the West.[3] In their view, the more established Western members have not forgotten their past. Rather, they had the opportunity to reassess it and thus have found more common values to share. Since Eastern Europeans did not participate in the process of "constructing Europe," their experience of the shared values of Europe is bound to be thinner and so is their understanding of the informal rules and meanings. If Europe wants to unite, questions such as "What is the full history of Europe?" or "How do we deal with different histories within Europe?" have to be asked.

From the perspective of citizens of the new Europe, building European identity on strategies of forgetting appears ill-suited. On the one hand, the shaping of collective memory is required as a moral imperative and as a political necessity aimed at appeasing identity-conflicts between ethnic groups or social classes while also acknowledging wrongdoings against minorities. On the other hand, memory appears helpless against the challenge to commemorate crimes of absolute evil, to remember as "it truly was." Precisely because memory is inherently contentious and partisan, authors, such as Tony Judt, argued that only the historian can assure that Europe's past can furnish Europe's present with admonitory meaning and moral purpose.[4] In the center should be an "austere passion for fact, proof, evidence."

Both positions share a central characteristic: evaluations of the past limit memory to a function of the present, an affair of the living. Moreover, any possible evaluation of Eastern European memory works within conceptual paradigms, which are hegemonically "Western."[5] The proposition I am going to defend is that if we want to understand dynamics of memory in the new Europe, we first have to examine the conditions under which narrative commitments have been made across the political evolution of postwar Europe. The shaping of memory and the perception of historical legacies are not opposites. Rather, they operate through complex interactions between biological renewal, social experience, and the search for meanings by new generations. Thus, the past is to be considered not as a bygone and well defined period but rather as a social organism in gestation.[6] Following distinct but interrelated interpretive traditions established by José Ortega y Gasset, Karl Mannheim, Reinhart Koselleck, and Paul Connerton, I argue that historical judgments and political identities are culturally transmitted across generational memory. This process of cultural transmission is not simply about the construction of narratives by political elites or by professional historians. Societies are historical individuals who are initiated into memories. Societies, like individuals, "learn" habitual acts of performance by forgetting the exact circumstances. However, such practices are not always "learnt" by processes that are institutionally ordered, consensual, legally bounded, or normatively structured. Fundamentally, the renewal of generations is a source of opposition, a force of conflict, rejecting established conventions, traditions, and habits. As Reinhart Koselleck put it, "there is no collective memory but there are collective conditions of potential memories."[7]

The case for generations as collective conditions for potential memories calls for the integration of biological, social, and cultural conditions of memory. Generations are carriers of ever-changing and mutually reinforcing formats of social memory and cultural memory. Only individual beings remember, yet memories can also be transmitted beyond the death of individuals. Across history, carriers of memory grow old and die whilst new people are born and enter the social world. Despite the disappearance of individual carriers of memory, there is remarkable continuity over time. This relationship between biological decline and cultural connectivity across the *longue durée* raises an important question: how is the perception of historical continuity communicated across biological changes? In a seminal essay on the links between the transformation of language and event-history, Reinhart Koselleck argued for the meta-historical biological preconditions for history, which precede and remain outside language.[8] The time span between birth and death determines human finitude. Diachronically, the constant transitions between earlier and later are constitutive for any history to be perceived as a sequence of occurrences. This perception of temporalities is structured by the sequence of generations, often entailing different overlapping spaces of experience, which mutually exclude each other. The passing away of people (the deaths of individuals) and the rise of new generations are the anthropological preconditions for the search for meanings.

Initiating Generational Memory

Generational memories clearly contain a synchronic dimension, which refers to the contemporaneous time frame of formative experiences. Jay Winter, for instance, attributed the flourishing of cultures of memory in the twentieth century to two generations.[9] The first generation was a cohort of men and women born between the 1860s and 1880s who made an impact in academic, literary, professional, and public prominence between approximately 1890 and 1925. The second generation of memory framed the period between the 1970s and 1980s, characterized by the witness of the Holocaust. However, local proximity, similar age group, and temporal congruity are not enough to achieve what Karl Mannheim called connectivity *(Generationszusammenhang)*.[10] The knowledge of one's birth date is not sufficient to know which generation one belongs to. Class divide or ethnic differences in the same city may cause same age groups to diverge completely on their intentions. Interpretive responses to World War II, for instance, entailed atonement in Germany but denial in Japan.[11] According to Mannheim, the formation of a generational unit *(Generationseinheit)* depends primarily on a sense of common purpose and spiritual likeness.

Generations are not only biographical, demographical, or social facts but also existential communities. Born into an existing environment with established hierarchies and prevailing conventions, members, and specific events makes people reciprocate feelings and conceive of their co-existence in social environments as a problem for which they have to find a common spiritual purpose in order "to make sense of" it.

Before taking up leading positions in politics, society, or the economy, i.e., before becoming an elite, people enter wider society through adolescence, early adulthood, and maturing. According to Karl Mannheim, important occurrences during these formative years of individuals are absorbed and stored, thus becoming "the historically oldest stratum of consciousness, which tends to stabilize itself as the natural view of the world."[12] Such initiations may become socially and politically relevant because they cannot be forgotten. It is through the encounter with the social world that people make career choices, adhere to worldviews, develop aspirations, and adopt certain lifestyles. By doing this, they not only discard other career options but also critically engage with the actions and moral attitudes of the previous generation. Such "choices" are sometimes more in tune with their social environment, sometimes more radical, but always more unconscious than one would admit.

Social identities of future political elites are formed at particular junctures of individual lifecycles. Revolutionary elites seize power, for instance, when they are middle-aged men and women. Yet, what "makes" revolutionaries is the decisions underlying their absolute commitment to the revolutionary cause. Such decisions are often made in the face of deep crises of personal self-definition in the formative years of their youth—crises resolved by the selection of a subversive identity.[13] The average age of the Bolshevik leadership in 1917 was thirty-nine, but most of them committed themselves totally to revolution as a way of life due to the situations they experienced at ages between fifteen and twenty.[14] As Sebastian Haffner pointed out, the birth cohort 1900 to 1910 would become the genuine generation of National Socialism.[15] This cohort of young Germans schoolboys absorbed the reports from the frontlines of World War I on an almost daily basis. For these boys, war was not the front experience, but consisted of the great exciting adventure; the struggle between nations loaded with strong emotions; and a positive vision of values such as honor, fatherland, and sacrifice for the nation.

Thus, it is not sufficient to focus on the specific chronological location of a generation, a cohort so to speak. A generation is not only a matter of the biography of individuals, but it requires the connection between individual consciousness and the passing of social time. As Ortega put it, one cannot really know what happened at a certain date if one does not ascertain to which generation it happened. The stakes for the young and adolescent—when confronted with social oppression, revolution, or war—are different from those for the established social elites or even the old. The same event happening to two different generations is a vital and hence historical reality which is completely different in each case.[16] No major historical event can determine historical stages, political identities, or generational succession. The reason for this is that events are experienced and appropriated by people depending on the generation to which they belong.

Thomas Mann, the literary master of time, argued that biological age not only unfolds within the passing of time and the transformations of social conventions, but also with the relentless appearance of events. Mann claimed that transitions *(Übergänge)*, not ruptures, were the essence of history. His own life span stretched over two epochs, which allowed him to experience how the seeds of the new were already alive and spiritually active within the old regime.[17] Born in 1875—in the late period of the liberal epoch of peace in Europe—he confessed to have an "advantage" with regard to those born in the contemporary disintegration of order, values, and morality marked by the European civil war between 1914 and 1945. Mann's own experiential background allowed him to understand what equilibrium, stability, and a long-lasting system of values actually meant. The meeting in Munich in 1938 between Chamberlain, the Victorian gentleman at the age of sixty-eight, and Hitler, the young warrior of World War I at the age of forty-eight, epitomizes how this discrepancy in generational capital resonated in attitudes to keep peace and to push for war.

Each generation accepts events according to their own way of life. Ortega distinguished two fundamentally different types of historical change: first, when something in our world changes, and second, when the world itself changes. The latter type of change occurs normally with each generation, bringing about a greater or a lesser variation in attitudes towards the prevailing moral codes and social values. However, when such change is quantitatively very pronounced, leaving people without beliefs and orientation and hence without a world, one may speak of a "historical crisis." Major social transformations may have such an impact on individual, social, and national consciousness as to make the mediation of generational conflict through institutions and established hierarchies next to impossible. In Ortega's view a "decisive generation" is one that, "for the first time thinks the new thoughts with full clarity and with complete possession of their meaning, a generation that is neither still a precursor nor any longer bound by the past."[18]

Generational Memory between Past and Future

The forward-looking orientation of new generations may oppose old values and lifestyles but still may be bound by performative rituals that refer to some kind of foundation. Decisive generations are founding generations who initiate societies in a particular form of commemorative practice, imposing social conventions, and new validities *(vigencias)*. Ortega's concept of *vigencia* points to a system of binding social conventions that may last for a certain stretch of time, during which it exercises its conventionalizing influence. It is the characteristic of a founding generation that the validity it established is remembered across time. A founding generation will become a strategic generation in that it will inscribe and incorporate its experience into national consciousness through literary expression, semantic symbols, and ritual performance.[19] Representations of the past and aspirations for the future overlap, so to speak. According to Hans-Georg Gadamer, this tension appears as a hermeneutic process where achieving self-awareness of the horizons of the past is based on the engagement between old and new, the past and the present.[20]

The tension between two fronts can be expressed in the concepts of bonding and social memory.[21] According to Nietzsche, bonding memory *(Bindungsgedächtnis)* concerns the will to remember engagements and promises made. Without such bonding memory, there could be no mutual trust, no reliability in keeping promises, no predictability of human interaction, and no "longsightedness" in human and social life. Conversely, horizons of the past in complex societies are never an individual's "natural view" of the world but are socially constituted. Formative historical experiences, such as revolutions or wars, will urge people to produce a variety of testimonies that they will communicate to their kin, the wider public, and even across national boundaries. If, according to Maurice Halbwachs, our individual memories are socially constituted, how can such generational units bind future generations?

Let us briefly dwell upon how collective, inter-individual communities can be bound to commitments made. The key idea of a wide range of recent studies in memory is that memory can no longer be seen as a reflection, a transparent, or cognitive record of the past; rather, it should be seen as performative.[22] It comes into existence "at a given time and place through specific kinds of memorial activity."[23] Personal memories play a huge part in the recollection of people who belong to generations whose spiritual likeness was established in war situations or other contexts of socially disruptive events that formed individual consciousness. We recall revolutions, wars, or major transitions in a country's history in literary expression, autobiographies, memorials, or semantic symbols. Yet, a far more important claim to memory is that social experiences create ritualized habit memory. Habit memory is the capacity to make acts of performance. We remember how to ride a bike, mow a lawn, or assemble furniture. The memory of these performative acts is like learning a lesson. As Paul Connerton put it, "the better we remember this class of memories, the less likely it is that we will recall some previous occasion on which we did the thing in question."[24] This type of memory sustains by far most of our actions in daily life but it is based on forgetting, i.e., on disconnecting with the personal memories of when it was learned or the cognitive memories of how to do it. Unless we encounter a problem and have to consult a manual, we would not necessarily recall when, how, or where we learnt it.

Authors such as Connerton and Jan Assmann have provided strong accounts of how commemorative rituals, bodily practices, and the coding of memory allows for remembering such bodies of generative mythology. Specific socially experienced memories will remain fundamental bonds by which individuals or communities will habitually remember. Assmann suggested that Judaism—in an age of extreme uncertainty—established memory techniques in the service of bonding memory.[25] As exemplified in the book Deuteronomy, symbolic representations and ritual commemoration bind people through techniques such as learning by heart, conversational remembering, oral transmission, or canonization of the text of the covenant (Torah) as the foundation of "literal" adherence.

Such coding of memory can become culturally hegemonic. It can outperform, if not entirely efface, the values and ideas of previous generations. In liminal conditions, individuals may go through formative inventory experiences that coincide exactly with major socially comprehensive and dramatic events. Some protagonists of flourishing Athenian democracy such as Sophocles, Pheidias, Anaxagoras, or Pericles were born between 500–495 BC, making their coming-of-age coincide with the battle of Salamis in 480 BC, which was the crucial moment of the forging of democratic consciousness. The Founding Fathers of the United States of America can also be seen as a strategic generation. Here, the Declaration of Independence and the War of Independence were turned into commemorative strategies and ritualized coding of memory that has pervaded national consciousness, political identity, and cultural memory. For many key members of this generation, such as Alexander Hamiliton (born 1755), James Madison (born 1751), or John Marshall (born 1755), the initiation into adulthood coincided with the Revolution and the War of Independence.

According to Connerton, commemorative ceremonies engage members of the community by enacting cults, encoding gestures, and ritually repeating movements. The aim is to remind the community of its identity. Revolutionary periods leave an extraordinary impact both on the self-definition the regime and on the social memory of citizens. The emotional intensity of the French Revolution would, as Kant realized at the time, never again be forgotten. On the one hand, the Revolution ritualized the break with the monarchical sacred. The trial and execution of Louis XVI was enshrined in a ritual performance of extraordinary power, which not only killed a king but revoked a ruling principle.[26] On the other hand, it established the symbol of popular sovereignty. The political emancipation of the people would be remembered across rituals of triumph, such as the storming of the Bastille, but also public festivals.[27]

This reflexivity between the past and the future makes even acts of forgetting an act of performance based on memories that are "learnt" and internalized. Thus, "blessed acts of oblivion" are acts of self-consciousness and identity-formation that are rooted in habit memory. When democracy in Athens was re-established in 403 BC, a double forgetting occurred. The democrats renounced vengeance by swearing an oath to forget the disasters of the past.[28] Not only was memory of faction, division, and conflict repressed but the political–as the very essence of the original democratic regime–was stifled. Despite this double forgetting–by not only "forgetting" resentment and vengeance but also one's own victory–the democrats nevertheless performed an act of nobility based on the habits and the memory of the former aristocratic regime. Narrative commitments in a nation's history can also take the form of semantic symbols. In Italy, for instance, the term *mezzogiorno* is a powerful semantic symbol for the widespread idea of a failed nation *(nazione mancata)*. It stands for the persistent condition of backwardness, anarchy, and the structural incapacity of Southern Italy to achieve progress and freedom. Against common assumptions, the *mezzogiorno* is not the result of Italy's political unity in 1861. It is rather a narrative made popular by the revolutionary generation of Italian liberals who had to make sense of the failed revolution in the Kingdom of Naples in 1848.[29] The ruthless response by the Bourbon regime after 1848 dispelled the elites and banned half of the literate population from any administrative work in the restored state. As a reaction to the failed revolution, the exiled Neapolitan intelligentsia lost all hope in any reform movement in the near future.

Constituting Narrative Commitments in Europe

The outline of a framework of generational memory so far has suggested that historical legacies in Europe are not only "learnt" and conveyed by dispassionate and critical scrutiny of historical facts. Rather, the very perception of historical legacies requires the transmission of memories across generational conflict. In this sense, narrative commitments that supported identification with Europe have been constituted by the search for meaning against established conventions. Subsequently, this proposition will be illustrated by aspects of Europeanization in the context of postwar West Germany and Italy as well as post-Franco Spain.

In West Germany, the period 1945–1957 can be seen as dominated by the victim syndrome. This was based on a clear separation between the crimes against humanity committed by the Nazi regime and the German people, attributing the role of perpetrator to the former, that of the victim to the latter.[30] How could West Germans in the decades to come develop a self-critical view of the *Shoah*? How could its commemoration become supportive of West German democracy and integration into Europe? As Norbert Elias suggested, the usual competitive situation of a generational conflict between younger outsider groups and older established groups was particularly polarized after 1945.[31] Paradoxically, the young generation would "rebel" against the older generation at a time when the economic miracle had given West Germans economic wealth and new confidence. However, material security and prosperity may not satisfy a generation's desire to realize a personally fulfilling purpose which can be experienced as meaningful.[32]

The aftermaths of each of the two World Wars were followed by emancipatory spurts and the extension of political rights, yet the scenarios differed radically. Despite the radical regime change in 1918/19, the generational divisions after World War I were not as pronounced as they would become in post-World War II West Germany. Many German army officers who resisted the Weimar Republic were deeply frustrated by the loss of Germany's greatness. Not surprisingly, the stab-in-the-back legend after 1918, suggesting that the German army—unbeaten in the battlefield—had been a victim of defeatist forces, found great popular support among young adults. After World War II, however, West Germans not only had to face the consequences of military defeat but also the stigma of a nation responsible for barbaric acts of violence.[33] The fathers' generation—who had held responsibility during Weimar and the Nazi regime—had to cope with individual guilt and self-blame. The young generation that was born during or right after the war, however, grew up with a greater sensitivity towards the charge of collective guilt leveled at Germany by the outside world. Thus, the young outsiders of the post-World War II generation fought most fiercely against what their fathers and grandfathers had regarded as most sacred and meaningful: national greatness. The destruction of the German state and the catastrophe of a divided nation rendered patriotic glory absolutely meaningless. Unlike the stab-in-the-back legend after World War I, West Germany's self-blame would now promote initially latent but progressively more insisting claims for the responsibility of the perpetrators.

The case of the Italian *Resistenza* illustrates a different mode of performing generational memories. The foundation of the Italian Republic in 1946, the second *Risorgimento,* derived its moral force from social memories about the resistance movement. In many ways, the *Resistenza* was a formative experience for those young Italians born just on the eve of fascism's ascent to power in the early 1920s.[34] These cohorts had been quite indifferent politically until Mussolini's fall in the summer of 1943 and the effective onset of a civil war that would divide Italians between 1943 and 1945. While after September 1943 the Fascist regime continued to exist at Hitler's mercy in the Republic of Salò, the German occupation and the Allied invasion in Southern Italy forced many young Italians to take sides and to make existential choices of the most basic kind. The ritual of the Feast of Liberation, the Italian national holiday on 25 April–celebrated since 1946–commemorates the *Resistenza* as both a "chaos" and a "golden age" simultaneously.[35] It might sound paradoxical to see a civil war as the source of republicanism. Nevertheless, the reconciliation of the deep contradictions between supporters of fascism and partisans required some consensus about the unity of conflicting memories and identities. The Italian national holiday represents a double funeral of sorts. It relates to physical burials, reburials of partisans, and arrangements of cemeteries but also to symbolic burials, commemorating, tautologically, that the dead have died.

Generational conflicts lead to a moral urge to denounce one's own country for crimes, backwardness, or faded national glory. They can push for "progressive" moves in the sense of closing the gap with what they imagine as a superior form of political organization or culture. In Italy, the sons of war *(figli della Guerra)* were infatuated with "democracy," standing for America.[36] The immediate sources for images that saw America as synonymous with modernity, freedom, and prosperity were the individual memories of relatives and friends who emigrated in masses to the United States in the early twentieth century. The cluster of ideas and symbols on which the *Democrazia Cristiana* based their power in postwar Italy made skillful use of the "American dream." Fascism was eventually regarded as a parenthesis, a contrast consciously promoted by sometimes quite interventionist policies by successive U.S. governments.[37] Yet, both in West Germany and in Italy narrative commitment to ritualistic representations of the communist threat testifies to the importance of the fear of contagion with totalitarianism as a driver for European integration.

The Spanish transition to democracy after 1975 drew considerably on the social imaginary of "Europe" as iconic marker of identification in Spanish cultural memory. The trauma of losing the last overseas colonies in 1898 gave rise to the "generation of 1898," a group of young writers and intellectuals who voiced the outrage about the failure of Spanish elites and launched an appeal for regeneration. Ortega, born in 1883 and aged fifteen in 1898, argued that Spain was not a nation-state but a series of sterile compartments such as the monarchy, the church, and the army. Each of these was mostly interested in turning their own concerns and ambitions into truly national issues.[38] Eventually, the "generation of 1898" in Spain was to translate the backwardness of the country *(atraso)* into the desire for regeneration, the powerful aspiration of Europeanization. In Ortega's words, "regeneration is the desire; Europeanization is the means to satisfy it."[39]

The Spanish Civil War became almost instantaneously a "global" event. It drew tens of thousands of volunteers from all over the world in what was seen as a universal fight between human solidarity against nationalist-fascist reaction. Franco's victory was constructed in official political memory as a clear divide between *vencedores* (winners) and *vencidos* (losers). The Franco dictatorship was intransigent towards the defeated. It executed many leaders of national movements and prohibited the public use of language, literature, folklore, flags, and hymns. However, by the 1960s, the official transcript was progressively replaced by alternative versions informed by clandestine literature, families, or schools.[40] In the deep uncertainty of the months after Franco's death in November 1975, many Spaniards "knew" that "we have met the enemy, and the enemy is us."[41] Often, the success of the Spanish transition to democracy was attributed to a collective amnesia. The more persuasive argument, however, is that it was not based on a pact of oblivion *(pacto de olvido)*, but rather on a pact of remembering *(pacto de recuerdo)*.[42] The memory of historical fratricide would disseminate fear and even panic of the danger of radicalization. Harking back to the regenerationist aspirations of 1898, this identification of Europe with modernity acquired enormous power in post-Franco Spain. The new political elites associated "going to Europe" with a promotion of Spain aiming to achieve democracy, modernity, freedom, and a civilized and European status.[43] Unlike Britain, for instance, the dominant paradigm of Spanish cultural memory has incorporated the concept of belonging to Europe as it has essentially symbolized the quasi-mythical success of the transition to democracy.

Shifting the Centre of Gravity of Memory in the New Europe

As Jay Winter suggested, the study of memory in Europe needs to shift its center of gravity.[44] A shift from Paris to Warsaw would make "European memory" look very different, but the mechanics and passions of such a relocation are very complex, if not messy. If we go even further east, that is, from Warsaw to Moscow or Kiev, memory would look very different again. And would we all agree that it is still "European"? Who measures and with what kind of tools? If history lessons are to be learnt, who is the master and who is to be taught? "Coming to terms with the past" or "dealing with the past" are clumsy translations of the German terms *Vergangenheitsbewältigung* or *Geschichtsaufarbeitung*. The phenomenon probably exists everywhere but the weight of the Nazi past and its fundamental role for the postwar order was quite unique. Under Western eyes, East European memories appear as a social pathology, a constant trauma, an inability to forget, to mourn, to acknowledge crimes, even to bury the dead. Apologetic forms of memory have been rare in this part of Europe. When confronted with the pogrom at Jedwabne, where in 1941 more than three hundred Polish Jews were killed by Poles, the reactions ranged from incredulity to outrage. Despite widespread efforts by organizations, such as *Memorial,* the recognition or rehabilitation of victims of political repression in Russia has remained rudimentary.[45]

Given the malleability of memory, historians such as Timothy Garton Ash and Tony Judt have warned of the excesses of cults of commemoration. As Judt argued, Europe has been constructed upon a "compensatory surplus of memory" since 1989. The focus was on institutionalized public remembering as the very foundation of collective identity. For Judt, this will not endure. Some measure of neglect and even forgetting is the necessary condition for civic health.[46] Ash suggested that the path of history lessons and "truth-telling" may be more promising than trials or purges. Historians would be the professionals best equipped to teach these lessons.[47] He advocates putting texts into historical context, applying intellectual distance, but also essential imaginative sympathy with all the men and women involved.

Yet, if the period between injustices and trials that address these injustices stretch over a long timespan, resentment can remain part of cultural memory over a century or more.[48] The divided memories, which resonated in the escalation of violence in Yugoslavia, were consolidated by historians.[49] The anti-fascist myth was one of the pillars for memory regimes in Tito's Yugoslavia, which were anchored in the symbol of "Brotherhood and Unity." In order to glorify the Partisan experience, Yugoslav historiography portrayed the state as a victim of fascism. A central "fact" in history books was to fix the total number of Yugoslav dead during World War II at 1.7 million, considerably higher than the historically more accurate 1 million. In the climate of growing tensions amongst the federal republics and after Tito's death in 1980, the second postwar generation, especially in Serbia, would use these numbers to "prove" the huge numbers of Serbs killed by Croatian *Ustascha*. In the memorandum of the Serbian Academy of Sciences of 1986, Yugoslav history was portrayed as a systematic persecution of the Serbian minority threatened by physical annihilation.[50] The different expectations of Poles and Jews after 1945 led to competing and often conflicting accounts of sufferings during the Nazi occupation. Essentially, "the Poles competed with the Jews for a palm of martyrdom. Both sides accuse each other of the heinous theft of suffering."[51] After 2003, Polish public opinion was deeply critical of tendencies in Germany to create a *Zentrum gegen Vertreibungen* (Center against Expulsions). It was felt that these commemorative efforts by some Germans signified a grave form of historical revisionism or relativism that would turn "perpetrators into victims."

Meike Wulf and Patti Grönholm provided an important study on the generational background of historical meanings in the case of post-Soviet Estonia.[52] They used generational group identities among Estonian historians in order to examine how professionals engage actively in the transformation processes and support nation-building processes. They elaborated on four different strategies Soviet historians used in response to the new conditions of historical research—conformism, opportunism, withdrawal, and passive resistance—and relate these strategies to different generational groups of Soviet historians. Looking at some of their post–1991 biographic accounts, they show how various modes of talking about their past experiences, such as glorification, denial, self-justification, apologetics, distancing, resignation, and destiny, reveal strategies of coping with loss and of generating new meaning.

Teaching history afresh with each passing generation, as Judt suggests, is unlikely to be a guarantee for "the austere passion for fact, proof, evidence, which are central to his vocation."[53] It can safely be assumed that historical legacies are interpenetrated by cultural forms of memory. Even forgotten and repressed forms of memory resonate in particular cultural formations and official transcripts. As students of memory, we are products of our stored mental archives of images and terminologies that respond to dominant narratives of social memory. In the modern communication age, national scandals can resonate worldwide as semantic symbols. A political scandal, such as Watergate in the United States, should not be confined to its political legacy. Given its unprecedented scope, the memory of this scandal entered semiotic practices and political symbolism to an extent, which allows political elites only marginally to control it.[54] A French teenager still associates the *Résistance* with the *Libération* in August 1994, while young Poles associate the *Armia Krajowa's* resistance and the Warsaw uprising in summer 1944 with a heroic but also suicidal endeavor. In a similar vein, a student of memory claiming to observe empirical facts cannot leave subjective value judgments at the doorstep.

History lessons based on an austere passion for facts and proofs, which would resist the malleability of makeshift pasts through memory, are wishful thinking. Historians, much like political leaders, are products of cultural memory, which can be likened to the storage capacity in a granary.[55] This storage memory *(Speichergedächtnis)* contains meanings and knowledge of the past that are stored extensively in libraries, museums, or archives. They contain a reservoir of potential meanings across the *longue durée* in a country's history, which persist as artifacts such as literary texts, pictures, and sculpture but also as spatial compositions such as monuments, architecture, landscape, and temporal orders such as feasts, customs, or rituals. Cultural forms of memory are amorphous, often discarded, or forgotten. A large part of our memories are unconscious. In a Proustian twist, they "sleep" within our bodies until they are awakened or triggered by some external, often haphazard, stimulus.

In Eastern Europe, the available pasts of the revolutions in 1848 but also of 1956, 1968, and 1980 have considerably constrained official politics of commemoration in countries of Eastern Europe.[56] The long stateless existence of Poland between 1795 and 1918, for instance, bequeathed a political meaning to the term society (*społeczeństwo*), which also highlighted the moral authority of the Catholic Church as the carrier of the continuity of the nation against foreign domination. Literary works and religious faith have been crucial for maintaining a cultural memory of national self-determination. The monument to Polish victims of Ukrainian massacres,[57] for instance, bears the inscription of a quote by Adam Mickiewicz's drama *Dziady*: "*Jeśli zapomnę o nich, Ty, Boże na niebie, zapomnij o mnie*" (If I forget them,

God in heaven, do forget me). The massacre at Katyń is the most obvious *lieu de mémoire*–recently reinforced by Andrzej Wajda's film–to substantiate the Polish status as victims. In April 2010, a plane carrying the Polish president Lech Kaczyński and almost a hundred high-ranking Polish civil and military dignitaries crashed very close to this site on its way to commemorate this event–a tragedy that only heightens the resonance of this memory place.

In pre–1989 Hungary, the memory of Imre Nagy and the 1956 revolution had survived in counternarratives defying the system of organized forgetting. Imre Poszgay's official acknowledgement that the 1956 events were not a counter-revolution but a popular uprising offered a powerful symbolic resource to emerging political opposition. Popular representations of the memories of the failed revolutions in 1956 and 1968 sustained communicative memory of acts of defiance and resistance. The Prague Spring, for instance, did not arise as a spontaneous happening but was the result of a gradual awakening, a sort of creeping opening of the "hidden sphere" of society.[58] In Poland, the spirit of defeat in victory after 1945 led to intense efforts to reconstruct historical memory as a narrative of active heroism against the humiliating memory of defeat. In Poland, the *Solidarność* generation relied upon a spirit of silent, daily, and obstinate resistance based on social memories of sacrifice and suffering that emerged in the crises of 1956, 1968, 1970, or 1976.[59] The eruption of unofficial or independent symbols during *Solidarność's* self-limiting revolution in 1980 strongly suggests that there was no need to define the meaning of an independent society. Remembering the tragedy at the workers' unrest in Gdańsk back in December 1970, for instance, Polish workers "knew" that they had to stay inside their factories rather than go outside in order to present their strike demands. In post-martial law Poland after 1981, the memory of the Solidarity experience was kept alive under the shelter of the Catholic Church but also in rituals of celebrating mass services, exposing Solidarity's symbols, and by individual life-conduct.

The transmission of generational memory in wider cultural memory gives a further but decisive twist to the idea of a "common European memory." This one we may characterize as a quest for recognition across what can be called the civilizational divide in Europe: Few "Westerners" conceived of the "enlargement" of the European Union other than in terms of a generous gift offered by Europe. "Europe" here means "Western" Europe, the free and civilized part, which was not the Europe behind the Iron Curtain. As Croatian writer Slavenka Drakulic put it:

> Europe ... describes only one part of it, the western part, in a geographical, cultural, historical and political sense. Europe has been divided by the different historical development of its component parts, communism and most of all by poverty ... Now it looks as if all the ex-communist, Eastern European countries have the same almost palpable wish to push that dividing line as far to the east as possible, so that eventually Europe will be a whole, undivided continent. Yet it is this desire itself which forms the current dividing line. The West does not feel the need to belong (it just is) or to allow the countries standing at its threshold to enter.[60]

Generational succession not only generated self-representations of victimhood but also self-representations as European, Western, and democratic.[61] One example here is the concept of "cultural trauma," which has been applied to slavery, the Holocaust and also to 9/11, all of which appear as wounds that resonate in the identity formations of African Americans, Jews, and all Americans.[62] In cultural trauma, direct experience is not a necessary condition of trauma. It is through time-delayed and negotiated recollection that cultural trauma is experienced, a process that places representations and ritual performance in a key role. Vindictive mythologies of retribution and vengeance are particularly pervasive in parts of Central and Eastern Europe, which was characterized by territorial instability, forced migrations, and traumatic experiences.[63] Conversely, the marginality of Eastern Europe has not been an obstacle but rather a condition for new generations to aspire to return to Europe. The traumatic experiences that shaped communities of fate in the confusion between victory and defeat after 1945; in the failed East European revolutions in 1956, 1968, 1980; or the unaccomplished processes of achieving full recognition by the "West" have generated meanings that have provided identification with Europe.

Therefore, from the "inside" perspective, Poles, Czechs, Latvians, and others felt subjectively an integral part of (Western) Europe. If they already belonged "naturally," the notion of enlargement was either offensive or nonsensical, and possibly both. When Alexis de Tocqueville claimed that Americans are "born equal" he meant that a democratic people transcended the inequalities based on class antagonism.[64] Similarly, Eastern Europeans would transcend effective inequalities and political antagonism between East and West by a powerful imagination of sharing values and commitments inherent to (Western) Europe; here many people were under the spell of Europe, which they considered a synonym for paradise. The fall of the Iron Curtain, however, laid bare the realities. Evoking the betrayal of "Yalta" in 1945, the cultural memory of many Central Europeans "remembered" the historical debt "Europe" seemingly owed them. The former Hungarian prime minister, József Antall, summed up in 1992 the overwhelming convictions of politicians, intellectuals, and other elites of Eastern Europe when he said that Eastern Europe had won the third world war for the West without firing one shot and that this achievement was greeted with unrequited love.[65] The recovering of the lost moment of 1989 may indeed be precisely centered on this desire for recognition by Europe. Vaclav Havel argued that with the distance of time a new generation comes of age, which gradually begins to lose patience and may indeed perform a kind of "second-generation revolution" which could complete the original revolution. Overcoming *Mečiarism* in Slovakia or staging colorful revolutions in Ukraine would give a clear answer to the open questions: "Where does one of the major spheres of civilization in the world today (the so-called West) end, and where does the other sphere (the so-called East, or rather Eurasia) begin?"[66]

Collecting and Transmitting Generational Memory

It could be objected at this point that the concept of generation has a collectivist bias, presupposing more consistency than there really can be. Not everybody belongs to a generation. Lines of conflict in society are defined by social classes, ethnic divisions, religious factors, or by forms of cultural capital. Yet, generational memory can be grasped by what Jeffrey Olick calls "collected memory."[67] Rather than assuming an identity as collective, one needs to ascertain how memories are collected over time, space, and across different generations. As individuals grow up in a specific cultural and historical context, their aim is to become aware of an identity. Different historical legacies in post–1989 Europe need to be seen through the prism of transmissions of generational memory.

This process of becoming aware of an identity often occurs in family settings. Traditionally, the family had been the most important carrier of knowledge transformation but also the main provider of meaning in the inter-generational memorial fabric. In less complex societies, the natural cycle of death and birth was mediated by rites of initiation into adulthood or positions of power that were relatively well-defined and quick affairs. The specific inter-generational construction of traditionalism in peasant societies was examined by Marc Bloch.[68] He pointed out that in rural societies—with the parents working all day—it was the grandparents' task to bring up children, rather than being under the influence of the next chain, i.e., the parents, children's education relied on a backward step. The most malleable minds were under the influence of the least flexible. Still Tocqueville could argue that nations do not grow old as men do and each fresh generation is new material for the lawgiver to mold.[69]

The growing pace of modern life—urbanization, industrialization, as well as bureaucratization of the modern service economy—has shifted the weight from tradition and kinship towards the primacy of social conventions, a fact captured in Bloch's suggestion that human beings are more the sons of their times than of their fathers. Precisely because of this increased impact of the social environment—including the demands of education, personal skills, and social learning in modern complex societies—generational shifts have become a more drawn-out process.[70] While, for instance, the young postwar generation in Germany after 1945 grew up with much fewer social constraints than any previous generation, its initiation phase before taking up leading positions in society was much longer than it would have been for aristocratic or higher middle-class members before 1914. In more complex societies, adolescence is prolonged and new generations take much longer to penetrate the establishment.

This does not prevent a young generation from absorbing the world as its own "natural" world. Evoking the mass migration of people from old, tribal Africa into cities and towns as a pivotal moment of South Africa's history, writer J.M. Coetzee suggested that his parents' generation misread this migration. They assumed that African children born in the cities would carry the memory of that migration within themselves,[71] as if they were conscious of being a transitional generation linking the old, tribal with the new urban Africa. In reality, however, the world into which we are born is our world. "Trains, cars, tall buildings (three generations back), mobile telephones, cheap clothing, fast food (present generation)—these constitute the world as it is, unquestioned, certainly not a gift from strangers, a gift to be marveled at and felt thankful for." In this sense the city-born black child bears no mark of the bush.

However, beyond the demands of division of labor, the reshaping of social structures, and the need for high qualifications, new generations are in search of meaning. Strategic or founding generations bequeath their memories in inter-generational processes. As Eva Hoffman argues with reference to the *Shoah,* children of the "second generation" are the "hinge generation." Such hinge generations can either arrest the meanings of awful events and "fix" them at the point of trauma or help processing them towards a new understanding.[72] While survivors were too traumatized to begin the work of mourning, let alone overcome the events, the second generation has a second chance to do this processing. Against the repression of memory but also the symbolic reductionism of "founding" generations, the "hinge" generation can enter a critical relationship, often rejecting the interpretive frameworks established by the previous generation. The quest for meaning across generational chains has resonated in family settings as well as in societal dynamics of identity-formation. As Marianne Hirsch argued, the second generation is connected to the past not by recall but by "imaginative investment, projection, and creation."[73] Post-memory is not an identity or collectivity but a structure of trans-generational transmission of traumatic knowledge and experience embedded in family life and mediated through photographic images. In the case of traumatic interruption, exile, or diaspora, embodied connections with the past are lost. Post-memorial work strives to "reactivate and reembody more distant social/national and archival/cultural memorial structures by reinvesting them with resonant individual and familial forms of mediation and aesthetic expression."[74]

Generations as Transitions

Thomas Mann once suggested that the essence of history is not in ruptures, but in transitions between historical configurations. To take up similar propositions by Ortega and Elias,[75] such identity formation across trans-generational memory is engaged on two fronts. One front concerns the lived experiences, such as communities of fate, which bequeath ideas, value judgments, and memories of people who are initiated into the social world. The other front is constituted by the way generational memory sustains the imagination of hypothetical futures, by how it seeks the orientation towards new validities. Yet, these two fronts are in constant conflict. As historical configurations, generations are in-between, liminal entities, who create new images, symbols, and utopias.[76] When people undergo fundamental social transformations, such as revolution, these rites of passage shape recollection and individual consciousness, but also create mythical representations.[77] From a generational perspective, forgetting and commemoration are no opposites but require the painstaking work of relating horizons of the past and expectations of the future across two fronts.

The unprecedented scope of bloodshed and suffering during World War I in Europe decisively shifted attention from glory to trauma. The memory of the Great War stressed the healing language of tradition, referring to nationhood, sacrifice and patriotism.[78] The social carriers of commemorative practices in France after 1918 were often non-state associations who kept private or family memories by listing concrete names. This tendency would then be taken over by the official state monuments in remembrance of the war dead. The commemoration of human losses in World War I would be used by "late" nations such as Italy to ritually perform cults of nationhood. Memorials and statutes in every town and village commemorated the ultimate sacrifice for the unity of Italy's territory and soul. Conversely, the disillusioned and marginalized generation of Germany's imperial army assembled in the *Freikorps* became a source of ideological and concrete support for the rise of Nazism.

Generational identities of political leaders that were "learnt" in the "remote" past can resonate in a new founding generation across generational change. Key leaders of the European integration process after World War II, for instance, came from marginal regions in their respective home states and, generationally speaking, from the far distance having been initiated into adulthood before the end of World War I. Konrad Adenauer (born 1876) was from the Rheinland, a western border region, Robert Schuman (born 1886) was of mixed Luxembourg and Lotharingian origin, Alcide de Gasperi (born 1881) was from the Trentino and had been a subject of Austria-Hungary in his youth.

In Spain, losers of the civil war decided not to settle accounts, while the winners agreed to support a democratic system quite similar to the one they had rejected in 1936. When, on 23 February 1981, a group of *guardias civiles* under the command of Colonel Antonio Tejero stormed the Spanish parliament, two major political figures defied the military coup. Ironically perhaps, both of these had in their youth taken up arms against the legitimate democratic Republic. Gutiérrez Mellado, the vice-president of the extant government, had followed Franco in 1936 (aged nineteen in 1931 and twenty-four in 1936) in revolting against the democratic Republic but in 1976 had accepted to join the Suárez government committed to promote democracy. The leader of the Communist Party, Santiago Carrillo, had already taken part in the Asturias revolution in October 1934–also directed against the legitimate Republic. Aged sixteen in 1931 and twenty-one in 1936, he was a prominent leader in republican Madrid and became the villain of Franquism. Both committed to rebellion in their formative years, Carrillo decided not to settle accounts with the past, whereas Gutiérrez Mellado strongly disapproved of the conventional practice of military coups.

Generational conflict is also crucial for the reassessment of master narratives of nation-building. Two major cases of nation-building after World War II are very instructive here. Both the official interpretations of the partitions of India and Pakistan in 1947 and the creation of Israel within Palestine in 1948, for instance, would be challenged in the wake of generational divides over the memory and meaning of each nation's past.[79] While the generation of the founders of Pakistan, Muhammad Ali Jinnah and David Ben-Gurion for the Zionists, claimed to lead a heroic struggle for freedom and the people's self-determination, the hinge generation has developed a number of counter-narratives to the official transcript of national glory. Essentially, the traumatic component of the nation's establishment could no longer be successfully repressed for patriotic goals. Against the official collective memory of the foundation of the Israeli state, the generation of new historians in Israel has pointed to the dimension of colonial exploitation and ethnic cleansing in the occupation of Palestine.

In the German Democratic Republic, it was members of the generation born in the first ten years of the country's existence who were most important in creating the political upheaval of 1989.[80] As Bärbel Bohley–often referred to as the mother of the revolution–explained, she was born in 1945 and always lived in Berlin. Bohley's most important problem was the confrontation with the human problems of life in a divided city. For her, the workers uprising of 17 June 1953 in East Germany, the Hungarian revolution in 1956, and the Prague spring of 1968 were factors that made her sympathetic to the building of the Berlin Wall in 1961. While a sizeable proportion of East Germans (some 41 percent) who left in 1989 were between twenty-two and twenty-nine years old, most leading members of the opposition were in their forties.

Generational memory can be culturally meaningful across diachronic ruptures and resonate in political choices. The strong polarization of generational conflict in postwar West Germany decisively contributed to the narrative commitment that bound Germans to the political recognition of responsibility. The Polish writer Gustaw Herling-Grudziński deplored the fact that Poland in 1989 lacked a cathartic rupture with the past such as occurred in post–World War II Europe. Purges, such as in postwar France or Italy, or trials, such as Nuremberg, were impossible. The only systematic trials occurred in reunified Germany, a special case given the "colonization" of East by West Germany. In this sense, the peaceful transition from communism blurred the dividing lines between friend and enemy, victim and perpetrator, judge and accused. It has often been argued that the founding generation, the "class of 1989"–unlike that of 1917, 1945, or 1968–was nowhere to be found. Yet, it could also be argued that the negotiated revolutions in Poland and Hungary in 1989 were the culmination point of a series of performative acts that incorporated memories of confrontation, humiliation, and violence. Habits are learnt as a relational process, where individual psychology is part of a wider group existence, and *vice versa*. The formation of generational memories is, in Ortega's words, based on "interindividual" reality.[81] The Polish dissident Adam Michnik described his arrest by the communist authorities in 1965–at the age of nineteen–as the guiding motive for his entire "career," as a dissident entirely to the communists. "If there had not been communists in Poland, I would not have known what to do."[82] The Polish roundtable of early 1989–the terminal point of *Solidarność* generation–engaged in a particular form of ritual, a liminal *communitas*, in Victor Turner's terms. Physical proximity and a common sense of purpose led to mutual forgiving, reconciliation, and understanding. The participants "forgot" their former antagonism, not so much despite but rather *because of* the diametrically opposed personal trajectories and divided memories.

Concluding Remarks

As these examples suggest, carriers of political power and of historical interpretation are themselves products of generational chains. They are not "free" or autonomous present-oriented agents strategically planning for the future or dispassionately evaluating facts. Rather, their interpretive judgments are collected and transmitted–beyond their individual experience–across their wider cultural existence. This cultural existence includes the phenomenological background of their inventory experiences but also the habit memory they acquire. The generational perspective on dynamics of memory in the New Europe transcends a synchronic and presentist position. It is in the tension between two fronts that generational conflict constitutes narrative commitments, habits, and performative acts that have been transmitted across historical change. From a perspective of generational memory, political elites as well as historians are not confronted with models, values, or facts that they adopt, reject, or evaluate. Such groups have made their identities in generational conflict through opposition and antagonism with previously dominant values. Memory and history, therefore, are not two independent forms of confronting the past. Rather, perceptions of the past and aspirations to the future are two constantly changing fronts by which societies make sense of the world.

Notes

1. See Henry Rousso, *The Vichy Syndrome: History and Memory in France Since 1944* (Cambridge, MA: Harvard University Press, 1991); Aleida Assmann and Ute Frevert, *Ge-*

schichtsvergessenheit, Geschichtsversessenheit. Vom Umgang mit deutschen Vergangenheiten nach 1945 (Stuttgart, 1999).
2. Representative here are the Holocaust Memorial in Paris that opened in 2005 and the Berlin's Memorial to the Murdered Jews of Europe.
3. Wojciech Roszkowski, Gyoergy Schoepflin, Tunne-Valdo Kelam, Girts Valdis Kristovskis, and Vytautas Landsbergis, "United Europe–United History: A Mission to Consolidate a Common Memory."
4. Tony Judt, *Postwar, A History of Europe Since 1945* (London, 2005), 830–1.
5. Jay Winter, *Sites of Memory, Sites of Mourning: The Great War in European Cultural History*, new edition (Cambridge, 1998); Jan-Werner Müller, *Memory and Power in Post-war Europe* (Cambridge, 2002); Jeffrey Olick, *The Politics of Regret* (London, 2007). Timothy Synder, *Bloodlands: Europe between Hitler and Stalin* (New York, 2010).
6. For such attempts see Harald Wydra, *Communism and the Emergence of Democracy* (Cambridge, 2007).
7. Reinhart Koselleck, "Gebrochene Erinnerung? Deutsche und polnische Vergangenheit," in *Deutsche Akademie für Sprache und Dichtung,* Jahrbuch 2000 (Göttingen 2001), 19–32, 20.
8. Reinhart Koselleck, *Begriffsgeschichten* (Frankfurt/Main, 2006), 38.
9. Jay Winter, "Notes on the Memory Boom. War, Remembrance and the Uses of the Past," in *Memory, Trauma, and World Politics,* ed., D. Bell (Basingstoke, 2006), 56–60.
10. Karl Mannheim, "The Problem of Generations," in *Essays on the Sociology of Knowledge* (London, 1997).
11. Erna Paris, *Long Shadows: Truth, Lies, and History* (New York, 2002).
12. Karl Mannheim, *Essays on the Sociology of Knowledge,* 296.
13. Philip Abrams, "Generations in Conflict," *Journal of Contemporary History* 5, no. 1 (1970): 175–190.
14. The execution of Lenin's brother because of the assassination attempt against Tsar Alexander III in 1887 is reported to be the single most important motive for Lenin (aged sixteen at the time) to become a revolutionary.
15. Sebastian Haffner, *Geschichte eines Deutschen, Die Erinnerungen 1914-1933* (Stuttgart, 2000), 21–22.
16. Jose Ortega y Gasset, *El tema de nuestro tiempo* (Madrid, 1923), 55.
17. Thomas Mann, *Über mich selbst. Autobiographische Schriften*. 5th edition (Frankfurt/Main, 2002), 8.
18. Quoted in Julian Marias, *Generations. A Historical Method* (Birmingham, 1970), 99.
19. For an analysis of generations of English poets and writers as makers of national consciousness, see Bryan S. Turner, "Strategic Generations: Historical Change, Literary Expression, and Generational Politics," in *Generational Consciousness, Narrative, and Politics,* eds., J. Edmunds and B. Turner (Lanham, 2002), 13–29.
20. Hans-Georg Gadamer, *Philosophical Hermeneutics* (Berkeley and London, 1976).
21. Jan Assmann, *Religion and Cultural Memory* (Stanford, 2000).
22. Paul Connerton, *How Societies Remember* (Cambridge, 1989); Mieke Bal, Jonathan Crewe, and Leo Spitzer, eds., *Acts of Memory: Cultural Recall in the Present* (Hanover, 1999).
23. Nancy Wood, *Vectors of Memory. Legacies of Trauma in Postwar Europe* (Oxford, 1999), 2.
24. Connerton (see note 22), 23.
25. Assmann (see note 21), 16–21.
26. Connerton (see note 22), 7–9.
27. William H. Sewell. *Logics of History* (Chicago, 2005), 225–70.
28. Nicole Loraux, *The Divided City: Forgetting in the Memory of Athens* (New York, 2002), 251.
29. Marta Petrusewicz, "A *Nazione Mancata*: The Construction of the Mezzogiorno after 1848," in *Myth and Memory in the Construction of Community,* ed., Bo Strath (Zürich, 2000), 281–305.
30. Assmann and Frevert (see note 1), 144–5.
31. Norbert Elias, *The Germans* (New York, 1996), 251–77.
32. Ibid., 237.

33. Ibid., 229–31.
34. Giuseppe Carlo Marino, *Le generazioni italiane dall'unità alla repubblica* (Milan, 2006), 814–22.
35. Cristina Cenci, "Rituale e memoria: le celebrazioni del 25 aprile," in *Le memorie della Repubblica,* ed., L. Paggi (Florence, 1999), 338–49.
36. Marino (see note 34), 814.
37. Christopher Duggan, "Italy in the Cold War Years and the Legacy of Fascism," in *Italy in the Cold War: Politics, Culture, and Society 1948–1958,* eds., C. Duggan and C. Wagstaff (Oxford, 1996), 13.
38. Jose Ortega y Gasset, *España invertebrada* (Madrid, 1964), 52.
39. Pablo Jáuregui, "National Pride and the Meaning of Europe: a comparative study of Britain and Spain," in *Whose Europe? The Turn towards Democracy,* eds., D. Smith and S. Wright (Oxford, 1999), 275.
40. Paloma Aguilar Fernández, *Memory and Amnesia: The Role of the Spanish Civil War in the Transition to Democracy* (Oxford, 2002), 31.
41. Laura Desfor Edles, *Symbol and Ritual in the New Spain* (Cambridge, 1998).
42. Javier Cercas, *Autonomía de un instante* (Madrid, 2009), 180.
43. Jáuregui (see note 39), 280.
44. Keynote address to the inaugural workshop of the project "Memory at War," Cambridge University, 4 June 2010.
45. Nanci Adler, "The Future of the Soviet Past Remains Unpredictable. The Resurrection of Stalinist Symbols Amidst the Exhumation of Mass Graves," *Europe-Asia Studies* 57, no. 8 (2005): 1093–1119.
46. Judt (see note 4), 829.
47. Timothy Garton Ash, "Trials, Purges, and History Lessons: Treating a Difficult Past in Post-Communist Europe," in Müller (see note 5), 265–82.
48. Jon Elster, Closing the Books: *Transitional Justice in Historical Perspective* (Cambridge, 2004), 77.
49. Wydra (see note 6), 232.
50. Ibid., 201.
51. Piotr Wróbel, "Double Memory: Poles and Jews after the Holocaust," *East European Politics and Societies* 11, no. 3 (1997): 560–74.
52. Meike Wulf and Pertti Grönholm, "Generating Meaning Across Generations: The Role of Historians in the Codification of History in Soviet and Post-Soviet Estonia," *Journal of Baltic Studies* 41, no. 3 (2010): 351–382.
53. Quoted in Judt (see note 4), 830.
54. Michael Schudson, *Watergate in American Memory: How We Remember, Forget, and Reconstruct the Past* (New York, 1992).
55. Aleida Assmann, *Erinnerungsräume. Formen und Wandlungen des kulturellen Gedächtnisses* (Munich, 1999), 130–145.
56. Rogers Brubaker and Margit Feischmidt, "1848 in 1998: The Politics of Commemoration in Hungary, Romania, and Slovakia," *Comparative Studies in Society and History* 44, no. 4 (2002): 700–44.
57. The number of Poles killed by Ukrainian nationalists during World War II varies between 60,000 and 100,000.
58. Vaclav Havel, "The Power of the Powerless," in *The Power of the Powerless: Citizens Against the State in Eastern Europe,* ed., J. Keane (London, 1985), 43.
59. Wydra (see note 6), 175–176.
60. Slavenka Drakulic, *Café Europa. Life After Communism* (London, 1996), 12–13.
61. For an extensive analysis see Harald Wydra, "The Power of Second Reality: Communist Myth and Representations of Democracy," in *Democracy and Myth in Russia and Eastern Europe,* eds., A. Wöll and H. Wydra (London, 2008), 60–76.
62. Jeffrey C. Alexander, Ron Eyerman, Bernard Giesen, Neil J. Smelser, and Piotr Sztompka, *Cultural Trauma and Collective Identity* (Berkeley, 2001).

63. Vladimir Tismanenau, *Fantasies of Salvation* (Princeton, 1998).
64. Alexis de Tocqueville, *Democracy in America* (New York, 2000), 624.
65. Quoted in Harald Wydra, *Continuities in Poland's Permanent Transition* (Basingstoke, 2001), 138.
66. Vaclav Havel, *The Castle and Back* (London, 2008), 22.
67. Olick (see note 5), 23–5.
68. Marc Bloch, *The Historian's Craft* (Manchester, 1954), 40–1.
69. Tocqueville (see note 64), 95.
70. Elias (see note 31).
71. J.M. Coetzee, *Diary of a Bad Year* (London, 2008), 103.
72. Eva Hoffman, *After such Knowledge: Memory, History, and the Legacy of the Holocaust* (New York: 2004).
73. Marianne Hirsch, "The Generation of Postmemory," *Poetics Today* 29, no. 1 (2008): 103–128.
74. Ibid., 111.
75. Elias's concept of dual front strata *(Zweifrontenschicht)* goes beyond a static conception of class, focusing on how the tensions between a stratum above and a stratum below is constitutive for class consciousness. See Norbert Elias, *Die höfische Gesellschaft,* 8th ed. (Frankfurt/Main, 1997), 387–90.
76. See the special issue on "Liminality and Cultures of Change," *International Political Anthropology* 2, no. 1 (2009), especially Harald Wydra, "The Liminal Origins of Democracy," 89-107, and Arpad Szakolczai, "Liminality and Experience: Structuring Transitory Situations and Transformative Events," 141–172.
77. Wydra (see note 61).
78. Jay Winter, "Forms of Kinship and Rememberance in the Aftermath of the Great War," in *War and Rememberance in the Twentieth Century,* eds., J. Winter and E. Sivan (Cambridge, 1999), 40–60.
79. Jonathan D. Greenberg, "Generations of Memory: Remembering Partition in India/Pakistan and Israel/Palestine," *Comparative Studies of South Asia, Africa, and the Middle East,* 25, no. 1 (2005): 89–110.
80. Molly Andrews, "Generational Consciousness, Dialogue, and Political Engagement," in Edmunds and Turner (see note 19), 82–83.
81. Marias (see note 18), 79.
82. Adam Michnik, *Diabeł naszego czasu* (Warsaw, 1995), 398.

Chapter 2

Time-out for National Heroes?

Gender as an Analytical Category in the Study of Memory Cultures

• • • • • • • • • • • • • • •

Helle Bjerg and Claudia Lenz

> To be honest I don't think she has much to say. I mean, I don't find it very interesting. She can probably talk about particular episodes, like how a Norwegian sits in a treetop shooting at a German, but … that is not so interesting. I'd rather have the whole picture than the small pieces. When I find anything of importance, I'll ask and dig further… And I'm almost 90 percent sure that she doesn't have any information of that sort. Therefore I have to say I have no interest in bothering to ask her anything.
> (Gunnar Solstad, thirty-three years old)

> I always admired Grandmother because she didn't regard the Germans as enemies but as human beings.
> (Eivind Ness, thirty years old)

In these two contradictory statements of young Norwegian men, grandmothers are valued as transmitters of memories, providing understanding and/or knowledge of the history of World War II. In one case, the grandmother is completely devalued as a bearer of relevant *knowledge;* in the other case she is highly valued for her *attitudes* and her wisdom. Both positions are closely related to gendered scripts, according to the intergenerational transmission of memories. The aim of this chapter is to introduce gender as an analytical category into the study of historical consciousness,[1] memory culture, and history politics,[2] as we shall suggest an analytical model for understanding how gender makes sense in various ways when the meaning of the past is negotiated in the present. The empirical analysis underpinning our model is concerned with the transition of historical consciousness and the formation of cultures of memory of World War II in Danish and Norwegian families in three generations. The findings developed within this particular study can also work as fruitful analytical perspectives when compared with other national case studies or fields of research where questions of the formation of cultures of memory are at stake. Our argument is that looking at gender as an analytical category within studies of memory enhances our knowledge of the uses of history, the transition and formation of historical consciousness in a generational perspective, the family as a space of commemoration, and not least private and public cultures of commemoration.

The work to be presented in this chapter is based on the findings of the European research project "Traditions of Historical Consciousness."[3] The focus of the overall project was a comparative study of how memories of World War II have been passed on and reinterpreted in families over three generations. The project started off as a single project focusing on Germany and was later extended to include Serbia, Croatia, the Netherlands, Denmark, and Norway. Gender was not included as an analytical concept in the original outline of the project, but in our later work with the empirical material from Denmark and Norway it has proven very fruitful to look at the transmission of memories from a gender perspective.[4] In the following, we shall draw in particular on our analysis of the material from Denmark and Norway, but some of the general findings from the larger project will also be included in the analysis.

In light of the overall findings of the study, the following observations can be placed within a process of transformation of nationalist master narratives about World War II into memory cultures in which national and global/cosmopolitan traits can be observed, partly re-informing each other. This process, enforced by the emerging and expanding field of Holocaust education, can be said to have replaced an emphasis on heroism with a focus on suffering and victimization in Western Europe, whereas Eastern European memory cultures went through very different transformative processes after the end of the Soviet Union. Here, nationalism, and with it, heroism, has experienced a renaissance rather than a dissolving into a rather amorphous form of global mourning.

The Svendsen Family—a Glimpse into the Family Archive

Before venturing further, we present another interview excerpt, this time from a group interview in a Danish family. In this interview all three generations were present: grandmother Ida Svendsen (born 1920), daughter Karin Esman (born 1948), and granddaughter Susie Jones (born 1971). As a methodological rule in the overall project, each person was first interviewed individually about his/her memory/historical consciousness about

World War II, and afterwards the family members were gathered for a joint interview.

Just before the excerpt presented below, Ida, aged eighty-four at the time of the interview, told a story from the war period. During the war, she was employed as a maid by the Blendstrup family. Mr. Blendstrup was active in the Resistance, and one day the Gestapo arrived at the house in order to arrest him. The whole family had fled the house, and Mrs. Blendstrup and the maid Ida were hiding in some bushes in the garden, carrying the small baby Kirsten in a laundry basket. Afterwards, Ida had to remain alone in the house taking care of the baby for about a week, before she was able to take the baby to Copenhagen, where she and the baby hid again for some days until the child could be reunited with her parents. After Ida had finished her story, the interview evolved in the following way:

> Interviewer: [To Karin (daughter) and Susie (granddaughter)] Have you ever heard these stories before?
>
> Karin and Susie: No.
>
> Interviewer: About the ones who were taken?
>
> Susie: Not at all.
>
> Ida: No, you definitely wouldn't have!
>
> Susie: Only that part about the bushes and ... and Kirsten. But till now I never got that about the laundry basket, and that Ms. Blendstrup went as well.
>
> Ida: Oh yes. She was with me, because at that point she didn't know what to do. The question was if they would catch Blendstrup, because he was supposed to be smuggled to Sweden and they didn't know when that could happen.
>
> Interviewer: [to Susie] But are you really surprised to hear this?
>
> Susie: No, I'm surprised that... No, I think that it is strange that grandmother didn't tell... that she didn't feel the need to tell this at any point. And then I think that it was so awful that you wouldn't want to [talk about it] at all.
>
> Ida: It's been so long.
>
> Susie: And then I immediately wonder what my grandfather didn't get to tell, because I'm sure he experienced a thing or two.

In the following discussion, this excerpt will be used to exemplify the general features we want to point out, because the patterns to be presented are widespread in both the Danish and the Norwegian material, as a whole. We shall suggest three analytical dimensions in order to contextualize and elaborate on the diverse ways in which the gender category plays a part in the culture of memory, both when it comes to investigating the *content* of memories and the *transmission* of memories throughout generations. The analytical dimensions suggested are: the family as a site of commemoration, national cultures of memory, and discourses of the past.

The Family as a Site of Commemoration

The family often represents a community with strong emotional ties between its members. Furthermore, research shows that making sense of the past within the family and in relation to family history often seems more relevant to people than public or national history as, for example, presented in schools.[5] Making sense of the (family) past often plays an important role in creating and maintaining the family as a community as well as constituting an important space for building and forming historical consciousness.[6] Yet, engaging with the past within the family does not take the form of "formalized" situations where family members gather and tell complete narratives of "what happened." Instead, the past seems to slip into the present in glimpses or as short references to episodes. In that sense, the family archive consists of a collection of narrative fragments rather than a whole set of fixed, linear stories. This fragmentary form keeps the "family archive" open to joint processes of (re)constructing episodes from the past, and in a way this practice of joint recollection is what defines the family as a group with a specific history and common identity, processes which have been described as "communicative envisioning."[7] The openness allows listeners to fill in the narrative gaps with their own individual interpretations. At the same time, there is an ongoing adjustment between narrator and listeners, in order to ensure that the story told or referred to is adjusted to the expectations and situational necessities within the family constellation. This allows individual family members to maintain what, at times, can turn out to be quite different versions of the "family story" without threatening the sense of unity within the family–as long as their interpretation fits into the shared normative frame of reference of other family members.

In this context, the Svendsen interview illustrates the fragmentary form of the family archive. The comment of granddaughter Susie on what was new to her in the story of the grandmother's escape points to how this story had been stored away as what one might call "iconic fragments" in her version of the family archive:

> Susie: Only that part about the bushes and … and Kirsten. But till now I never got that about the laundry basket, and that Ms. Blendstrup went as well.

There is also her odd comment that, in one way, she already knew this story, yet, on the other hand, she wondered why her grandmother never told it, using a kind of popular psychology of repression of bad memories as her frame of explanation. Still, her comment may point to the fact that her grandmother never really told this version of the story, with such detail and coherence regarding what happened after they had hidden in the bushes. However, at the same time, fragments of the story have managed to find their way into the imagination of the granddaughter. As diverse and fragmented as it may seem, we shall now argue that the content of the family archive is by no means incidental or arbitrary.

The National Culture of Memory

Another significant feature of the family as a site of commemoration is how it can be positioned as an intersection between public and private memory. As we argued above, family memory is bound up with emotions, personal meaning, and identification, and it is connected to individual or biographical memories of family members. Simultaneously, family memory is deeply inscribed into collective discourses of the past, in the sense that the more widespread public or national cultures of memory constitute an interpretative framework for the memories maintained in the family archive. This framework can be characterized as consisting of publicly circulating images conveyed through education, the media, public acts of commemoration, etc.[8] From this perspective, memory work in families not only negotiates family identity and unity amongst family members, but it also positions and balances family memory within a broader community—in this case, first and foremost, the nation. Our analysis shows how this negotiation most often seeks to bring family memory into accordance with broader societal patterns of interpretation.

In both Denmark and Norway, the national culture of memory of World War II can be summed up in what has been termed the "basic narrative" of the occupation in Denmark and Norway respectively. The concept of the "basic narrative" and the elaboration of its content have been developed by the Norwegian ethnologist Anne Eriksen and the Danish historians Claus Bryld and Anette Warring.[9] Thorough analysis of the public culture of memory and commemoration of World War II in Norway and Denmark shows that in spite of very different courses of events in the two countries during the German occupation, the storylines created in the aftermath of the war are almost identical. The concept of the "basic narrative" refers to the way the history of the German occupation in both countries has been reduced to a mythically loaded storyline. It is a storyline about a small country in a state of emergency, which is presented as a "dark parenthesis" in the history of this nation. Yet, the dark times are loaded with positive signification for the nation, for they are characterized as times when the whole people gathered in defense of their national values against the powerful external enemy. This defense took the form either of open or of discreet resistance. Here, a national imaginary arises out of a symbolically and morally re-created national community where political and social differences are overcome and omitted. The construction of this uplifting narrative comes at a price, and it keeps on drawing lines in the culture of memory of World War II in both countries. First, this national compromise has meant harsh stigmatization and exclusion of any person or group branded as a traitor or internal enemy. This branding has been applied not only to various groups such as members of the National Socialist parties volunteers for the German army but also to any form of behavior understood as collaboration, from doing business with Germans to having romantic/sexual relationships with them. Second, the idea of the united nation has suppressed other political and social conflicts and differences that existed before, during, and after the occupation.

Turning back to our empirical example, we see how the story of the escape and rescue of Mr. Blendstrup and his family—as well as the way Ida takes part in this story—is more than just a dramatic and exciting narrative. It also connects the private memories of the family with the national culture of memory, and it positions the family on the "right and bright" side within the national community. Two conclusions can be drawn from this very widespread feature of the intersection of the family and national culture of memory: Even though family history can be seen as intimate and personal history in opposition to "official history," it is still the national culture of memory which defines what counts as history at all, i.e., what is considered worth remembering, telling, and retelling within the family setting. Moreover, it is also within the national framework that the moral coordinates of history are set and family history is told and attuned in accordance.[10]

Discourses of the Past

While national cultures of memory can be said to set the stage for what is represented as "real history," we also want to draw upon a more general analytical perspective that we have chosen to call "discourses of the past." What is decisive here is the fact that cultural representations of the past only become meaningful when used and attached with meaning by individuals and groups. Drawing on Michel Foucault's analysis of power-knowledge relations as well as on the concept of hegemony as outlined by Ernesto Laclau and Chantal Mouffe, we want to highlight how negotiation of the meaning of the past can also be seen as related to the negotiation of both what that meaning *is* and who has the authority to define what the historical truth is as well as what its consequences are.[11] Following Foucault, power is to be understood as the power to interpret and define what counts as relevant stories and interpretations of the past, meaning not only what counts as relevant knowledge about the past but also who can occupy a subject position of "knower." Negotiating what should be retained from the endless supply of past events and how these events should be interpreted also means negotiating who "we" are and what should be passed on to future generations for orientation. For example, the "basic narratives" of World War II elided political and social differences and conflicts during the war, thereby making it harder to articulate these differences afterwards without running the risk of being excluded from the national community. In that sense, this "authorized" storyline can be understood within the concept of "dispositive"[12] as constituting an overarching framework of what can be thought and said about the past within a certain period. Furthermore, bringing the concept of hegemony into play, we can see how holding a position of power means occupying a position in which one can articulate or even rearticulate meaning that is considered relevant and valuable within a certain context. Positioning oneself and/or being positioned as powerful can be termed as being either authorized or de-authorized as narrator and interpreter of the past. To sum up, understanding the meaning-making processes related to the past as "discourses of the past" allows us to focus on these processes as relations of power and knowledge through which what counts as relevant stories and relevant knowledge is defined. It also makes it possible to view subject positions as either "authorized" or "de-authorized."

Gendering Memory

What about the gender perspective? Our argument is that looking at how memories are transmitted in the memories of families vividly shows how gender plays its part in defining what and who is positioned as relevant to history. A wide range of research into history and memory has shown how national historiography and memory are gendered in different ways.[13] Our goal here is to show not so much how the national culture of memory is gendered, but rather how the gender category plays out in various ways in the transmission of memories in families. The gendered structure repeats itself within family narratives in the way family members, above all the eyewitness generation, are positioned as agents of history and given possibilities of identification within history. In the following, we look at the Svendsen family in more detail, using it as a case study that typifies a larger number of families in our study in both Denmark and Norway.

The interviews with Ida Svendsen clearly show how there are several experiences through which she could not only attach her biographical memory to national history but also position herself as both an agent of history and an authoritative teller of the past. However, as it turns out, she neither inhabits this position herself nor is she ascribed this position by her daughter and granddaughter, a phenomenon which we shall come back to later.

Like most women of her generation—and admittedly some of the men—she takes the position that she does not really have anything to tell about the war. In that sense, she repeats a very significant feature of the memories within Denmark, a feature which to a certain degree characterizes the Norwegian material: namely the claim that "the war was somewhere else"—in the big cities, in Norway (from a Danish perspective), elsewhere in Europe, even in Germany. Of course, there is strong factual evidence in support of this position, especially in Denmark, the Danes were comparably little affected by the war and the occupation. Still, there is a much stronger tendency amongst women than men to draw on this fact in a devaluation of themselves as someone entitled to talk and express an opinion about the war, women do not see their experiences of shortage, rationing, and their everyday life in this period as "true" (war) history. Two points regarding the meaning of gender arise from the position adopted by grandmother Svendsen. First, it shows how she follows the gendered structuring of the national culture of memory in the differentiation of what counts as history; she ascribes historical significance to public actions, i.e. political or military action or actions of resistance perceived as "masculine," whereas the "feminine" spheres pertaining to everyday life and the work of the household are regarded as irrelevant. Second, she still does not position herself as an active subject of history even when she actually does take part in the first type of action by participating in the escape and rescue of the Blendstrup family as well as keeping the whereabouts of their arms' depot a secret.

This pattern is reinforced by the ways in which her daughter and granddaughter position the grandmother "outside" of history and how they inversely let the grandfather into the center of events. Looking at Susie's remark after the retelling of the escape story, we see how she not only dismisses her grandmother by not really taking her participation in these "dramatic" events into consideration but also in the way she brings her grandfather to the forefront:

> Susie: And then I immediately wonder what my grandfather didn't get to tell, because I'm sure he experienced a thing or two....

Furthermore, both Susie and Karin literally file anything Ida could possibly tell about this period under "rationing" or other issues relating to household activities. In so doing, they exemplify a threefold operation of gendering memory. They position Ida, first, in a "feminine" topos of collective memory; second, as a passive subject of history; finally, they deny her any authority as narrator or interpreter of the past.

At another point in the joint interview, granddaughter Susie refers to the fact that her ideas about her grandfather might actually be a trait of her imagination, but this does not lead her to dismiss him as an authoritative witness:

> Susie: And I also did tell in my interview how I've either experienced or have invented a belief that my grandfather was involved in something. And that there was something with a cupboard between the bedrooms and... And I'm pretty convinced that it is my imagination, but that's not totally certain.

Pushing this remark to its extremes, one could say that the gendered structure of memory inhabits her imagination contrary to the little factual knowledge she does have about the experiences of her grandparents during the war. This pattern is reiterated throughout the interview, as both Susie and Karin stress how much they might have learned about the time of the occupation from the grandfather. As daughter Karin puts it:

> No matter if he was in it [the Resistance] or not ... one could get to know so much more if he was still alive.

This overall pattern of gendered interpretation is to be found more or less explicitly throughout the material from both countries. We want to argue that gender intersects with the meaning-making processes within the family as a site of commemoration. Moreover, the national culture of memory, as well as discourses of the past within this gendered structure of memory, define relevant and irrelevant stories, allocate the roles of active and passive subjects of history, and authorize or de-authorize the preferred narrators of the past. The gendered structure of these processes generally means that women are assigned to, and assign themselves to, positions at one end of this continuum whereas men occupy the other end.

The Use of History

Finally, we would like to stress that the gender category intersects with the question of "using the past." Our question is to what extent the culture of memory of World War II offers gendered possibilities for identification and interpretation. As described above, men and women of the eyewitness generation position themselves along fairly traditional gender-specific lines in their own narratives—as either active or passive, as agents or bystanders of historical events. It should be added though that amongst the men there is also a general "modesty" in seeing the war as having taken place somewhere else, thereby suggesting that they did not take part at the center of things. However, gender differences come out more clearly when we take into consideration how the past is approached and used. Among the men, there is a stronger tendency not only to draw upon their own experiences but also to refer to knowledge about either military or political aspects of the war. Furthermore, it is more likely for men of the eyewitness generation to politicize and to put the war into a political and/or moral context than it is for women.

In the second generation, the picture is quite blurred. On the one hand, we find women who assign the position as an authoritative narrator of the past not specifically to the eyewitness generation but to their husbands by saying that the interviewer should "rather talk to Jorgen" as he would know much more about World War II. Here they reify the distinction between private and public—irrelevant and relevant—in seeing their own knowledge of "private stories" passed on in the family as less valuable than the "factual knowledge" of politics and military questions pertaining to the war. On the other hand, there is also a fair share of higher-educated women in the middle generation who do point to political and moral perspectives on the war, but at the same time, some of them reject the housewife experiences of their mothers' generation as particularly central to war history.

The politicizing perspective on World War II is even stronger amongst the male interviewees of the second generation. Especially when interviewed in relation to the experiences of their mother, there are quite a few examples of the son taking over the authority of interpretation by putting the experiences of the mother "into perspective" through drawing on other sources and other types of knowledge. As an example, we may cite Peter Jorgensen, who is clearly more interested in "big" history than the experiences of his mother and whose approach to the history of the war can be said to be fairly representative, not only for men of his own generation but also for the next generation, the generation of the grandchildren:

> Peter: I always read a lot. I wasn't particularly old when I started reading all these books on the Resistance; I was maybe 7-8-9-10-years-old then. And that was exactly in that period [in the 1950s] when all these books were written, as if we were all heroes... There was simply no discussion about the national spirit, that we had stood shoulder to shoulder. And of course as a boy, you look for adventurous stories for boys.

The general point to be made from this quote is that it shows an almost classical narrative of how boys are introduced to the history of World War II. They start by being fascinated by stories of acts of resistance or direct warfare. Gradually, more questions arise, which lead them to sources such as history books or documentaries in order to understand strategic matters. This might lead them to more politically oriented questions of which countries participated in the war, for what reasons and with which consequences. As they grow older, they get a more varied knowledge of the war, though still with a focus on military and political aspects. Putting this into a "use-perspective," one may say that they start off by using the past as entertainment and excitement, maybe even incorporating war themes into games. Gradually, they become fascinated with the accumulation of knowledge and may develop an understanding of the cause of events. This may finally be connected to a usage of the past as a frame of orientation in understanding events reaching into the present and as a reference point for moral orientation. It should be stressed though that there is no automatic "transition" from one use to the other.

Turning back to the question of gender, it seems that in the third generation some of the distinctive features of the earlier culture of memory merge. World War II is widely used as a reference point for more universalized moral questioning of right and wrong, both in the context of war and in a more general context of human rights, racism, democracy, etc. This can be illustrated by the example of the Norwegian Karlsen family, where grandmother Siri, daughter Margarethe, and granddaughter Grete were interviewed.

Siri Karlsen (born in 1911) was a young woman living on a farm in Eastern Norway, when heavy fighting between German and Norwegian troops took place in early April 1940. Her husband Ole and his brother joined the Norwegian army the day the German raid started and took part in the campaign for a few weeks until the Norwegian capitulation. Many years later, Ole wrote a report about his experiences at the front, which became a source of knowledge and a point of reference in the war memories of all generations in the Karlsen family. Before Ole died some years ago, he took his children and grandchildren on a trip to the sites of his war experiences in 1940. Siri, however, is the only one in the interview situation who has experienced war herself. In a striking similarity with the Danish Svendsen family, it is not her experiences but Ole's story which is a central element of all the interviews and even the conversation of the three generations. However, the more interesting observation for this context is the fact that Ole's story, serving as an ideal and positive point of reference linking family memories to the national master narrative, is interpreted in very different ways by the three generations. We will now present these changes by "using" the grandfather's story and relating it to contemporary phenomena and generalized normative orientations.

When Siri talks about the German invasion, pointing out that her husband and his brother went to the front immediately, she also positions herself in this patriotic framework. When telling about German soldiers coming to their farm and claiming food, she says that she refused to give them any because the bread should be saved for her husband and brother in case they came back from the front. This is her way of marking her patriotic attitude–being a female supporter of the boys fighting on the battlefield. In her story, there is a clear and gendered division of labor when it comes to the resistance against the occupiers: Men go out to fight and women keep the house and the resources away from the enemy. Anne Eriksen has described the extended concept of resistance which appeared in postwar memories.[14] This concept embraces even a "kitchen front." Everyone was ascribed their roles in the mythical play of the "nation-in-resistance." Siri's narrative seems to be shaped by this gendered postwar discourse.

In the interview with her daughter, Margarethe Rognes, Ole's participation in the war of 1940 is also a major topic, but her major interest is not Ole's heroic fight against the Germans–in fact, she does not even regard him as a resistance fighter. Quite the opposite is the case; she regards her father as a person traumatized by the experience of the battles in April 1940 and explains that this must be the reason why her father did not join the Resistance movement afterwards. Even if he was not a resistance fighter during the five years of occupation, Margarethe is sure that he would have been one had he not been so horrified by his war experience. In this way, he is constructed as a "good Norwegian," due to his patriotic attitudes, and even the fact that he did not carry out any resistance activities is depicted as the result of a patriotic sacrifice. Regarding her father as a patriot, she concurs with Siri, but beyond that the differences begin. While Siri talks about "them" and "the Germans" as the enemies, constituting her brother and herself as patriotic subjects, Margarethe stresses that after the war she was taught not to regard all Germans as enemies:

> Margarethe: With regard to the Germans, we always learned that they are nice people with the same needs as us ... and no problem, but he [Ole] was very afraid of power-hungry persons ... democracy meant that everyone should be heard.

For Margarethe, belonging as she does to the second generation which had grown up in a period when Germany was a NATO ally, her father becomes a role model in his democratic attitude—not in the anti-German sentiment which still shines through Siri's war stories. Both of them seem to be proud of Ole's commitment, but with contradictory consequences. There is a turn from a heroic, nationalist interpretation to a more universalistic one, attached to the idea of suffering and sacrifice and oriented toward ideas of tolerance and reconciliation. This tendency becomes even more evident when we look at the grandchild, Grete.

Ole's story is placed in the center of her interview. She knows many details of the campaign he participated in, which means she constitutes herself as an "expert," even though her only source of knowledge seems to be the report of her grandfather. In between, she turns to a position of the commentator, which can be very emotional. This is the case when she relates that Ole shot some German soldiers from close range, something that does not fit into her picture of the nice grandfather. Her solution for the dilemma is to define him as an object and a victim of the warlords. She describes him as a naïve, young man drawn into the war without any control over his own situation. This stands in stark contrast to Siri's proud portrayal, according to which Ole joined the army because of his patriotic spirit. However, Grete needs to avoid seeing him as a perpetrator, which would be the consequence of her pacifist attitude. For her, war—not the Germans—in itself is the real evil. Since the fact that he joined the army voluntarily does not fit in with her image of her grandfather, she has to construct Ole as a victim. She does this when she explains the fact that he did not write the report about his war experiences until fifty years later by suggesting that he was deeply traumatized. Evidently, she does not care too much for Ole's patriotic attitudes; her interpretation has completely moved out of the nationalistic framework into a universalistic one, oriented towards peace and humanity. By "knowing" her grandfather's story and claiming the authority of interpreting it in line with psychological theories of trauma,[15] Grete constitutes both him and herself as moral subjects.

The picture which emerges in the attitudes of the third generation shows that young men seem to connect more easily with the "fact-based" representations of war, and this may work as a point of entrance into a more diversified reservoir of knowledge about the war. This certainly does not mean that girls of the third generation are not fascinated by the action and excitement of tales of resistance, heroism, and rescue, but they seem to draw more explicitly on their family stories and less on other sources or types of knowledge. When it comes to using the past as a reference point for more universal questions of morality, human rights, racism, democracy, war, and conflict, this form of usage is shared by both young men and women, as is the tendency to refer to themes outside the national framework, especially the Holocaust and the Third Reich. This is also the case for an approach to the past based on empathy and identification; several of the young men do show an interest in their grandmothers' memories of daily life and see it as part of history, while young women also identify with stories of (male) resistance fighters. Finally, they are also influenced by the ongoing renegotiation of the national narrative. This more nuanced perspective is both welcomed and used by the third generation to open up space for more reflection on how "right and wrong" may not always be such a simple matter. As one young Danish man has described it: "These dilemmas with the liquidation of informers [committed by resistance fighters] and German girls and soldiers on the Eastern front and the collaboration government on which different opinions exist today and where you can discuss forever what was right or wrong. I don't think I can sit back, rationalize it and say: This is what they should have done. But it has made a great impression, because it tells about how much dissent there is amongst people. And I think it is interesting to see how it can create totally different patterns."

Here, the past is used as a space for reflection where the younger generation often asks the question "what would I have done," without having a clear answer. In that sense, they view the past from a moral, but not a moralizing, perspective.

Conclusion

Traditional, patriotic narratives, authorizing male heroes and placing patriotic women in the second row of silent supporters, are used by the third generation in radically new ways. Drawing on the same stories that their grandparents have told, heroism and patriotism are replaced by universalistic values and a tendency towards moralization, if not victimization. Here, young men and women share almost "equal opportunities," when it comes to the authority of speaking about and sometimes even "in the name of the past," drawing parallels, comparisons, and conclusions with regard to contemporary problems. One might—reasonably—argue that the fascination of and interest in "hard facts" constitute another, deeper authority of truth-definition and interpretation than more empathy-based ways of relating to the past. However, history culture, as it appears today in Western European societies, is influenced more and more by the media which produce empathy, the "authentic voice," creating identification and proximity and promoting a tendency to "learn lessons from history," even though the past is hardly ever treated in a manner that is critical toward sources. What we see is that young women and men are prepared to play the "truth-power game" in contemporary societies.

As indicated in the introduction, these findings might be contrasted by observations from Eastern European memory cultures. Here, the impact of a cosmopolitan memory culture, related to Holocaust education and carrying along "feminine" virtues of empathy and mourning, stands in stark contrast to a reinforced nationalism, cultivating virility and heroism. However, media representations of World War II and the Holocaust become transnational references of memory cultures. Young people from all over Europe visit memorial sites as a part of exchange programs and student encounters, something Bodo von Borries describes as an important and maybe the most powerful element of historical reconciliation in Europe.[16] This means the influencing factors of memory cultures start to merge and with them, possibly, gendered scripts of "heroes," "villains," and "victims." As such, it would be interesting to conduct longitudinal comparative studies investigating the impact of European integration on the gendered scripts of memory cultures in Eastern and Western European countries.

Notes

1. We use the concept of historical consciousness coined by the German historian Ernst Jeismann and the cultural scientist Jörn Rüsen saying that every understanding of the past takes its starting point in present needs for orientation, identification, and future perspective. So, the past has no meaning in itself but has to be made sense of in constant narrative and interpretative processes. See Karl-Ernst Jeismann, "'Geschichtsbewußtsein.' Überlegungen zur zentralen Kategorie eines neuen Ansatzes der Geschichtsdidaktik," in *Geschichtsdidaktische Positionen. Bestandsaufnahme und Neuorientierung*, ed., Hans Süßmuth (Paderborn, 1980), 179–222.
2. History politics or the politics of history/the past (*Geschichtspolitik*) is a concept coined by the German political scientist Edgar Wolfrum saying that references to the past serve as a

means of legitimation for political decision makers. This goes beyond the concept of the politics of commemoration (*Gedenkpolitik*) saying that public and official rituals of commemoration are an essential part of the construction of national identity and therefore heavily politicized.

3. The comparative project was based on an already finished German project. This project triggered a lot of interest and discussion with the publication of the book "Opa war kein Nazi." See Harald Welzer, Sabine Moller, and Karoline Tschuggnall, *Opa war kein Nazi: Nationalsozialismus und Holocaust im Familiengedächtnis*, Unter Mitarbeit von Olaf Jensen (Frankfurt, 2002); More information on both projects can be found on this homepage: www.memory-research.de; accessed on 14 September 2011.

4. See Claudia Lenz, *Haushaltspflicht und Widerstand. Erzählungen norwegischer Frauen über die deutsche Besatzung 1940-45 im Lichte nationaler Vergangenheitskonstruktionen* (Tübingen, 2003); Claudia Lenz and Isabella Mattauschek, "Geschichtspolitik und Erinnerungskultur in Dänemark und Norwegen aus der Perspektive intergenerationeller Tradierung," in *Wissenschaftszentrum Nordrhein-Westfalen/Kulturwissenschaftliches Institut Essen (KWI) Jahrbuch 2004* (Essen, 2004), 65–78; Claudia Lenz and Harald Welzer, "Zweiter Weltkrieg, Holocaust und Kollaboration im europäischen Gedächtnis. Ein Werkstattbericht aus einer vergleichenden Studie zur Tradierung von Geschichtsbewusstsein," *Handlung, Kultur, Interpretation. Zeitschrift für Sozial- und Kulturwissenschaften* 2 (2005); Claudia Lenz, "Zwischen nationalem Verrat und romatischer Liebe. Zur diskursiven (Ent-)Politisierung sexueller Verhältnisse zwischen norwegischen Fauen und deutschen Soldaten," in *Politische Gesellschaftsgeschichte im 19. und 20. Jahrhundert*, eds., Henning Albrecht, Gabriele Boukrif, Claudia Bruns, and Kirsten Heinsohn (Hamburg, 2006), 133–147.

5. See Roy Rosenzweig and David Thelen, *The Presence of the Past: Popular Uses of History in American Life* (New York, 1998) quoted in Bernard Eric Jensen, *Historie–livsverden og fag* (Copenhagen, 2003).

6. Welzer et al. (see note 3).

7. Harald Welzer, Sanine Moller, and Karoline Tschuggnall, *Familiengedächtnis. Über die Weitergaber der deutschen Vergangenheit im Gespräch zwischen den Generationen* (Frankfurt/Main, 2002); Olaf Jensen, *Geschichte machen. Strukturmerkmale des intergenerationellen Sprechens über die NS-Vergangenheit in deutschen Familien* (Tübingen, 2004).

8. See Jensen (see note 5).

9. Anne Eriksen, *Det var noe annet under krigen. 2. Verdenskrig i norsk kollektivtradisjon* (Oslo, 1995); Claud Bryld and Anette Warring, *Besættelsestiden som kollektiv erindring. Historie- og traditionsforvaltning af krig og besættelse 1945–1997* (Roskilde, 1998); See also Anette Warring, "Køn, seksualitet og national identitet," *Historisk Tidsskrift* 2 (1994).

10. This mechanism was shown very strongly in the German part of the project "Traditions of Historical Consciousness." See Welzer et al. (see note 3).

11. Michel Foucault, *Dispositive der Macht. Über Sexualität, Wissen und Wahrheit* (Berlin, 1978); Ernesto Laclau and Chantal Mouffe, *Hegemonie und radikale Demokratie. Zur Dekonstruktion des Marxismus* (Vienna, 2000).

12. Foucault (see note 11).

13. Sylvia Paletschek and Sylvia Schraut, eds., *The Gender of Memory Cultures of Remembrance in Nineteenth- and Twentieth-Century Europe* (New York, 2008).

14. See Eriksen (see note 9).

15. "Trauma" is maybe one of the most popularized theoretical concepts framing the interpretations of the members of the third generation in our study.

16. Bodo von Borries, "Coping with Burdening History," in *Historicizing the Uses of the Past. Scandinavian Perspectives on History Culture, Historical Consciousness and Didactics of History Related to World War II*, eds., Helle Bjerg, Erik Thorstensen, and Claudia Lenz (Bielefeld, 2011).

Chapter 3

THE MEMORY-MARKET DICTUM
Gauging the Inherent Bias in Different Data Sources Common in Collective Memory Studies

● ● ● ● ● ● ● ● ● ● ● ● ● ● ●

Mark A. Wolfgram

Collective Memory and Political Science

"Building the new Europe" has been a buzzword for many decades and—like the construction of national political systems before it—necessarily entails the creation of numerous new narratives and symbols, all buttressed by emotive collective memories and disseminated through dominant media and technologies. Scholars working in the field of culture, symbols, identity, and memory often assume the a priori importance of their subject matter, but there is still extensive skepticism—beyond this intellectual community—that any of this matters or, if such importance is recognized, that methods and data necessary to substantiate the hypothesized impact exist. Studying culture and memory is like trying to nail a pudding to a wall—as someone once quipped—perhaps especially when one devotes attention to the still ambiguous Europeanization of these collective memories.

In this chapter, I take a step back from the normal political science approach toward culture, memory, and European studies to examine more basic conceptual and methodological dynamics. I intend to provide an intellectual justification for the importance of a culturalist approach to the study of politics that also encompasses a focus on collective memory dynamics, and after a brief methodological critique of many existing studies, I offer a more promising way forward. The utility of the memory-market dictum, which highlights supply and demand issues, consumption of media products, the role of capital, and the construction of collective memories as inherently social processes and not mere social objects, is demonstrated through an empirical analysis of several television productions in postwar Germany. This theoretical discussion and case study demonstrate a way to capture identity and collective memory formation at the European level—or at the least, an indication of where to look.

Let me begin with a brief defense of collective memory studies in the discipline of political science. While this may not be necessary for many other disciplines such as anthropology, sociology, and history, political scientists have placed their discipline at a distinct disadvantage when it comes to dealing with culture because of the way in which many in the discipline conceptualize power. For this reason, the culturalist perspective remains somewhat on the margins of the discipline.

I take as my starting point Abner Cohen's discussion of what he calls the "two major variables" with which social scientists need to concern themselves: "symbolic action and power relationships."[1] Writing in the early 1970s, Cohen noted specifically that political scientists were reluctant, unsure, or—more likely—uninterested in studying symbolic action.[2] According to Ross, by 1997 there was little evidence that the culturalist tradition had done much to establish itself in political science except on the margins, although he now correctly notes that progress has been made over the past decade.[3] Indeed, the work of Murray Edelman, Richard Merelman, Andrei Markovits, Marc Howard Ross, Michael Schatzberg, James C. Scott, and others has been followed more recently by a couple of edited volumes by Edward Schatz, Eric Langenbacher and Yossi Shain, which highlight the scholarship of those working to bring cultural analysis to comparative politics and international relations.[4]

Writing in 1974, Cohen said of political scientists and their attempts to deal with culture, "Above all, they suffer from an implicit assumption that political symbols are consciously intended symbols and when some of them write of 'political socialization' their accounts are mechanical and unidimensional."[5] Thus, we can see part of the reason for the title of Cohen's work, *Two-Dimensional Man,* the two-dimensions referring to both symbolic action and power relations. What Cohen is pointing to is the dependence of political scientists on viewing all human action through the pursuit of goals guided by conscious and intentional action—in short rational choice. In his most recent work, Ross is moving in the same direction as Cohen, toward a two-dimensional view of human action, by noting that such rational choice and intentionalist explanations lack, "thoughtful consideration of where interests come from in the first place, how interests get defined in specific cultural contests, and the ways that culture structures appropriate ways to pursue them."[6] By ignoring the symbolic action part of the equation, a good deal of political science risks resting on the tautological argument of answering, "Why did they do that?" with "It was in their interest to do so."

The culturalist approach wants to answer yet another question, "Why did they come to view their interests in that manner?"

One way in which we can think about Cohen's distinction between symbolic action and power relationships is to highlight the difference between the immaterial (symbolic) and the material (power). As Cohen argues, humans can be driven to action by either symbols or material power, and by conscious and nonconscious processes. Political scientists tend to focus primarily on material power, and treat its pursuit as a process of conscious reflection, largely to the exclusion of nonconscious processes.

Myths and stories about the past matter, and nonconscious processes and decisions fill our lives. The neuroscientist Antonio Damasio, in writing about the development of human consciousness as an outcome of an evolutionary process, notes that storytelling is the central means through which collectivities of conscious minds come together and give meaning to human suffering and also attempt to regulate that suffering. It is through stories and myths that these communities create norms of behavior, which allow culture and civilization to take form.[7] And what is the process of collective memory formation if not a specific type of storytelling? Anthropologist David Kertzer puts it nicely when he writes, "In short, people are not merely material creatures, but also symbol producers and symbol users. People have the unsettling habit of willingly, even gladly, dying for causes that oppose their material interests, while vociferously opposing groups that espouse them. It is through symbols that people give meaning to their lives; full understanding of political allegiances and political action hinges on this fact."[8] By going back to ancient Greece and looking at their explanations of human behavior, Richard Ned Lebow has argued that social scientists need to consider both the appetite for material wealth as well as the nurturing of the spirit or self-esteem.[9] Lebow argues that Western societies, especially since the Enlightenment, have tended to focus on appetite to the exclusion of spirit.

We can see parallels in the work of all these authors. Cohen's use of the words "symbolic action" and "power relations" is somewhat unfortunate, because it suggests that "power" only exists in the form of physical coercion and control, which is not what he means at all. Rather, as with Ross, Lebow, Kertzer, Edelman and others, Cohen wants to emphasize that both the symbolic order and material power relations can drive people to action.[10] Victor Turner, drawing upon the work of Wilhelm Dilthey, also wrote about social drama, myth, and narrative as a symbolic force in the lives of individuals; I'll return to Turner in the next section.[11] For Turner, as well as all of these other authors, storytelling and narratives are an essential component of understanding and explaining human motivations and behavior.

Meaning and Death

Collective memory studies should play a central role in how we think about the creation of meaning in human societies, because it is through an understanding of the past that humans generate meaning and quite often political legitimacy. One's right to rule or to speak in public is often based on one's claim to be descended from or connected to the dead ancestors. For the modern social scientist, this may appear more obvious in more so-called primitive societies rather than his own,[12] but think of how often modern politicians reach back into history to try and legitimize current policies. In American politics, to call upon Washington, Jefferson, the "Founding Fathers," Roosevelt, or Reagan is to invoke the symbolic power of the dead ancestors. This is especially true following massive loss of life in modern warfare or in preparing a country for those sacrifices in a new war. The dead are some of the most powerful and ambiguous symbols in both primitive and modern societies.

Although Victor Turner probably did not have the field of collective memory studies in mind when he wrote the following passage, his work is quite relevant to this field: "If a given human collectivity scans its recent or more distant history—usually through the mediation of representative figures, such as chroniclers, bards, historians, or in the liminal lens of performative or narrative genres—it seeks to find in it a structural unity to whose total character every past, culturally stressed, collective experience has contributed something."[13] He then goes on, again drawing on Wilhelm Dilthey's work for inspiration, to state, "the category of *meaning* arises in *memory*, in *cognition* of the *past*."[14] We generate meaning by pulling all the pieces together into some meaningful whole.

It is significant that Turner links this process of reflection to human mortality. "Meaning is connected with the consummation of a process—it is bound up with termination, in a sense, with death. The meaning of any given factor in a process cannot be assessed until the whole process is past."[15] I would disagree with Turner only in so far as he seems to define a specific point of complete termination before the assessment of the past can begin. While this may be truer for an individual human life, even there the meaning of that life is interpreted and reinterpreted again and again. This is especially true for the lives of prominent political figures.[16]

I want to pursue the significance of these relationships among death, other kinds of endings, the past and meaning. First, I will take a look at how different scholars have talked about the relationship between meaning and death. Bronislaw Malinowski writes: "The study of 'The Golden

Bough' shows us that for primitive man, death has meaning mainly as a step to resurrection, decay as a stage of re-birth, the plenty of autumn and the decline of winter as preludes to the revival of spring."[17] We will, of course, want to dispense with this distinction between so-called primitive man and modern man, in keeping with Abner Cohen's work and what Mary Douglas has denounced as "spiky, verbal hedges that arbitrarily insulate one set of human experiences (ours) [the modern people] from another set (theirs) [the primitive people]."[18] Nonetheless, Malinowski points to a fundamental human need to assign some meaning to death, a need that is uniform across so-called primitive and modern societies. Douglas J. Davies refers repeatedly to the relationship between death and meaning in his recent book, *A Short History of Death,* addressing the question in the opening and closing. He opens his work noting, "To perfect life's obvious flaws and resolve the persistent search for the meaninglessness of things has been a constant feature of afterlife beliefs."[19] And then closes: "When it comes to the meaning of life, human beings live strange lives. Day by day, society functions on values and beliefs that, at one moment, seem so solid and, at another, can dissolve into emptiness. Grief can produce that switch, as can philosophical reflection or loss of faith … Yet all live, and the drive for meaning impels us to live creatively. As social animals, our sense of life as players in the cosmic game is potentially powerful in challenging us to live knowing that we will die."[20]

As suggested by Damasio above, storytelling is an evolutionary survival strategy for beings that have become aware of their own mortality. It is not by chance that Cohen also addresses death in his work noting: "Two sources of the obligatory that are common to both 'primitive' and industrial man are discussed. The first is the continual struggle of man to achieve personal identity or selfhood. The second is his concern with the perennial problems of human existence, like life and death, fortune and misfortune. On both fronts man resorts to symbolic action, in the course of which he continuously creates and recreates his oneness, and also develops solutions to the big, essentially irresolvable, questions of existence."[21]

It is the struggle to find meaning in life and death.

Collective Memory as a Social Process

If we go back to Turner's comment about a human society scanning its recent past, we see an example of how we should think about the study of collective memory as a study of a social process. What this approach demands is that we need to avoid generating research of "the" collective memory for some group by looking at their cave drawings, television programs, or paintings and then say that this is their collective memory of some past event.

Rather, we should study the process of collective memory formation by looking at the interrelationship of three factors: (1) an individual encounters; (2) a representation of the past; (3) in a given social, cultural or political context. What we are after is the meaning that is generated through the interaction of these three factors. We need to avoid writing collective memory scholarship that tries to find the meaning and memory in the representations of the past alone. These are empty symbols until human interaction with them breaths life and meaning into them.

Looking briefly at each factor and then thinking about its relationship to the other two, I will begin with the individual who is embedded in a network of social relations. We need to keep the individual in our analysis as a unique factor; for each individual, even if part of a group and a shared culture is capable of generating their own understandings of symbols. In answer to the question, "what do you think about that," each individual can generate their own understanding. They may keep this to themselves, or they may begin a discussion–through symbols–with others about the meaning of a given representation. And this discussion will take place in a given social, cultural and political context. The individual will have drawn upon their cultural context as a baseline for interpreting and generating meaning, but they then engage in the transformation of the same context by answering the question.

Second, the representations of the past can take many different forms. I want to give special attention to the political struggle over the generation of these representations in this essay. By way of a brief introduction, it is useful to think of these representations of the past coming to us in different forms. Perhaps the first useful distinction to be drawn is between that of text and language based representations of the past and non-textual forms. Obviously, the two can be combined in many standard ways of engaging the past such as that of a memorial, which often includes a representational structure and then a text to help anchor the potential meaning of the object.[22] The text and language based forms can include oral history, epic poems, books, and language on the internet. The non-textual forms can include physical use of the body in dance or the creation of images through painting, drawing, or digital photography, to name just a few examples.

Third, we can think about the social, cultural, and political context within which people create these representations of the past and within which people encounter them and debate their meaning. Taking each in turn, the social context may involve the location of the individuals and groups in different hierarchies in the society, which can be defined and maintained through both Cohen's symbolic actions and political relations. We might expect that elites in many societies have more control over the processes by which representations of the past are generated. Second, we have the cultural context, and here we can find the shared norms and behaviors of the society, which inform individual behavior but do not necessarily determine it. Last, we have the political context within which individuals and groups struggle for control over the interpretation of the past. Perhaps we could think of each society being located on a continuum from democratic pluralism through authoritarianism to totalitarianism. One probably associates these different forms of governance with different modern types of state regimes, but I would encourage us again to broaden our historical framework and to try and theorize beyond the division between the primitive and modern. In the end, we may still want to draw some distinctions between the two–based upon different levels of technology and how technology may be changing the way we relate to the past. What is important is that we distance ourselves from prevailing thought, which argues that symbols and ritual matter less in modern technological societies and that meaning and meaning creation, by extension, is not nearly as important in modern societies.

The Memory-Market Dictum

With this introductory material in mind, how can we combine all three factors (individual, representation, and context) in research on the process of collective memory formation. The most difficult part of the three-way relationship is to capture that of individuals and the meaning that they take away from different representations of the past. Unless this inner world of the individual manifests itself in some notable behavior or discussion with others, we have no access to it. In certain limited instances, the technology of the later half of the twentieth century offers us some insights into this process on a mass scale. For example, with the arrival of television and radio, we have different quantitative and sometimes qualitative attempts to measure the satisfaction and meaning that the audience takes away from these productions. We may have the attendance figures for certain films or how their popularity compared to others. We also have access to numerous opinion polls, which sometimes draw the individual's attention to questions of what the past means. In short, we may be able to detect trends in how different social groups view the past over time through patterns in their consumption of books, television programs, newspapers, films, museums, etc.

Wulf Kansteiner, following the work of Margaret Archer, has argued that, at a minimum, one can expect some sort of fit between the mass consumption of representations of the past (books, television programs, films) and the views of individuals: "this approach acquires some validity if the representations in question are carefully contextualized, that is, if it can be shown that specific representations found large audiences and faced little competition from other media."[23]

This is a useful assumption and starting point. By studying patterns in mass consumption, we can assume that the consumers are finding something useful and meaningful, something that reconfirms their worldview. This is supported by further research into cognitive dissonance and the general reluctance most people express in engaging with material that disrupts or confuses their worldview.[24] Remember that the worldview is the basis for generating meaning, without which we cannot live and function. Material that threatens to overthrow or disrupt one's worldview will be used sparingly, if at all. This will be especially true if the established interpretation of a war is drawn into question. If one tries to disrupt a well-established meaning for a war and the war's dead, the response can be strong, as we will see in the examples below.

One point upon which we need to reflect further regarding the Archer-Kansteiner assumption about the link between consumption patterns and the views of individuals is the social, cultural, and political context. This assumption works well in an affluent democratic-pluralistic society in which the ability to consume beyond the most basic needs is widespread and there is more or less open access to the mechanisms that allow various carrier groups and individuals to engage in competition over the production of representations of the past. As we move away from this ideal setting, the assumption comes into ever-greater difficulty. For example, if the ability to consume is highly skewed toward specific classes or only a very limited portion of the population is literate, then the buying of books may tell us less and less about the society as a whole. At the same time, the consumption data about books will tell us a great deal about the attitudes and orientation of the educated elites. If we combine a limited ability to consume with low literacy and then place all of this within an authoritarian state, the consumption preferences in books may tell us still less about the society as a whole, as the choice of consumption is further limited. For example, we can expect a better fit between consumption patterns of films and mass attitudes in West Germany than East Germany, during the Cold War division of the country.

We should not abandon the Archer-Kansteiner assumption, as it can be very useful; rather, we need to reflect further on how that assumption might need to be modified in different social, cultural, and political contexts, such as at the European level. We need to think about how that context shapes and perhaps limits the production of certain representations of the past. Let me propose the following generalizable dictum, the memory-market dictum: "As memory makers need access to 'capital' to reach the market, the more market dependent and capital intensive a given mode of representation is, the more likely one is to find it in tune with the times, either with mass attitudes (democratic regimes) or state ideology (authoritarian regimes). The 'capital' will take primarily a financial form in a democratic-capitalist system, and primarily a political one in an authoritarian-command economy system."[25]

The Archer-Kansteiner assumption about consumer desires needs to view the process of consumption as a dialectic, in which producers will seek to meet the wishes of consumers and consumers will reveal their preferences through consumption. We need to not only think about how consumers are behaving but also how producers are making their choices.

Staying with a democratic-pluralistic regime based on a capitalist economy, think of the different production costs and risks that Capitalists take in producing a pamphlet or a book, compared to a theater play, a television program or a film. Following the memory-market dictum and knowing that film is the most capital intensive of all these ways of representing the past, we would expect film to be more conservative, that is to say more in touch with mass attitudes, than perhaps pamphlets passed out on the street. There is a reason why low cost forms of communication have long been associated with underground cultural movements. Although it goes beyond the boundaries of the current chapter to discuss this in detail, it is important to point out the fact that the digital world of the internet has driven many of these production and distribution costs toward zero. The ways in which communication and power function in the pre-digital and digital world of the internet requires a separate discussion.[26]

Returning to the pre-digital world, which is where most collective memory scholarship has been based, we have an excellent example of the memory-market dictum from the West Germany with Carl Zuckmayer's play *Des Teufels General,* which was later turned into a popular film by the very well known German director Helmut Käutner. In Zuckmayer's original play, which opened in Zurich in 1946, the character of Oderbruch faces a serious moral dilemma. Having decided to resist the Nazi war machine, Oderbruch is forced to realize that his actions will result in the death of German soldiers and eventually his own best friend. Along with others in a resistance group, he sabotages warplanes that are being sent to the front. In the film, Käutner transforms Oderbruch's resistance dilemma to make his actions more acceptable for the audience when General Harras prevents the sabotaged planes from being sent to the front and the test pilots are able to parachute to safety.[27] The producer of a theater play could take risks with resistance themes that might offend many potential audience members, whereas the producers of a film sought to take fewer risks. Themes of resistance are very difficult to deal with because they may come to be seen as a moral challenge to the soldier in the field. An uncomfortable question begins to arise—if resistance was justified, then the cause of the war might not have been legitimate; the war sacrifices may, in fact, have been meaningless. The need to find meaning in those wartime deaths will lead to pressure to reject the legitimacy of the Resistance.

This same memory-market dictum helps us to understand and explain the choices made by some West German, public television stations in contrast with the film industry. As public broadcasters, the station managers were not wholly dependent upon revenue from advertising dollars, and they were therefore able to take greater risks with their audience. They still had to be careful not to offend their political bosses as public broadcasters, but the public broadcasting system in West Germany was federalized, giving pockets of control to more liberal and conservative political forces. They were given a mandate to operate outside of explicit political control. As a result, West German, public television was responsible for bringing important and challenging narratives about Germany's Nazi past to the public.

Take, for example, the regional West German Television's (WDR) presentation of the film *Das Haus in der Karpfengasse* (The House in the Karpfengasse) from Kurt Hoffmann.[28] Despite being one of Germany's best-known directors with numerous awards for his previous work, Hoffmann was only able to find the small "neue filmform" distributor to release the film. But this distributor was unable to find any movie houses interested in showing the film.[29] Only after the WDR broadcast the film on television, did a small film distributor again try to bring it to the cinemas.

Karpfengasse was based upon M.Y. Ben-Gaviel's 1957 novel of the same title.[30] Given the context within which Hoffmann was making the film, it is fairly easy to understand why he faced these difficulties. First, the film deals with the plight of Prague's Jewish population during the German occupation; it tells the story from a Jewish perspective rather than a German one. Unlike most other West German films that tried to deal with the Nazi persecution of the Jews, there are no "good Germans" seeking to help the Jews. Furthermore, Hoffmann decided to film the movie in Prague during the Cold War, which greatly upset many in the German expellee community as well as many conservatives. The only resistance against the German oppression and occupation in the film comes from young Czechs. As we have seen above with the example of Zuckmayer's theater production, the subject of resistance was extremely sensitive in postwar West Germany. The harsh German occupation tactics were not something German audiences wanted to learn or be reminded about.

The Cannes Film Festival was also supposed to show the film in the competition, but the organizers had the film withdrawn because of "technical-esthetic" considerations.[31] We now know that the film was withdrawn after the German Foreign Ministry placed extensive pressure upon the French government.[32] Resistance against the film's presentation came from the highest levels of the West German government as well as from below. In my archival research on the film, I found a report from the Filmgutachtungskommission für Jugend und Schule (The Film Expert Commission for Youth and Schools) in Berlin, which voted 5:2 against recommending the film because of its "artistic shortcomings."[33]

This is far from the only example that exists in postwar Germany. The WDR was part of the public television federation housed under the ARD that worked to bring the American television mini-series *Holocaust* to German public television.[34] The WDR was prepared to purchase the mini-series and show it only in its own regional network as there was resistance to showing the film in the entire ARD public television network, especially from Bavarian Television (BR), which is located in a more conservative part of Germany.[35] In the end, there was a majority of support amongst the ARD regional directors, and the showing of *Holocaust* became one of the single most important events in postwar West Germany history in terms of opening up a public dialogue about the Holocaust. Indeed, most Germans, as was the case amongst Americans at the same time, were unfamiliar with the term Holocaust. When the program hit the West German public in January 1979, the reaction was immense.[36] I mention it here simply as another example of how public television played an important role in helping German society confront the crimes of the Nazi regime and that this was made possible in part as a result of their decreased reliance on the market expectations.

Conclusion

Collective memory studies are at their root about how different individuals and groups compete over different interpretations of the past. It is a social process and one that involves contentious politics in which individuals and groups make claims against each other.[37] What is important for us to realize, especially those in political science, is that this competition over symbols and ritual is not epiphenomenal. It is not simply a game played by political forces seeking to instrumentalize symbolic worlds for their own advantage, although this too can be part of the story. Not all that occurs in these struggles is primarily about material power or wholly conscious. As Cohen, Edelman, Kertzer, Ross and others have argued, humans are motivated and driven by both symbolic and material power, or as Lebow argues, spirit and appetite. Dead ancestors can be particularly powerful, if ambiguous, symbols. This means that political scientists, in particular, should give more attention to the culturalist perspective and engage what Jeffrey Alexander has called the "strong program" for cultural sociology.[38]

What the examples of *Des Teufels General*, *Karpfengasse*, and *Holocaust* show us is that while we can start with the Archer-Kansteiner assumption about some sort of fit existing between patterns of consumption and the general view of the masses, we also need to take into consideration the memory-market dictum. We need to think not only about patterns of consumption but also patterns of production and how the two interrelate in different cultural, social, and political contexts. Quite often because of any given scholar's area of expertise, works on collective memory frequently focus on one specific media for representing the past. In our different departments and professions, we tend to focus on painting, photography, theater, literature, oral history, newspapers, television, or film, although we may sometimes combine these in different ways. There is nothing inherently wrong with this, and it makes sense for us to develop areas of expertise within our professional fields. Our scholarship would be impoverished if we only focused on the mass media.

What we need to take into consideration is that the different slices of the represented past that we work with may have a varied correspondence with the attitudes and views of the broader society. We should avoid claiming that any specific set of representations in a given medium represents the "memory" of Germany or the Germans, for example. First, we should reflect on how any given medium relates to the Archer-Kansteiner assumption and the memory-market dictum. Then we can better gauge how the broader public, or a specific subgroup of the society, uses and makes sense of these representations. We need to reflect on collective memory as a process embedded in social relations, which is constantly in motion and ever changing, rather than a fixed social object that is captured in specific representations.

Engaging in such analysis is difficult in any context–even in one as comprehensively studied as the German case or Holocaust memory across Europe. This process will be even more challenging as scholars study an emerging and ambiguous level of political organization, such as "Europe" or the European Union. I do not claim to have a definitive answer. One way forward, however, is clearer. We must identify the various actors who claim to speak for the new Europe or who have attempted to influence European-level identities and representations of the past. We need to study the political and cultural products that such interested actors create, looking also at the dynamics of consumption and reception. Finally, we will probably want to give special attention to how a more Europeanized and transnational process of collective memory formation deals with its dead ancestors, especially those that have died in Europe's wars and revolutions of the past century.

Notes

1. Abner Cohen, *Two-Dimensional Man: An Essay on the Anthropology of Power and Symbolism in Complex Society* (Berkeley: University of California Press, 1974), 13.
2. Ibid., 7.
3. Marc Howard Ross, "Culture and Identity in Comparative Political Analysis," in *Comparative Politics: Rationality, Culture and Structure,* ed. Mark I. Lichbach and Alan S. Zuckerman (Cambridge, 1997), 42-80; Marc Howard Ross, "Culture in Comparative Political Analysis," in *Comparative Politics: Rationality, Culture and Structure,* ed. Mark I. Lichbach and Alan S. Zuckerman, 2nd ed. (Cambridge, 2009), 134–161.
4. Murray Edelman, *From Art to Politics: How Artistic Creations Shape Political Conceptions* (Chicago, 1995); Richard M. Merelman, *Partial Visions: Culture and Politics in Britain, Canada, and the United States* (Madison, 1991); Andrei Markovits and Lars Rensmann, *Gaming the World: How Sports are Reshaping Global Politics and Culture* (Princeton, 2010); Marc Howard Ross, *Cultural Contestation in Ethnic Conflict* (Cambridge, 2007); Michael G. Schatzberg, *Political Legitimacy in Middle Africa: Father, Family, Food* (Bloomington, 2001); James C. Scott, *Seeing Like a State: How Certain Schemes to Improve the Human Condition Have Failed* (New Haven, 1998); Edward Schatz, ed., *Political Ethnography: What Immersion Contributes to the Study of Power* (Chicago, 2009); Eric Langenbacher and Yossi Shain, eds., *Power and the Past: Collective Memory and International Relations* (Washington, 2010).
5. Cohen (see note 1), 7–9.
6. Ross (see note 4), xiv.

7. Antonio Damasio, *Self Comes to Mind: Constructing the Conscious Brain* (New York, 2010), 293.
8. David I. Kertzer, *Ritual, Politics, and Power* (New Haven, 1988), 8.
9. Richard Ned Lebow, *A Cultural Theory of International Relations* (Cambridge, 2008).
10. Cohen (see note 1), 23.
11. Victor Turner, *The Anthropology of Performance* (New York, 1987).
12. David Lan, *Guns & Rain: Guerrillas & Spirit Mediums in Zimbabwe* (Berkeley, 1985), Chapter 4.
13. Turner (see note 11), 95.
14. Ibid., 96.
15. Ibid., 97.
16. Barry Schwartz, *George Washington: the Making of an American Symbol* (New York, 1987); Katherine Verdery, *The Political Lives of Dead Bodies: Reburial and Postsocialist Change* (New York, 1999).
17. Bronislaw Malinowski, *Magic, Science and Religion and Other Essays* (Glencoe, 1948), 6.
18. Mary Douglas, *Natural Symbols: Explorations in Cosmology* (London, 1996), 7.
19. Douglas J. Davies, *A Short History of Death* (Oxford, 2005), 1.
20. Ibid., 173.
21. Cohen (see note 1), 14.
22. For a playful discussion of how images and texts may interact see, Michel Foucault, *This Is Not A Pipe,* trans. and ed. James Harkness (Berkeley, 1983).
23. Wulf Kansteiner, "Finding Meaning in Memory: A Methodological Critique of Collective Memory Studies," *History and Theory* 41 (2002): 179-197.
24. For a recent work on cognitive dissonance, see Carol Tavris and Elliot Aronson, *Mistakes Were Made (But Not by Me): Why We Justify Foolish Beliefs, Bad Decisions, and Hurtful Acts* (Orlando, 2007); Leon Festinger, *A Theory of Cognitive Dissonance* (Stanford, 1962).
25. Mark A. Wolfgram, "The Process of Collective Memory Research: Methodological Solutions for Research Challenges," *German Politics and Society* 25, no. 1 (2007): 102-113; See also Mark A. Wolfgram, *"Getting History Right": East and West German Collective Memories of the Holocaust and War* (Lewisburg, 2011), 21-22.
26. Manuel Castells, *Communication Power* (Oxford, 2009).
27. Wolfgang Becker and Norbert Schöll, *In jenen Tagen… Wie der deutsche Nachkriegsfilm die Vergangenheit bewältigte* (Opladen, 1995), 88-90.
28. *Das Haus in der Karpfengasse,* Dir. Kurt Hoffmann. WDR 7, 9, and 11 March 1965.
29. Several of these historical details are drawn from Peter Daniel, "Kurt Hoffmanns 'Das Haus in der Karpfengasse,'" *Die Andere Zeitung* (Hamburg). Landesbildstelle Berlin (LBS) newspaper clippings archive.
30. M.Y. Ben-Gaviel, *Das Haus in der Karpfengasse* (Berlin, 1957).
31. Klaus Sigl, Werner Schneider, Ingo Tornow, *Jede Menge Kohle? Kunst und Kommerz auf dem deutschen Filmmarkt der Nachkriegszeit* (Munich, 1986), 47.
32. Inge Deutschkron, *Leben Nach Dem Überleben* (Munich, 1995), 130-131.
33. *Filmgutachtungskommission für Jugend und Schule* Berlin 21, Levetzowstr. 1-2. The document is marked "confidential" and is undated. LBS newspaper clippings archive.
34. *Holocaust,* Dir. Marvin Chomsky. Robert Berger, 1978.
35. "Fernsehen: Gaskammern a la Hollywood?" *Der Spiegel,* 15 May 1978.
36. "'Holocaust': Die Vergangenheit kommt zurück," *Der Spiegel,* 29 January 1979; Wieslaw Kielar, "'Niemand kommt hier raus,'" *Der Spiegel,* 5 February 1979.
37. Charles Tilly and Sidney Tarrow, *Contentious Politics* (Boulder, 2007).
38. Jeffrey C. Alexander, *The Meanings of Social Life: A Cultural Sociology* (Oxford, 2003), 3-26.

Chapter 4

Remembering World War II in Europe
Structures of Remembrance

●●●●●●●●●●●●●●●

Christian Gudehus

Every time Europe or European remembrance is spoken about, the underlying assumption seems to be that there is something like Europe, that European countries somehow belong together, and that references to the past, at least in their manifestation as history, are somehow significant, if not of central importance, to create a so-called European identity.[1] This approach is quite normative, since it affirms Europe as a sphere which is re-created time and again in mostly communicative acts pertaining to economic, cultural, legal, geographical, and political issues. Hence, any such affirmative speech about European remembrance is an integral part of its very creation. In this sense, Europeanization is understood as the fabrication of a shared history or, respectively, as shared values rooted in a shared past. An analysis of such discourses quickly shows that they revolve around two closely interrelated aspects: What should the content of such remembrance be? What are the borders of Europe? In other words, which history, which countries, and which human beings are included in this "New Europe," and—here the downside of affirmative discourse shows—which are not?

An excellent example of such affirmative discourse is provided by Hans-Ulrich Wehler, one of the most well-known German historians, who has been using history as a resource to construct a Europe without Turkey, thus arguing against Turkey's entry into the European Union.[2] On the other hand, the historian Karl Schlögel, with his focus on Eastern Europe, expressly wants to give the experiences of the GULag and Stalinist crimes center stage in European remembrance.[3] In contrast to Wehler, Schlögel does not conduct a European identity project based on history. Rather, he is concerned with the attempt at restitution, as W.G. Sebald put it with regards to European Jewry.[4] From this vantage point, the narration of history and stories is a way of compensation and for many victims of past persecutions the most important one. Therefore, it is of an eminently political nature.

In contrast, Claus Leggewie, a well-known political scientist featuring prominently in German newspapers, takes a more analytical stance when critically investigating issues surrounding the national and European politics of history. Although he also discusses what belongs here and what does not, he ultimately advocates—in a very political scientific manner—the development of a culture of historical debate and, thereby, introduces the possibility of negotiating the content of European remembrance. Thus, what is considered to be European is not defined by specific historical issues but by the culture of negotiating such questions.[5] Wehler, Schlögel, and Leggewie all choose their individual approaches to the issue of Europe and European remembrance, and they vary considerably in the degree to which they rely on an affirmative mode of speaking that, in turn, is responsible for the criteria of inclusion and exclusion they develop.

In this chapter, I would like to take the discussion another step forward by analyzing the modes of speaking that constitute structures of remembrance. This requires a step backwards, as far away as possible from any contemporary political discussion. The aim, then, is not to construct an image of Europe of any particular nature whatsoever. Neither is this chapter meant to contribute to the success of a European project. Far more modestly designed, it is rather a review of various modes of speaking about the past.

My argument is based on empirical studies investigating how World War II is remembered, since this event was a meaningful, if not central experience even for allegedly neutral countries, such as Switzerland. Clearly, it has left its mark on politics and culture all over Europe as well as in the minds of many people, even after such a long time. I am thus interested in how the history of World War II is approached in different European countries.[6] The usually central reconstruction of the respective national histories of memory in this article serves as a background for the discussion of various uses of history in private rather than public contexts of communication. Apart from the comparison of national patterns of memory, the relationship between the official politics of history and the less official and more private references to history constitutes a decisive dynamic of remembering. I draw (among others) on the findings from a number of projects with related research questions that were conducted at the Institute for Advanced Study in the Humanities (Essen) until summer 2007. The countries analyzed are

Denmark, Germany, the Netherlands, Norway, Croatia, Austria, Poland, Switzerland, and Serbia.

The concept of a private memory is designed to conceptualize how human beings put the official and public memory of their culture's stories and interpretations of the past to their very own use.[7] The fact that certain issues of memory officially declared to be taboo are kept alive, for instance, in the family memory, is often acknowledged, yet all too often very little empirical data is available in order to validate this surely plausible claim. I agree with Claus Leggewie when he states that a European remembrance cannot emerge by way of determining a specific set of historical events and personages as representative for Europe. Rather, more important are the narrative modes used in order to approach the past. It is in this respect, and this is my proposition, that the different nations vary. This discrepancy between narrative modes, which, I believe, is a more appropriate term than remembrance, is the real obstacle within the political debates about a European memory.

Here, I argue that these narrative modes reside between national remembrance and meta-narrativity. Both approaches describe ideal types that, accordingly, cannot be found in their pure forms in reality, at least not in the countries analyzed. It does not, however, seem to be too adventurous to speak of more or less dominant narratives promoted by institutionalized historical culture as well as the media. The empirical research clearly shows that specific narrative modes dominate political discussions, a fact that was especially evident in Germany and Poland.

The material presented below is based on a comparative study analyzing the possibilities and conditions for European remembrance in Austria, Germany, and Poland.[8] Group discussions with twenty differently composed groups were guided by moderators from particular regions of the three countries. At the beginning and during the discussions, which lasted an hour, six photos were presented. On the one hand, the researchers wanted to know how people who receive products representing cultural memory, and who are the addressees of the efforts made by education policy, speak about World War II and European remembrance. We, therefore, questioned families and different age groups in cities, in the countryside, and, in the case of Germany, in the eastern and western part of the country. On the other hand, the researchers were interested in so-called agents of memory culture, i.e., persons whose profession it is to *make history,* such as history teachers, people working at memorial places, politicians, historians, journalists, but also expellees (in Germany) or Catholic clerics (in Poland). Just as the first category–the families and age groups–is not merely the passive recipient of a message, so does the second group–people concerned with making history–certainly draw on available representations of the past when re-creating history, be it sources, books, films, or monuments.

Germany: Between Meta-Narrativity and Minotaurs[9]

I begin with an extract taken from a group discussion among German university students:

> Moderator: So when you think about European history, what, in your opinion, should under no circumstances be forgotten but remembered in the future?
>
> Jürgen: This suggests to me that I had the chance that whatever I don't want to be forgotten, that this will work.
>
> Moderator: Well… it's a personal question.
>
> Heide: This originates simply from the media. The media make some movies about it. Well, I–Hollywood–Hollywood produces a movie and everyone knows. Well, even fifteen-year-olds then know.
>
> Otto: But, now there is Munich [the movie] somehow. I haven't seen it yet, and movies about rubble women (*Trümmerfrauen*) or something like that.
>
> Heide: Martin Luther [the movie]; well, there everything is again/we're downright being trained. Hollywood trains us.
>
> Frank: Hm. Yes, but that is finally, because it happens there, is a form of constructing a collective memory because all of a sudden these are events which–about which–everyone is talking, and which, at least for a short period of time, exist somewhere.

In the discussion the question posed by the moderator remained unanswered. Nobody talked about events that should or should not be forgotten within the framework of European history. Even when the moderator added that he was interested in the opinions of each participant, the students stayed on a meta-discursive level. It is not that the discussants were not able to focus on the topic; to the contrary, these very clever students of a private university were talking in a "state of the art" manner. As the research material showed, there were more sequences on this meta-level than plain answers like "I think World War II should be remembered, because …" These sequences were also considerably longer and dominated entire discussions, so that the recurrence of meta-narrativity turned group discussions into a "discussion" about the discussion itself. This is evident once more in the following example taken from a discussion among historians (students and a lecturer):

> Sebastian: But maybe it's more about uncovering how these automatisms work which we recognized as valid for ourselves that is, how one's conditioned for pictures which are located somewhere, first of all, and how much this immediate act of locating, this automatic and also non-reflective locating depends on the cultural context one belongs to, including the national context.

Sebastian, it seems, completely abandoned the initial question and instead reflected on the intentions and methods of the research group. This shift generated a new theme that fueled the contributions of all the participants in the minutes that followed. They began, for example, to speculate how Poles and Austrians would probably discuss similar scenarios. Later in the same discussion, when reminded of the core research question on European remembrance, Christoph, a student, responded:

> And one can create some narration from it–that the war was the starting point and then this Europe grew together from it. And one can also approach it differently. Or there are people who do this and then, for example, determine Europe, ehm–the beginning of Europe–to be Charlemagne.

Christoph, too, did not take a point of view, did not express his opinion. We do not know which contents of a European remembrance might be of importance to him. Presumably, he could not answer the question. Instead, he spoke of the ways of constructing the past which, at the bottom line, are arbitrary. One can tell the story either way. With this argument, he is on level with the current academic discussions and the tenor of most German newspaper articles on the subject in the literary and arts sections. History itself, or rather its content, is merely a marginal subject; what is spoken about is rather the character, the structure of the narration. In this way, the content, namely what happened and why it happened, is made redundant in the process of reflection. Accordingly, an opinion on the events is not needed anymore. These examples already illustrate some features of the ideal-typical mode of meta-narrativity. Such narrations: (1) reflect on every form of representation of the past, thus speaking about their functions; acknowledge that selection processes take place and that the discrepancy between an event and its representation can be reduced, yet is irreconcilable in the end. History is, therefore, a construct; (2) have the tendency to regard so-called grand narrations or master narratives with skepticism. Accordingly, they are not embedded in a more or less complex ideological context of interpretation. Especially in academic contexts such a–at least at first sight–neutral approach can be observed; (3) are resistant to fostering the national. History is not a resource to be exploited for the foundation or strengthening of national self-confidence; (4) are fundamentally anti- or post-heroic. The history narrated is negative, dealing with the guilt of the remembering collective.

Thus, meta-narratives tend to be skeptical, anti-heroic, and not nationalistic. This estimation, however, only applies as long as it is made about negative history, and even here restrictions have to be made. The German state, for example, indeed takes responsibility for the crimes of National Socialist Germany, yet does the same only very hesitantly for the colonial crimes carried out during the period of the German Empire (Kaiserreich). Along with this attitude goes the attempt to distance oneself from the crimes, as when using the term "Nazi" (also used in compounds, such as "Naziverbrechen"–Nazi crimes) and thereby indicating, "It was not us, it was the 'Nazis.'" This is hardly objectionable in moral terms, even more so as there is some truth in it. Nevertheless, this attitude relativizes the assumption that the collective would face up to its history, since it is, rather, the history of the respective others. These observations may at first seem to be hair-splitting, but an attitude like this has many consequences within the field of private, historical narration. This is, for example, the case when grandchildren simply do not perceive the anti-Semitism or racism of their grandparents, ignoring their statements dealing with the crimes carried out by them or even turning them into positive stories (cumulative hero-ization).[10]

But what do narrations dealing with history look like? The aftermath of National Socialism is narrated as a success story on different levels, no matter whether this approximation is correct or not.[11] From the West German perspective democratization, reintegration into the (at first Western) international community, economic development, and, since the 1990s, also the societal, political, and cultural treatment and "coming to terms" with World War II are composed as stories of success. In this combination, German history can once more be used as a foundation for the national, and, in this way, the function of history as a resource for the establishment of cohesion, meaning, and moral orientation remains untouched. However, and this constitutes the meta-narrative mode, this happens on the basis of the negatively composed, anti-heroic, anti-national, and skeptically narrated previous history. This is, in short, the description of the currently dominant way of addressing issues of the past in Germany. It goes without saying that this model has a history and emerged from fierce arguments, as it became apparent that these fights might never be resolved and that other discourses might, under different circumstances, become dominant.[12] Later, I turn to the factors that influence these processes. But first, I would like to show, with a second excerpt taken from the German material, that beyond the culture of public memory, many different layers of the construction of history do exist. Only by way of this contrast does it become apparent just how inappropriate it is to speak of a German remembrance or a German memory. Transferred to the European context the German example indicates how highly artificial and, above all, elitist the concept of European remembrance actually is.

The excerpt is taken from a discussion in a family living in a large city in northern Germany. The grandmother, Marlene Marx (born in 1937, hospital nurse, now retired), a German expellee coming from a territory which today belongs to Poland, dominates the discussion with long narratives of her fate. In addition, her daughter Hilde Schneider (born in 1960, accountant), her son Jörn Schneider (born in 1985, chef apprentice), and her niece Iris Grugal (born in 1992, student) are present. The following conversation took place after the moderator asked the participants to describe which aspects of the past were important to them:

> Jörn: I am really interested in the Middle Ages.
>
> Moderator: Tell us a bit about it.
>
> Jörn: Yes, the Middle Ages. The castles, how they were constructed, the architecture, former firearms, crossbow, arrow and bow, swords, clubs, maces, sledgehammer, everything. Mythical creatures, too. [*laughter*] Dragons, Minotaurs, Centaurs.
>
> Iris: They used to exist.
>
> Jörn: What do you mean, Minotaurs used to exist? When was this? In Atlantis?
>
> Iris: Yes, ehm. No, that was the Greek/ labyrinth of Kamos, Minos/ of Minos / I believe.
>
> Hilde: Yes, Minos, I believe.
>
> Iris: Yes.
>
> Moderator: So you have a soft spot for the Middle Ages. It seems as if you are mostly interested in details, technical stuff, but not in history itself.
>
> Jörn: Yes, I also like medieval role-playing.
>
> Moderator: Yes, okay.

After speaking almost exclusively about the grandmother's post–World War II experience, Jörn changed the subject to a completely different experience of history: role-playing. It is remarkable that real historical references (the Middle Ages, Antiquity) and mythical narrations (Minotaurs, Atlantis) are treated as equal during the conversation. Hilde then abruptly changed the topic. A moment before she commented on localizing Minotaurs, but the whole time seemed to have her mind on something else.

> Hilde: What really bothers me and what really ehm is not worth discussing is this memorial in Berlin. I think that ehm...
>
> Moderator: Have you seen it?
>
> Hilde: No! I think it's simply outrageous. What for? Why that/the the memory also lives on partly within people, in history and so on and so forth. People don't live up to it much anyway, I think it's nonsense, I really think it's nonsense because it doesn't get us anywhere. It doesn't get us anywhere; people are not warned or reminded that there was something back then. That's the way it is.
>
> Iris: The memorial? What exactly is it?
>
> Hilde: These blocks that were put up, these stone blocks, you know, that were put up.
>
> Jörn: You mean those from the Wall?
>
> Marlene: No, now these blocks.
>
> Hilde: These black blocks.
>
> Marlene: These blocks for the–for the Jewish memorial (*Judenmahnmal*) and such, such a large...
>
> Moderator: Yes, yes, exactly.
>
> Hilde: Well, such things, you know.
>
> Marlene: These are provocations, too.
>
> Hilde: Yes exactly. Why would anyone do that?
>
> Marlene: That's the way I feel about it.
>
> Hilde: To talk us into a guilty consciousness, to say: you were that once? Well, that's the way I feel about it.

After a brief and carefree excursion to a diffuse and romanticized past the discussion returned to the present. Like her mother, Hilde was against the "Jewish memorial" in Berlin. They focused their criticism on the assumed intention of the monument to talk them "into a guilty consciousness." Since there are no grammatical subjects in their statements, it remained unclear who might be behind this intention. At first, it seemed as if the conversation was changing to a meta-narrative level, since they were speaking of a monument as a presentation and realization of the past. This presentation, however, was rejected due to its negative impact on self-perceptions and its nature of a skeptical narrative, which are characteristics of meta-narrativity. In the following discussion, it should be noted how Jörn dismissed the accusations he felt were unfair:

> Jörn: Well, but then there is still a contradiction continuing to exist from World War II until today. Our, ehm, former Führer in quotation marks, ehm, he wasn't German.

> Hilde: He was an Austrian.
>
> Jörn: There you go. And then the Germans always are the ones to blame, always. Why don't they go to Austria and tell them, yes, you started the war. No, it's always the Germans. That's how it always is.

This is an example for a particular mode of speaking about history which mainly consists of fragments of historical knowledge interspersed with highly emotionalized, interpretive horizons. It is far from the goal of meta-discursive didactics of history to critically deconstruct historical narratives, which, by the way, is implemented in many German curricula.[13] Minotaurs, Atlantis, role-playing, the "Jewish memorial," and "our former Führer" are parallel or interlinking fragments of references that belong to a historical consciousness not yet mapped. This layer of addressing history coexists with the meta-narrative mode of referring to a past mentioned above. The latter mode can be described as dominant in the public sphere, for example, in politics and education, but it is neither the only approach nor even the most widespread in German society as a whole.

Poland: Acceptance[14]

At the time this survey was carried out during the Jarosław Kazcinski government in 2006–2007, Poland was a country whose politics of history represented, in many ways, the opposite of the German model.[15] We can observe stronger analogies than in Germany between institutionalized historical culture and the statements of Poles of quite different origin, gained in our group discussions. The following excerpt is from a discussion with students from Poznan:

> Kamil: I don't know if you know what this is about. It is about the change of name to "Hitlerist concentration camp Auschwitz Birkenau" instead of "Camp in Poland." The attempt to call these camps "Polish camps" just because they were in Poland is a pure lie.
>
> Paulina: A shift of blame by using this name.
>
> Kamil: Absolutely. We do still know it, but the next generations won't know that history was like this and not different.
>
> Paulina: And they will say: there were these camps in Poland.
>
> Tomasz: And since they were in Poland, they then belonged to the Poles, thus the Poles have…
>
> Kamil: Built them.
>
> Tomasz: Yes and that is wrong. One has to say that there are a lot of people, for example, outside of Europe, who, when they hear the term "Polish con-

centration camps", don't have a clue that they were not built by Poles, but that Poles were incarcerated there. They are only Polish because they were in Poland. Such people just don't have a clue about that. When they hear something like that, it is obvious they think the Poles were the bad ones and the camps were not built by the Germans. This definitely has to be changed!

The topos "Polish camps" plays a decisive role in the politics of history of the Polish government. According to the homepage of the Ministry of Foreign Affairs, "Polish camps" is "false terminology in the foreign media used in reference to former German, Nazi concentration camps in Poland."[16] On this page, the ministry chronicled the use of the term by foreign politicians and in the international media. The argument behind this campaign is that, by using the term "Polish camps" as a designation for concentration camps built and used by Germans, there is a great danger that sooner or later history might be changed and Poland might, at least in the eyes of the uninformed international public, be connected to the crimes that were carried out there.[17] The fear that Poland could, in principle, be considered by the world public to have built and conducted the extermination camps Birkenau, Chełmno, Sobibor, Majdanek, Treblinka, and Bełżec is not entirely absurd. Some years ago, the ethnologist Jackie Feldmann found an example for this tendency among visitors from Israel.[18] When analyzing such discourses as the one on "Polish camps," though, the point is not whether they are legitimate, but how they are composed. As the example illustrates, the Polish discourse cannot be described as a meta-narrative in the way it is applicable to the German one. I chose this example, because it was, in fact, the formulation "Polish camps" that was frequently used in the group discussions we carried out in Poland.

As all three narrators in the example above developed the argument with all its detailed phrasing in complete accordance, it shows how strong this topos is and how easily it serves to create communality. Moreover, the Polish material is full of criticism, especially regarding the Germans' lack of knowledge of Polish and European history, which, incidentally, is mainly justified. The Poles questioned definitely had a broader historical knowledge than the Germans and Austrians with whom we spoke. But, most importantly, the Poles spoke differently about history for a number of reasons. It is important and certainly not wrong to assume that Poland as a nation is shaped by the feeling of not being adequately accepted by others (and other nations), and this feeling is experienced also by individuals.

Correspondingly, a strong incentive of Polish foreign and domestic policy, on the one hand, has been and still is the continuous effort to be politically accepted. On the other, a strong national self-confidence is sought to be created. Considering memory from a functionalist perspective, the question why the sphere for skeptical, critical, anti-national, anti-heroic, in short, meta-narratives should be so narrow, can be answered quickly. These modes of narration certainly exist and can also be traced in the data; after all, Poland is a democracy. Yet, at the time of the survey those modes simply had a limited functionality. Consequently, these modes of narration remain (as yet) marginal and are even legally challenged, as reactions to Jan T. Gross' book on Polish anti-Semitism, published in 2006, demonstrate.[19]

A Panorama of European Discourses about World War II

The two dominant modes of narration prevalent in Germany and Poland at a certain point in time, namely in 2007, draw near to the ideal-typical modes of narration: meta-narrativity and national historiography. As mentioned before, these modes of narration are neither the only ones (as demonstrated with the German examples), nor can they ever be defined conclusively, but are constantly changing. Accordingly, every description is just a snapshot that always has to account for two dynamics: first, the dynamics at work in the field of public discourses, especially in politics, the public sphere and education; and, second, the tension-filled and alternating relation between the continuously shifting official interpretations of history on the one hand, and the private adaptations of the past, on the other. Both dynamics are central variables when talking about the possibility and the form(s) of a European remembrance. While there are sufficient, increasingly even comparative, studies in the field of a politics of history, in the broadest sense of the word, for a number of European and non-European countries, so far the private adaptation of history, which is often shaped by the family, has by no means been fully researched. Nevertheless, I now briefly expand on a general panorama of European remembrance of World War II.

Austria, the third country investigated in the study on European memory-scapes, is one of the most interesting cases, since here, as Heidemarie Uhl points out, two seemingly quite contradictory modes of narration and interpretation of the past coexist.[20] On the one hand, when taking a look outward, so to speak, at Austria's relations to other countries, it has for a very long time (and some people, including politicians, still argue correspondingly) regarded itself to have been the first victim of the National Socialist policy of expansion, an assessment warranted by other states that officially acknowledge this position via various treaties. On the other hand, when taking a look inwards at Austria's domestic memory culture, soldiers of the Wehrmacht and their achievements for the then-not-really-existent Fatherland have been and still are acknowledged, while other forms of political and military resistance are hardly ever addressed, if not fiercely criticized. In the 1980s, according to Uhl, a change of both perspectives began to show that came to dominate the discourse on Austria's manner of coping with World War II in the mid and late 1990s. Austria now recognizes that it plays a part in the crimes of National Socialist Germany. An important reason for this development is generational change that took place at different societal levels at this time. Uhl thus refers to a factor which is also very often said to be vital for the case of Germany whenever the changes in discursive modes of remembrance are discussed and to which I return below.

With regard to the Austrian group discussions among highly educated people, a similar finding as in the German material can be observed, namely the use of meta-narration. This is especially pronounced in the dialogues between historians. Andrea Wimmer, for example, when referring to the photos distributed as a basic prompt at the beginning of the group discussion and showing, among other things, dead bodies, said: "Yet, I find it interesting, you said that this does not appeal to you on an emotional level, me neither, and I believe it is symptomatic that the discussion has moved to a form of critical assessment of sources, since none of us have really been touched emotionally."[21] This is a reflection on one's own perception of visual representations of history, but history itself is not an issue. At the same time, and this mirrors historical developments, the seemingly ambivalent self-perception indicated above was addressed. Likewise, the student Paul Strobl commented on the question whether memories are nationally composed, thereby amusing his fellow students: "For us Austrians indeed, since we still don't know whether we are victims or perpetrators."[22] The so-called process of coming-to-terms with the past—that in the case of Austria set in at a later time than in Germany—was even more evident in the sequences that addressed, for example, the lack of memorials. At the same time, the Austrian material also contains sequences reminiscent of the German family, i.e., modes of narration to be located beyond public talking about history.

Another case, remarkable for different reasons, is Russia, where the national politics of history seems to be even more controlled by officials than in Poland. Interestingly, the Russian mainstream, namely those persons who, for example, define the design of schoolbooks, does not deny the narrative and therewith constructive character of history which designates a meta-narrative element. This does not, however, result in a skeptical, antiheroic, or even anti-national narration. Quite to the contrary, the political scientist Leonid Poljakov, a prominent representative of this mainstream, advocates a historical education that highlights positive events and is of a non-deconstructive/deconstructivist nature.[23] Neither should the pupils be unsettled by negative history, nor should their development to sound human beings be impaired by a type of historiography that questions their entitlement.[24] Only because of its originality is the statement of Poljakov worth mentioning. According to him, an unequivocal, positive historiography will challenge the students to develop a critical attitude and students exposed to this historiography, supposedly, are more likely to become critical citizens than, for example, students confronted with the German didactics of history. Nevertheless, quantitative studies paint a different picture. The popularity of Stalin, for example, continues to increase. In 2005, nearly a quarter of Russians would have elected him president.[25]

Even though private historical remembrance in Russia is not as uniform as one might assume, the tendency to tell a linear, heroic, and entirely positive story can also be observed.[26] Thus, the historian Irina Scherbakova reports on how young Russian citizens think and write about history, using material she gathered at a history competition for pupils carried out by the human rights organization Memorial[27] in 1999.[28] It shows that the sphere in which negative history is addressed by the students—and can, therefore, be traced back by the reader—is evidently becoming smaller. The family is of outstanding importance for the survival and, therefore, the transmission of alternative (hi)stories. In Russia, the stories serve as sources for a non-heroic image of the "Grand Patriotic War." The contributions of the students relate, for example, how "a great-grandmother was sentenced to eight years and died in a camp because of a loaf of bread which she smuggled from a factory for her starving children." "All these ... non-heroic family stories," Scherbakova continues, "are met by the unequivocal sympathy of the pupils."[29]

A comparative research project on the transmission of the past, carried out at the Center for Interdisciplinary Memory Research in Essen, analyzed the familial historical narrations and their relation to the so-called national basic narratives[30] about World War II in six European countries (Denmark, Germany, Croatia, the Netherlands, Norway, and Serbia) with a similar design structure.[31] The development of this basic narration—its structural composition—is quite similar for the Netherlands, Norway, and Denmark. They are more or less heroic, and, in the case of the Netherlands, quite factional narrations of countries in resistance that stood together in hard times. This narration underwent a crisis in all countries, was modified and—in an updated version—tends to become a part of a general discourse on human rights. The crisis basically started when critics argued that negative aspects of history, such as collaboration or the stigmatization of the so-called *Deutschenmädel* (women who had sexual and/or romantic encounters with German soldiers) during the postwar period, were hitherto not perceived as a part of the common history and should be included in the future. Even where, at least from the German perspective, almost unbelievable heroic deeds were reported—as in the case of the rescue of nearly all Danish Jews—all of a sudden something criticizable was found in the mainstream of non-heroic historiography. An impressive example of this in no way obsolete self-reflection is the currently best-known Danish actor Mads Mikkelsen. The background for his statement, made in an interview, was his—at that time—newest film. Mikkelsen plays a member of the resistance who is possibly misused for other criminal interests. It is obviously a very reflective and deconstructionist story. After the German interviewer pointed out that the Danes rescued a lot of Jews from the concentration camps, Mikkelsen responded: "This is correct. Yet some of them did earn money with this. Human beings quickly get used to things like war and then they make a deal, they benefit from it."[32]

A completely different constellation can be found in Serbia and Croatia. The violent collapse of Yugoslavia during the 1990s had two fundamental consequences for memory culture. First, the young generation can draw on its own experience with war and violence which, interestingly, does not make the experience of World War II any more accessible, but rather makes it seem more distanced, so that it is no longer used much as a point of reference. Also, narrations relating to either war are blended. Second, the states newly created after the war seem to rely on history as a source of self-justification. Above all, violent deeds from the past had to, and partly still have to, be justified. These goals cannot be achieved with skeptical narrations. Unstable self-perceptions are cured, as the example of Poland demonstrates, with a strong medicine of clarity, heroism, and nationalism. One consequence of the continuously changing official perceptions of history during the past twenty years is a lack of distinct and generally shared orientations. It comes as no surprise, then, that one hero of stories prominent among former Yugoslav families is the smart and not at all principled relative who cheats on and profits by everybody, fascists, communists, democrats. It is rather the structures of official and private narrations than the contents that resemble each other. A similar observation is made by the social psychologist Monika Palmberger when talking about young Croatians and Bosnians living in Mostar, Bosnia: "Although their lives are separated and points of encounters are rare, they speak of youth in Mostar (at times at least) as a 'we'-group. Observations indicate that we can speak of Mostar's youth as a 'mnemonic community' not with regards to their national historical consciousness but in the way they deal with the past in a more general sense."[33]

Factors Affecting Modes of Narration

Based on comparative analyses of the memory-history of World War II in Austria, Germany, Italy, Poland, France, Switzerland, and Russia, Claudio Fogu and Wulf Kansteiner identify the generation or rather generational change as an important factor influencing processes of change in the respective national remembrance cultures.[34] Yet, according to the authors, this does not apply to all countries analyzed. In Poland, Switzerland, and Italy, the generational dynamic is less or not at all developed. The authors hold that this gap results from the traditional way of dealing with history: "The politics of memory in these three national communities was shaped more by the persistence and popular diffusion of preexisting historical images, tropes, and paradigms than by the succession of different political generations."[35] In the case of Poland, it is "forever the unrecognized but self-conscious martyr," in Switzerland the narrative of "neutrality" and "humanity," and, in the case of Italy, "the eternal return of the myth of resurgence."[36] This second factor, therefore, comprises obviously stable cultural patterns in the interpretation and representation of the past which are handed down from one generation to the next, patterns which Robyn Fivush already has proved exist on the level of the individual.[37] Fogu and Kansteiner consider the influence of these patterns in addressing the past to be very strong in these three cases. This factor, hence, also points to the importance of structural aspects. What is relevant is it not the content of memory but rather its structural composition.

Claudia Lenz and Harald Welzer repeatedly have pointed out that within the European context, national narrations relate to European or even globalized modes of interpretation.[38] "Negative history" is, without doubt, such a universal pattern of interpretation that, in conjunction with discourses on human rights, may be incorporated into national and, as a matter of fact, also individual self-interpretations. This, however, occurs especially whenever these patterns and discourses can be related to already existing self-interpretations, namely when they can be used to confirm or strengthen the respective self-perceptions. Still, I would rather argue that these three factors—generation, cultural scripts, and universal patterns of interpretation—do in no way suffice to explain the observed dynamics. Memory is always just a secondary phenomenon, not the cause itself. The basic function of references to the past, commonly referred to as memory, is to provide interpretations and narratives, which codify a present behavior, so that it appears meaningful, coherent, and just. It is the respective behavior, the current views and the political decisions that, among others, are justified with reference to the past. Thus, as has been stated repeatedly, history is a resource for politics at the national level.

History is relevant for other reasons as well, yet its function as a resource for politics is of fundamental importance for the considerations analyzed here. That is, if we understand the specification of institutionalized memory to fulfill a societal function, completely different factors come to the fore, which are decisive for its elaboration. I propose extending the search for factors and also taking a closer comparative look at societies with regard to their political-moral composition. To give a hint regarding the direction such research could take, I propose a hypothesis that, however, cannot be further elaborated here: plural societies, namely those that show a high degree of tolerance for so called minorities, such as homosexuals, ethnic groups, or foreigners, and that have a free press, etc., address history in a rather meta-narrativistic way. In contrast, societies that are rather authoritarian, less tolerant, seeking a stable self-perception, and, primarily, acceptance, tend to lean towards the other type of narration.[39]

A European Remembrance of World War II?

My main argument in this chapter was that it is difficult, if not even improper, to talk about national memories, since the dynamic between institutionalized political and intellectual discourses, on the one hand, and the underlying, often only partly perceivable modes of narration of the private on the other, are not considered. One example of such a one-dimensional approach is provided by Etienne François who suggests that, since persons of different European countries consider Leonardo da Vinci, Columbus, or Martin Luther to be important historical figures, a common European memory must exist.[40] In contrast to this simplistic approach, I believe that, in the field of institutionalized memory, one can at best talk about dominant modes of narration. Until the present, the sphere of private remembrance and its relation to the basic narration have not been investigated sufficiently. At the same time, there are, as indicated, so-called transnational points of reference for historical narrations at the national level. In the different spheres of framing narrations of the past, namely private, national, and transnational, not only are different contents relevant, but they are also differently composed, having different subjects, functionalities, and media of representation.

As far as I know, these relations have as yet been analyzed mainly from a quasi-bilateral perspective, i.e., transnational to national and national/official to private. To give but one example, a research project could investigate the relationship between transnational (historical) issues, such as the Holocaust, compensation/restitution, and human rights to corresponding (but) changing basic narrations located at a national level as well as to the transmission of the past based on individual experiences and interpretations in the private sphere.[41] In this way, a statement on the composition of a European memory can be made, no matter what its exact nature could or should be, rather than through polls investigating whether Leonardo was or was not a significant European.

Notes

I would like to thank Sciences Po and especially Marie-Claire Lavabre for the opportunity to write a major part of this article during my time as *Professeur Invité* in Paris.

1. This is not the place to discuss other factors that might be equally important. A detailed discussion of different aspects can be found in the special edition of the *Kölner Zeitschrift für Soziologie und Sozialpsychologie* from the year 2000, http://www.uni-koeln.de/kzfss/archiv00-02/ks00shin.htm; accessed 22 August 2008.
2. Just to name one example: Hans-Ulrich Wehler, "Grenzen und Identität Europas bis zum 21. Jahrhundert," in *Europas Gedächtnis. Das neue Europa zwischen nationalen Erinnerungen und gemeinsamer Identität,* eds. H. König, J. Schmidt, M. Sicking (Bielefeld, 2008), 121–132.
3. Karl Schlögel, "Orte und Schichten der Erinnerung. Annäherung an das östliche Europa," *Osteuropa,* 6 (2008): 13–25.
4. W.G. Sebald, *Campo Santo* (Frankfurt/Main, 2006), 240–248.
5. Claus Leggewie, "Gleichermaßen verbrecherisch? Totalitäre Erfahrung und europäische Erinnerung," *Eurozine,* available at http://www.eurozine.com/articles/article_2006-12-20-leggewie-de.html; accessed 14 September 2011.
6. Every attempt to define Europe, even if only for a limited period of time, points to the constructive/construed character of these endeavors. Even geographically, the borders are not clearly defined.
7. Richard Ned Lebow, "The Politics of Memory in Postwar Europe," in *The Politics of Memory in Postwar Europe,* eds., R. N. Lebow, W. Kansteiner, and C. Fogu (Durham, 2006), 14–16.
8. I would like to thank Lars Breuer, Michael Heinlein, and Nina Müller for the collaboration on this project. I would also like to express my gratitude to Anne Katrin Lang and Jens Kroh for the critical reading of earlier versions of this chapter, and Jessica Holste for proofreading the English.

9. The following excerpts have already been discussed in an article with a focus on Germany: Christian Gudehus, "Germany's Meta-discursive Memory Culture: Skeptical Narratives and Minotaurs," *German Politics and Society* 6, no. 4 (2008): 99–112.
10. Harald Welzer, *Grandpa wasn't a Nazi: The Holocaust in German Family Remembrance* (New York, 2005).
11. One example is the introduction which Micha Brumlik wrote for the "Lexikon der Vergangenheitsbewältigung." Micha Brumlik, "Vorwort", in *Lexikon der Vergangenheitsbewältigung. Debatten- und Diskursgeschichte des Nationalsozialismus nach 1945,* eds., T. Fischer, M. N. Lorenz (Bielefeld 2007), 9–11.
12. Over the last few years one can, for example, observe the extension of German history over a period of 2000 years. Examples are the exhibition in the German History Museum in Berlin where German history begins in the year 100 BC: see http://www.dhm.de/ausstellungen/staendige-ausstellung/index.html; accessed 7 January 2009; the German magazine *Der Spiegel* with its title "Die Geburt der Deutschen. Vor 2000 Jahren: Als die Germanen das römische Reich bezwangen." *Der Spiegel* 15 December 2008; the widely acclaimed television documentary "Die Deutschen" which goes back only a thousand years: see http://www.zdf.de/ZDFmediathek/content/Die_Deutschen/9602/565650; accessed 7 January 2009. But all of these constructions of history are being commented in the meta-narrative mode over and over again.
13. Andreas Körber, "Die Dimensionen des Kompetenzmodells 'Historisches Denken,'" in *Kompetenzen Historischen Denkens. Ein Strukturmodell als Beitrag zur Kompetenzorientierung in der Geschichtsdidaktik,* eds., A. Körber, W. Schreiber, A. Schöner (Neuried, 2007), 89–154.
14. The following excerpts have already been discussed in Gudehus (see note 9).
15. Critical authors, such as Aleksander Smolar, even state that Polish politics, especially Foreign Policy, has been replaced by historical policy. Aleksander Smolar, "Geschichtspolitik in Polen," *Transit: europäische Revue,* 35 (2008): 50–67.
16. See http://www.msz.gov.pl/AGAINST,%E2%80%9EPOLISH,CAMPS%E2%80%9D,2076.html; accessed 12 September 2007.
17. I have to add that the campaign continues under the post 2007 government of Donald Tusk. Thus, the German newspaper *Die Welt* was criticized heavily for using the term. See Thomas Urban, "Geschichte für Populisten. Wie Polen mit Kritik an ausländischen Medien Politik" *macht,* available at http://www.transodra-online.net/de/node/3102 November 2008; accessed 7 January 2009.
18. Jackie Feldmann, "Marking the Boundaries of the Enclave: Defining the Israeli Collective through the Poland 'Experience,'" *Israel Studies* 7, no. 2 (2002): 84–114.
19. Jan T. Gross, *Fear: Anti-Semitism in Poland After Auschwitz* (Princeton, Oxford, 2006); See also *Spiegel online,* 18 January 2008, available at http://www.spiegel.de/international/europe/0,1518,529320,00.html; accessed 18 January 2008.
20. Heidemarie Uhl, "From victim myth to Co-responsibility Thesis: Nazi Rule, World War II, and the Holocaust in Austrian Memory," in Lebow et al. (see note 7), 40–72.
21. The original quote is: "Aber ich find's interessant, Du hast gesagt, des spricht Dich keines auf einer emotionellen Ebene an, mi nämlich auch nicht und ich glaub, des ist symptomatisch, dass die Diskussion da sofort in so eine Quellenkritische g'gangen ist, weil niemand von uns da wirklich emotionalisiert worden ist. Natürlich sind wir abgehärtet, aber es gibt immer Bilder, die mich ansprechen."
22. The original quote is: "Für uns Österreicher scho aa, weil wir bis heut net wissen, ob wir Opfer oder Täter san."
23. This happened during a conference in Moscow, among others. See Leonid Poljakov: "Kolloquium: die Gegenwart der Vergangenheit. Zum Umgang mit Geschichte und Erinnerung," Moscow 19–20 June 2008.
24. Another insight into this pattern of reasoning is provided by the documentation of the Friedrich Naumann Foundation of a Polish-Russian-German dialogue about the past. Dealing with negative history is denoted as dangerous on the part of Russia, since it

only leads to disturbances within societies and also between states. Moreover, if Poland should address Russian crimes even more pronouncedly, they would have immediately to expect the same from the Russian side. See Friedrich Naumann Foundation, *Gemeinsame Vergangenheit und die Gegenwart. Polnisch-russisch-deutscher Trialog der Historiker und Journalisten* (Moscow 2008), 38–39.

25. Lev Gudkov, "Die Fesseln des Sieges. Russlands Identität aus der Erinnerung an den Krieg, *Osteuropa,* nos. 4-6 (2005): 65.
26. As Orlando Figes has shown in his excellent book on private life in Russia, there is a long tradition of not talking about one's own past as a victim of persecution due to the fear that it might not really be over. Figes, for example, cited a woman who never spoke about her suffering in the labor camps. "All she would say, when her daughter questioned her, was:'I have a new passport. I am clean.'" Orlando Figes, *The Whisperers: Private Life in Stalin's Russia* (London 2007).
27. For the profile of Memorial see http://www.memo.ru/deutsch/ktomy/index.htm; accessed 15 September 2011.
28. Irina Scherbakova, "Landkarte der Erinnerung. Jugendliche berichten über den Krieg," *Osteuropa,* nos. 4–6, (2005): 419–433. Irina Scherbakova, "Erinnerung in der Defensive. Schüler in Russland über Gulag und Repression," *Osteuropa,* no. 6 (2007): 409–420.
29. Scherbakova, "Landkarte" (see note 28).
30. The term was coined by Anne Erikson, Claus Bryld, and Anette Warring. For this narration the inclusive and therefore harmonizing potential is of importance.
31. Harald Welzer, ed., *Der Krieg der Erinnerung. Holocaust, Kollaboration und Widerstand im europäischen Gedächtnis* (Frankfurt/Main 2007).
32. Rebecca Casati interviews Mads Mikkelsen, *Süddeutsche Zeitung,* 23–24 August 2008.
33. Monika Palmberger, "Distancing personal experiences from the collective: Discursive Tactics among youth in Post-War Mostar," *L'Europe en formation,* 357 (2010): 107–124.
34. Claudia Fogu and Wulf Kansteiner, "The politics of memory and the poetics of history," in Lebow et al. (see note 7), 284–310.
35. Ibid., 298.
36. Fogu and Kansteiner (see note 34).
37. Fivush speaks of "cultural life scripts." Robyn Fivush, "Remembering and reminiscing: How individual lives are constructed in family narratives," *Memory Studies* 1, no. 1 (2008): 51–52.
38. Claudia Lenz and Harald Welzer, "Zweiter Weltkrieg, Holocaust und Kollaboration im Zweiten Weltkrieg. Ein Werkstattbericht aus einer vergleichenden Studie zur Tradierung von Geschichtsbewusstsein," *Handlung, Kultur, Interpretation. Zeitschrift für Sozial- und Kulturwissenschaften,* 2 (2005): 275–295.
39. In the meantime, quite similar connections can be proved for the individual level. People who tend to react rather jumpily to, for example, spiders that have been placed in a row of pictures or to sudden noises in earphones, are in favor of more restrictive laws in contrast to those persons who are more relaxed in this regard: "Who reacted more strongly and were more frightened were against abortion, same sex marriage and in favor of house searches executed without a warrant," *Süddeutsche Zeitung,* 19 September 2008.
40. Etienne François, "Auf der Suche nach den europäischen Erinnerungsorten," in König et al. (see note 2), 85–103.
41. A successful example for a combined analysis of those levels is the contribution of Michael Heinlein on the so-called war children. Michael Heinlein, *Die Erfindung der Erinnerung. Deutsche Kriegskindheiten im Gedächtnis der Gegenwart* (Bielefeld 2010).

Chapter 5

✺ch(tung) Europa
German Writers and the Establishment of a Cultural Memory of Europe

•••••••••••••••

Hans-Joachim Hahn

The notion of a cultural memory evolved out of the broader concept of a collective memory that was initially conceived by Maurice Halbwachs,[1] during the interwar period. Halbwachs distinguishes between historical memory, based on clearly identifiable sources and established facts, and a collective memory, which belongs to a group and is associated with commonly perceived experience and shared values. It also differs from the Freudian idea of the unconscious and from strictly individual thought processes.

Whereas Halbwachs developed his concept as a disciple of Emile Durkheim, this chapter will approach the subject matter from a more epistemological approach, making use of Gadamer's hermeneutics.[2] I am indebted in particular to the work of Lutz Niethammer, Jan Assmann, and Wulf Kansteiner.[3] Deriving much of their impetus from Halbwachs, these authors' notion of a cultural memory avoids the proximity to the everyday, often oral, discourse, responding rather to published material.[4] Despite its excursion into literary forms of communication, the idea of a cultural memory nevertheless suggests—in common with Halbwachs—a belief that value judgments are subject to the passing of time and responsive to shifting opinions in a "mode of potentiality."[5] Taking this debate a step further, my chapter will also consider the extent to which such a memory can shape the political culture of a society, thereby contributing towards the establishment of some normative values. Within the framework of literary perception, one would generally assume that great writers and philosophers shape our perception of the world, thereby influencing our canon of values. In order to examine the interplay between a cultural memory and its effects on an existing political culture, I have focused on some of the outstanding

German writers and philosophers who have contributed to the European idea in the twentieth century.

The idea of a "common Europe" seized the collective mind of Europeans toward the end of World War I, when a period of nationalism and a class-based society dissolved into a general crisis of identity, shattering previously held convictions and distorting them as in a broken mirror. New experiences, forged in the trenches, and previously submerged values fused into our collective memory: a deep desire for peace, an awareness of frequently suppressed international traditions, such as humanism, and a common European culture came to the fore. The process of remembering also involved one of forgetting–some kind of collective amnesia[6]–with both developments competing with each other, affecting our highly complex perception of Europe. Most of the early references to Europe here are concerned with a search for new values, assuming that the existing order had become irreparable.

Oswald Spengler's *Decline of the West*[7] anticipated the end of European civilization as part of a new "global" development. The homeland of Spengler's Faustian man[8] is central and northern Europe, and this new type of man is noted for his creativity and willpower but also for a fatalistic attitude to life. He is neither Christian nor humanist and is opposed to liberal democracy. Spengler primarily influenced a conservative, rightwing, nationalist minority of intellectuals, but his critique of European modernism also met with opposition. Hermann Hesse viewed the decline of Europe as a moral and intellectual phenomenon, manifested in the young generation's rejection of Goethe's individualism and their enthusiasm for Dostoevsky and the all-embracing mysticism of his *Brothers Karamazov*.[9] Hesse advocated an immersion in Asian mysticism: "This [European] decline is a homecoming to the mother figure, returning to Asia, to the sources of life … Like all deaths, it will lead to a new life."[10] Other writers rejected Hesse's hope of a European regeneration via Asia's anti-individualism. Hugo von Hofmannsthal favored European individualism and was critical of the obsession with Dostoevsky, since Dostoevsky encouraged suffering as an antidote to human reason. Hofmannsthal contrasts such "oriental Christianity" with its European form based on "a purely intellectual and cultural understanding."[11] Thomas Mann adopted a different attitude to the Christian and humanist heritage, but favored the tradition of Goethe's neoclassical individualism. He wrote his essay "Europe Beware" (Achtung Europa)[12] in March 1935 for a meeting of the *Comité permanent des lettres et des arts* of the League of Nations at Nice. The essay title is ambiguous–it means "watch out!," "beware!," but it could also invoke the military command of "attention" or "falling in line." Mann's diary entries and correspondence indicate that the essay was written to alert Europe to the threat of Hitler's Germany and, in a wider sense, to warn against any irrational mass movements. In this latter respect, Mann was influenced by José Ortega y Gasset's bestseller *The Revolt of the Masses,* first published in German in 1931. Mann's essay hardly mentions Europe by name, but it expresses unease about a collectivist lifestyle of falling in line, with its implicit threat to any democratic political order. He attacks the petit bourgeoisie, since they foster neither an international attitude nor the inclination to defend democracy and republicanism. They despise the "European ideas" of "truth, freedom, and justice"[13] in favor of some ill-defined myth—some heady, collectivist intoxication, a "permanent holiday from individualism."[14] Both authors consider the new mass movements as the gravest threat to their civilization.

Since Mann is so obviously influenced by the Spanish philosopher, a few words about *The Revolt of the Masses* are germane. The masses, we are told, are content to view the state as a machine that provides them with material pleasure at the expense of a democracy, based on individual freedom.[15] Ortega paints a rather negative picture, reflecting the general pessimism of the decade after the end of World War I. He advocates a solution to the rise of the masses: while modern technology and the domination of international markets have rendered the nation state obsolete, diminishing the traditional identification of the individual with the nation, a unified Europe could fill the void left by dysfunctional nation states.[16] The time had come to convert the national into a new European identity.

By the time Mann wrote his essay, the threat from fascist mass movements had become infinitely more severe and there was no serious opposition from European governments. Disappointment over the League of Nations, the unresolved economic debacle, and the resulting mass unemployment had undermined the project of modernity that had only recently entered the cultural memory of Western Europe. The European idea was at this point still far too restricted to some liberal intellectual circles to gain a hold over the public mind in Germany; the old collectivist, racial considerations proved more effective, eventually forcing the Mann family into exile. Mann is particularly concerned about the threat to individualism, especially in Germany, where several youth movements had embraced various irrational messages based on a regeneration of race, class, or religion. These new movements no longer understood the German concept of *Bildung,* civilization in its true sense. The young were no longer interested in personal development, in "individual responsibility and care," seeking instead "comfort in the collective."[17]

Despite Mann's continuing conservatism, his essay points toward some similarities with the philosophy of the Frankfurt School, in particular with their fear of the development of a pleasure industry and mass consumerism. Mann hankers after an earlier epoch, "which not only believed in the blessings of liberal democracy, but also in a socialism ... that was committed to nurture and instruct the masses, to encourage their participation in scholarship, civilization, the arts, the benefits of culture."[18] Twentieth-century mass movements have abandoned this "purer humanism" in favor of "all kinds of secret sciences, demi-knowledge, and charlatanism," believing that "reason has been abolished and that intellect can be pilloried."[19] Mann speaks up for a Europe that is founded on the principles of "the Christian attempt to change the world and on the altruistic-humanitarian character of the French Revolution."[20] His position is indicative of a European form of modernism, as these elaborations on the normative principles of truth illustrate: "The problem of truth, i.e., of truth as an absolute concept and its relationship to life ... is a problem of the most serious moral gravity." With oblique reference to Nietzsche's philosophy, Mann accepts that truth has to stand "in the service of life."[21] His next sentence qualifies the earlier life-promoting statement, adding that "only truth can promote life. If truth is not a universal, absolute given, but is conceived as subject to change, then an intellectual's concern for truth must be the more profound, conscientious, and sensitive." Truth must "have no regard for the hate expressed by the insensitive, the fearful and obdurate, for those interested only in the preservation of that which has become evil or corrupted."[22]

Read in isolation, Mann's essay amounts to little more than a condemnation of the fascist mass movement and its adoption by the younger generation. Challenging this trend, Mann argues in favor of a "militant humanism,"[23] a new form of humanism that responds to the dangers of war associated with fascism. Traditional forms of humanism were too generous, too tolerant, but this new humanism should stand up to fanaticism in defense of the principles of freedom, genuine tolerance, and the right to question. For a better understanding of Mann's essay, it should be read in the wider context of the debate among writers and philosophers, concerned about the future of Europe.

We begin with the European debate within the Mann family. Thomas's brother Heinrich had long been a champion of the European Enlightenment, of an intellectual republicanism, and of reconciliation between Germany and France. Indeed, the famous quarrel between the two brothers preceded World War I. In an essay written in 1916, Heinrich traces a European tradition back to its roots in the Roman Empire, describing this foundation as the supremacy of reason over primitive emotions: "The revolt of reason, the dignity of the human spirit, has been our heritage since the days of ancient Greece."[24] Heinrich sees this heritage under threat from three directions, the "Asian chaos," racism, and social injustice. Only a spirit of reason, developed foremost in post–revolutionary France, can secure the European concepts of justice and freedom. Heinrich continued his pro-European stance during the war, despite the fact that only a few German intellectuals had the courage and insight to share his views—Albert Einstein, Hermann Hesse, and Stefan Zweig come to mind. He viewed the war as a temporary hindrance on the road toward a common European citizenship, a citizenship that could once again restore the principle of right over might: "Europeans already have freedom and self-determination; they now anticipate unity and inner peace."[25] Heinrich envisages the concept of a "European House"[26] that will abolish its internal borders once the catastrophe of the war is ended, and he develops this further in his 1924 essay, "The United States of Europe (VSE)." The old idea of the nation-state, a relic of the nineteenth century that had promoted political emancipation during the French Revolution, was now being replaced by a "common European spirit."[27] Reconciliation between France and Germany, promoted by intellectuals of both countries, would ultimately achieve a united Europe, for this is the only means of avoiding the fate of becoming either an economic colony of America or a military compound of Asia. Therefore, Heinrich is committed to the establishment of a United States of Europe, founded on a Franco-German economic union and anticipating a political union with Britain, once the British have withdrawn from their colonies.[28] A change in the intellectual climate after 1918 made reconciliation between the Mann brothers easier. The settling of their arguments in 1922 meant that, by and large, Thomas came to accept his brother's political ideas.

By 1925, however, the earlier Euro-enthusiasm began to fade away. Authors such as Robert Walser and Hermann Kasack ridiculed the Europhiles' idealism; a more sober and critical phase replaced postwar pacifism. One of Robert Musil's characters in *The Man Without Qualities* (Der Mann ohne Eigenschaften), the musician and Wagner enthusiast Walter, despairs about the old Europe which he believes to be "degenerate beyond hope."[29] His friend and intellectual opponent Ulrich, the man without qualities, takes an opposite but somewhat cynical view and gets involved in some kind of peace conference, which wishes to build Europe along the lines of the old "K and K" Austria (Habsburg Empire)– a concept which could be interpreted as a satirical comment on the European plans after 1918.[30] Whereas Musil could be seen as a precursor to postmodernism, aware that the Christian and humanist concept of Europe could not serve as the foundation for a new group identity, Thomas Mann's son Klaus took up the cudgel of modernism. His essay "The Youth and Pan-Europa" (Die Jugend und Paneuropa), published in 1930, championed the pro-European case. Anticipating his father's essay by some five years, he is alarmed that the young generation is so easily seduced by an anti-intellectual mysticism, which made fascism such a tempting attraction. "The fascination which fascism has for young people lies, so it seems to me, less in a need for 'new commitments' ... it emerges instead from the deep and ill-fated attraction with violence as such, with brutality as a principle. Both have the advantage over the intellect in that they do not have to convince with arguments."[31] Klaus equates a rational approach with Europeanism, warning that "whoever prefers violence against the intellect has himself ceased to be a European." Europe's young generation is in the grip of a Western intellectual crisis, which has a general crisis of faith at its root. Searching for a way out, he finds the solution neither in modern socioeconomics nor in the conservative neo-Catholicism of Henri Massis, nor in some inward-looking Euro skepticism, as displayed by the neoromantic generation and their preoccupation with matters of race. Klaus is critical of any definition that would restrict the European spirit to a medieval concept of the Christian-Latinate tradition that discharges its venom against communism and Russia. Through his criticism of Massis, Klaus develops his own vision of Europe, rejecting earlier sympathies with Dostoevsky's mysticism and the cultural pessimism of Keyserling and Spengler. Keen to extend Europe into Russia and Asia and opposed to the old European imperialism, as well as a reactionary Christian missionary spirit, Klaus pleads for a renewal of European cosmopolitanism: "the genuinely European spirit must open itself to outside influence and, at the same time, preserve its own nature, accept new ideas without losing its own identity."[32] He cites André Gide, whom he describes as "an intellectual adventurer without limitations," as a true European, for he conserves his French identity and at the same time explores other cultures. Klaus reserves his main criticism for Ernst Jünger, the very opposite of Gide. Jünger's hatred of civilization and bloodthirsty heroism have seduced the young generation. He charges Jünger with misapplying Nietzsche's philosophy in that he rejects all forms of charity and social concerns in the interest of right-wing radicalism. Klaus's analysis of German youth concludes that they reject existing democratic principles and portray a cynical attitude towards freedom, that they reject peace in favor of war and relish the opportunity to display a heroic barbarism. He reminds his readers that "politics is the terrain where reason must be given priority over feelings and sensations."[33] He is convinced that modern technology and the international market economy have rendered the concept of the nation-state obsolete. Like his uncle Heinrich, Klaus also accepts the need for economic unification, as long as it is supported by an intellectual, spiritual desire for political unification. He is in favor of a Pan-European Confederation, but only as a temporary bridge towards a far greater "European formula," equating this formula with European humanism, which distinguishes Europe from America and the Orient.

Klaus Mann remained faithful to this European idea, based on freedom, humanism, democracy, and cosmopolitanism. His "Affliction of the European Spirit" (Die Heimsuchung des europäischen Geistes), written in 1949, reiterates his prewar ideals, expressing unease with Freud's *Civilizations and its Discontents* and voicing reservations about T. S. Eliot's Europe essay[34] and its conservative Catholicism. He sums up his European credo:

> The true leaders of the European spirit, from Erasmus to Voltaire, from Montaigne and Spinoza to Heinrich Heine and Victor Hugo, were not only great skeptics and iconoclasts, but also great believers, believers in the dignity and moral mission of humankind, in the obvious supremacy of civilization over barbarism. They believed in progress. Without this belief, this conviction, they would have been unable to prepare for and bring into being such tremendous events as the Renaissance, the Reformation and the French Revolution.[35]

He recognizes clearly the great dangers of the twentieth century, a demonic obsession with irrational and barbaric forces, and he protests against the prevailing spirit of defeatism, which manifested itself in a wave of suicides among European intellectuals. This same defeatism and "absolute despair" drove Klaus Mann himself to suicide, shortly after he completed this essay.

While the Mann family could make little impact within Germany, despite Thomas Mann being awarded the Nobel Prize for literature in 1929, other intellectuals achieved wider publicity. One person, who became virtually synonymous with the pan-European idea, was Count Richard Coudenhove-Kalergi, the son of an Austro-Hungarian diplomat and a Japanese mother. In 1923, at the age of thirty-one, he published his "Manifesto" entitled *Pan-Europa* (Paneuropa. Das pan-europäische Manifest). Among its signatories were Albert Einstein, Thomas and Heinrich Mann, Sigmund Freud, Rainer Maria Rilke, Miguel de Unamuno, Salvador de Madariaga, Ortega y Gasset, and Konrad Adenauer. *Pan-Europa* held its inaugural congress in 1926; one year later, Aristide Briand became its first honorary president. The movement reflects a widely felt need for a Franco-German reconciliation after the chaos of World War I. Coudenhove-Kalergi was an unsentimental modernist, intent on developing new political initiatives. He considers nations to be man-made, artificially conceived spiritual communities, believing that the pursuit of nationalism has become an ersatz religion for the bourgeoisie. For all his liberal and tolerant stance, Coudenhove-Kalergi represented a strongly conservative group of Europeans with their roots in Catholic political associations, who had played a very considerable role in European politics. While on the one hand praising the unifying role of Napoleon, the liberalism of the 1848 revolutions, and the philosophy of Rousseau and Kant, he also extolled the unifying role of the Vatican and blamed Luther's Reformation for "a second period of European disunity,"[36] which had its legacy in contemporary chauvinism and bolshevism. Coudenhove-Kalergi's vision of a pre–Reformation Europe is reminiscent of the more reactionary views expressed by some German romantics: "One faith, one clerical organization, one spiritual overlord prevailed. There were common morals, festivities, and ceremonies, a common form of culture and life, a common architecture and a common speech–namely Latin, for the Church and for scholars."[37] The Pan-Europa movement provided important stimuli for the Locarno Treaty and the Kellogg-Briand Pact. In 1929, Briand, then prime minister of France, addressed the League of Nations and formulated the concept of a European Federation:

> I believe that a sort of federal bond should exist between the nations geographically gathered as European countries; these nations should, at any moment, have the possibility of establishing contact, of discussing their interests, of adopting common resolutions, of creating among themselves a bond of solidarity that allows them, on suitable occasions, to face up to serious circumstances, in case they arise ... Evidently, the association will take place mainly in the economic domain: this is the most pressing question.[38]

The economic depression of October 1929 put an end to Briand's hopes and the subsequent rise of Hitler rendered aspirations for a Pan-European Federation futile. Coudenhove-Kalergi continued his efforts to create a united Europe up to his death in 1972. His vision of Pan-Europa resembled the model of the Swiss Confederation: "Switzerland disproves the frequently stated assertion that a united Europe would destroy the cultural peculiarity of individual nations ... every Canton has its own distinctive and local patriotism."[39] The Count was an extremely industrious and skillful "networker," whose first wife, the famous Viennese opera singer Ida Roland, became instrumental for his propaganda machine. Among the many politicians he approached were the Austrian Chancellor Ignaz Seipel, Czech Prime Minister Tomáš Masaryk and his Foreign Secretary Edvard Beneš, Pope Pius XI, the French Prime Minister Edouard Herriot, the German Foreign Minister Gustav Stresemann, the President of the Reichsbank Hjalmar Schacht, and Baron Louis Rothschild. He sought to establish the broadest political spectrum, ranging from conservative Catholicism to international socialism, and, in 1922, he even contacted Benito Mussolini, whom he invited to save Europe "in the name of European youth."[40] He soon recognized the nature of fascism and moved over to the antifascist front, led by Benedetto Croce, Ortega y Gasset, and others. He sees his vision of Europe threatened by its own nation-states, but also by American economic competition and by Russian political expansionism.[41] He attracted German democrats and Center Party men as well as the left of the People's Party; the Pan Europa movement settled somewhat to the right of the political spectrum.[42]

When analyzing the European debate of the interwar years, today's more skeptical observer will consider it as somewhat high on pious ideals. It often lacked the popular appeal necessary to influence a broader public and hence has become part of a wider cultural or even collective memory. Nevertheless, these ideals survived the period of fascism and re-entered the public debate after World War II, at yet another crisis of identity. A new sociopolitical order had to be established for Germany and a new European order conceived within which a still rather unstable Germany could be embedded. As some of these ideals became reality, their resonance among a wider public in the original core Europe was strong enough for them to form part of a political–even cultural–energy, which has all the hallmarks of a cultural memory.

Winston Churchill's famous Zürich speech of 1946 (The Tragedy of Europe) reflected much of Coudenhove-Kalergi's concept, but itself became a watershed as Cold War ideology divided Europe and focused entirely on economic issues and on a militant, Christian reactionary antagonism towards communism. In view of Germany's division and cognizant of the growing ideological warfare, most German writers and intellectuals did not wish to be used as tools in the Cold War rhetoric. The common perception of Europe and its heritage of Christian ideals and humanist-enlightenment values could no longer hold; another change in our cultural memory was taking place. In this divided Europe, most intellectuals felt uneasy within this capitalist iron cage of teleological efficiency and industrial expansion at the cost of everything else–interviews by Heinrich Böll and Günter Grass clearly indicate this. Böll defines Europe in its traditional geographic dimensions, extending from northern Scandinavia to Sicily, from Ireland to the Ural Mountains, and into Siberia. He rejects a Europe that is no more than a military and economic giant in conflict with its eastern neighbors and pleads for a Europe that accepts these neighbors and Russia as partners. Referring to a time when Euro-communism had emerged as a consequence of the Prague Spring, Böll reminds us that the origins of Marxism lay in Western Europe.[43] He sees the great advantage of the European Community as liberating individual nations from their self-imposed isolation and bestowing upon them an international dimension. This should be the actual role of the newly elected European Parliament (1979), where members of individual national parties would talk to their friends from other countries, turning it into "a place for instruction and enlightenment."[44] Böll also warns against a monopoly of the big industrialized countries at the expense of smaller states.

The interview with Grass, conducted nearly two decades later, strikes a similar note. Although critical of the inadequate control that the Strasbourg Parliament exercises over the Brussels bureaucracy, he is in favor of a European constitution. Like Böll, he emphasizes the need to respect Europe's geographic borders and to recognize that Prague, not Paris, lies at the center of Europe. Unlike Böll, Grass believes that the notion of a common European identity is still utopian and could become reality only if we respect Europe's great diversity.[45] The influence of Böll and Grass in this debate is difficult to assess. Despite their leading role within the academic German youth movement of the late 1960s, they popularized, rather than shaped, the ideas of a prevailing Eurocommunism and therefore probably figure more as "memory consumers" than "memory makers."[46]

The last major author discussed here is Hans-Magnus Enzensberger, whose literary output reaches back almost as far as that of Böll and Grass, but who seems more attuned to the postmodern trend of our time. Enzensberger's travelogue, entitled *Europe, Europe: Forays into a Continent,* with its original German title *Ach Europa,* acts as a response to Thomas Mann's article. Enzensberger's position is diametrically opposed to the intellectual interwar search for a united Europe. His epilogue "Bohemia by the sea," itself an intertextual metaphor, transforms Europe into some kind of "chimera."[47] His Euroskeptic position is opposed to any form of a homogenizing superstructure. He defines Europe as a "fractal,"[48] a term–coined by Benoît Mandelbrot in 1975–denoting a fragmented geometrical shape which is mathematically unpredictable. *Europe, Europe* itself is a fractal or patchwork, consisting of observations on the specific characteristics of seven European countries, while deliberately ignoring the larger industrialized nations. His 1995 poem *Old Europe* (*Altes Europa*) amounts to a postmodern deconstruction in verse.

> In the warm aroma of bread outside the bakery,
> beneath the golden pretzel sign,
> a plump magician from Guinea
> sells key rings,
> in Graubrüdergasse
> (who were these Grey Brothers?)

> Small wiry dealers
> in enormous training shoes
> snap at each other in a language
> that no one understands, outside the wall
> of the Heiliger Geist cemetery
> (who was this Holy Ghost?)
>
> And then the old Bosnian lady
> stretches out her stiff leg,
> for a few minutes on a bench
> in the silent, dark-green yard
> behind the dark-green gate
> of the Elephant House, established in 1639.[49]

The poem has been described as a sonnet form, which has its origins in the Middle East, another instance of Enzensberger's multicultural and intertextual approach.[50] Its first two stanzas paint idyllic scenes that draw on foreign elements, but each last line develops rhetorical questions which explode the idyll. The author suggests that perhaps we no longer know or care about the true meaning of the "Graubrüder" or the "Heiliger Geist" and that therefore the foundations of Europe are undermined. The old Bosnian woman of the final stanza comes from the margins of Europe, the pain of her stiff leg possibly symbolizing the bloody conflict there. The double reference to the dark-green color suggests an Islamic environment and the Elephant House might be an allusion to Africa or India, the date 1639 coinciding with the foundation of Madras by the East-Indian Company.[51] Just like Jean-François Lyotard, Enzensberger proclaims the end of meta-narratives and consequently dismisses Europe as a spurious fantasy. Enzensberger is well known for his keen awareness of group perceptions but is far less attuned to ideological concepts than Böll or Grass. His observations seem more in tune with the new post–1968 generation which had lost its faith in ideologies and anticipated globalization as a possibility for reaching out to other, less familiar cultures.

Peter Schneider's "Plea for a Culture of Skepticism" (Plädoyer für eine Kultur des Zweifels), on the other hand, seems to strike a balance between Enzensberger's Europhobia and the modernist search for a European identity during the 1920s. In his address to a writers' conference in Berlin in 1988, Schneider anticipated that intellectuals would reaffirm the European cultural memory, a Europe that is primarily a cultural option, open to everyone who feels drawn towards Europe, either as a friend or an enemy.[52] Schneider disagrees with Enzensberger's anti-rational stance and celebrates a European culture of skepticism that developed on this small continent where, over the past millennium, some twenty different nations maintained their own languages, peculiarities, and follies. The "European project" must protect and promote this muddle and babble of voices—the utopia of a unity in diversity is Schneider's dream to be preserved at all cost.

This journey across twentieth-century Europe indicates shifting attitudes among (West) German intellectuals, sometimes promoting but more often reflecting changes in an existing cultural memory, usually responding to changes in political culture.[53] Although Jan Assmann's theory of a "clear system of values and differentiations"[54] seems rather utopian, it is probably too early to suggest that more recent developments amount to a "failed" collective memory.[55] The scope of this chapter does not allow for a detailed analysis of changes in cultural memories and their impact on the shaping of the dominant political cultures. I would suggest, however, that the latter is more stable and less dependent on the openness of the communicative process in its more populist form. While the cultural memory of our European vision, which has permeated the twentieth century, may show signs of "tiredness" or even failure, this is not the case as far as Western democratic concepts are concerned.

Notes

1. Maurice Halbwachs, *The Collective Memory,* trans. Francis J. Ditter Jr. and Vida Yazdi Ditter (New York, 1980).
2. Hans-Georg Gadamer, *Wahrheit und Methode. Grundzüge einer philosophischen Hermeneutik,* (Tübingen, 1990), in part. Part Two: "Ausweitung der Wahrheitsfrage auf das Verstehen in den Geisteswissenschaften," first published in 1960.
3. Lutz Niethammer, *Lebenserfahrung und kollektives Gedächtnis. Die Praxis der "Oral History"* (Frankfurt/Main, 1980); Jan Assmann, "Collective Memory and Cultural Identity," *New German Critique* (1995): 125–133; Wulf Kansteiner, "Finding Meaning in Memory: A Methodological Critique of Memory Studies," *History and Theory* 41 (2002): 179–197.
4. Kansteiner (see note 3), 181; Assmann (see note 3), 126.
5. Assmann (see note 3), 130; cf. also Kansteiner (note 3), 184.
6. Kansteiner (see note 3), 190–193.
7. Oswald Spengler, *Der Untergang des Abendlandes. Umrisse einer Morphologie der Weltgeschichte,* 2 vols. (Munich, 1923). The first version appeared in 1918 in an incomplete form.
8. Spengler completely ignores women in his deliberations, as do many other authors after him.
9. See Marco Schickling, "Hermann Hesse's Politics," in *A Companion to the Works of Hermann Hesse,* ed., Ingo Cornils (Rochester, 2009), 301–323.
10. Hermann Hesse, "Die Brüder Karamasow oder der Untergang Europas," in *Sämtliche Werke,* ed., Volker Michels, vol. 18 (Frankfurt/Main, 2002), 126. Unless stated otherwise, all translations are by the author.
11. Hugo von Hofmannsthal, "Blick auf den geistigen Zustand Europas," in *Gesammelte Werke in Einzelausgaben,* ed., Herbert Steiner, *Prosa IV* (Frankfurt/Main, 1955), 79.

12. Thomas Mann, "Achtung Europa!," in *"Achtung Europa!," Essays 1933–1938,* eds., Hermann Kurzke and Stephan Stachorski (Frankfurt/Main, 1995), 147–160.
13. Ibid., 157.
14. Ibid., 149.
15. José Ortega y Gasset, *The Revolt of the Masses,* an authorized translation (anonymous) (New York, 1993), 131f.
16. Ibid., 165, 176.
17. Mann, (see note 12), 149.
18. Ibid., 152.
19. Ibid., 155.
20. Ibid., 157.
21. Ibid., 158.
22. Ibid., 158.
23. Ibid., 159.
24. Heinrich Mann, *Essays,* ed. Alfred Kantorowicz, vol. 2 (Berlin, 1956), 256.
25. Ibid., 259f.
26. Ibid., 260.
27. Ibid., 277.
28. Ibid., 281–85.
29. Robert Musil, *Der Mann ohne Eigenschaften,* ed., Adolf Frisé (Hamburg, 1952), 63.
30. Note the involvement of the comical General Stumm von Bordwehr in this conversation.
31. Klaus Mann, *Auf der Suche nach einem Weg* (Berlin, 1931), 60.
32. Ibid., 71.
33. Ibid., 87f.
34. T.S. Eliot, "The Unity of European Culture," in *Notes Towards the Definition of Culture* (London, 1962), 110–124.
35. Klaus Mann, "Die Heimsuchung des europäischen Geistes," in Klaus Mann, *Auf verlorenem Posten, Aufsätze, Reden, Kritiken 1942–1949* (Reinbek, 1994), 526f.
36. Richard Coudenhove-Kalergi, *Europe Must Unite,* trans. Sir Andrew McFadyean (Glarus, 1939), 86–9.
37. Ibid., 86.
38. Address from 5 Novermber 1929, available at http://www.historiasiglo20.org/europe/anteceden.htm, accessed on 15 September 2011.
39. Richard Coudenhove-Kalergi, *Kampf um Europa* (Zurich, 1949), 23.
40. Richard Coudenhove-Kalergi, *From War to Peace,* transl. by Constantine Fitgibbon (London, 1959), 92.
41. Ibid., 90–93.
42. Ibid., 105f.
43. Politische Redaktion des Saarländischen Rundfunks, ed., "Ausweg aus der einzelstaatlichen Isolation, Interview mit Heinrich Böll" (Munich, 1979), 178–98.
44. Ibid., 186.
45. Wolf Scheller, "'Europa erweitert und was nun?' Ein Gespräch mit Günter Grass," available at http://www.heidelberger-lese-zeiten-verlag.de/archiv/online-archiv/schellereuropa.pdf; accessed 15 September 2011.
46. See Kansteiner (see note 3), 180.
47. Hans-Magnus Enzensberger, *Ach Europa! Wahrnehmungen aus sieben Ländern. Mit einem Epilog aus dem Jahre 2006* (Frankfurt/Main, 1987), 481.
48. Ibid., 2.
49. Hans Magnus Enzensberger, *Kiosk. Neue Gedichte* (Frankfurt/Main, 1995), 45.
50. Reinhold Grimm, "Altes Europa," in *Gedichte und Interpretationen,* ed., Walter Hinck Bd. 7 (Stuttgart, 1997), 48.
51. Grimm (see note 50), 51, relates the date to the Thirty Years' War and relates the "elephant" to slavery, but I cannot see enough evidence to accept such an interpretation.

52. Peter Schneider, "Plädoyer für eine Kultur des Zweifels," *Literaturmagazin* 22 (1988): 18.
53. Particularly important here are the fall of the Berlin Wall and the European Union's expansion into Eastern Europe. Jürgen Habermas seems to suggest that European liberal and democratic values will survive and bring about a change in the cultural memory or–as he would put it–the political culture of Eastern Europe. See Jürgen Habermas, "Europas zweite Chance," in *Vergangenheit als Zukunft* (Zürich, 1990), 100.
54. Assmann (see note 3), 131.
55. Kansteiner (see note 3), 192.

Chapter 6

Critiquing the Stranger, Inventing Europe
Integration and the Fascist Legacy

●●●●●●●●●●●●●●●

Mark Wagstaff

The European Union's integration of member states entails, in part, fostering a pan-national, social identity for its disparate citizens. This attempt at identity creation presupposes the existence of a shared sense of "being European." This chapter suggests that attempts to fashion a European social identity reflect the imperatives of nineteenth-century nation-building, while simultaneously attempting to supplant those imperatives through encouragement of new supranational identities and forms.

Substantively, I argue that identities are products of memory and that the substitution of external identities actively damages the techniques of memory that shape individual identity as part of the formation of national cohesion. I begin by theorizing about how individual identity is shaped while highlighting the reliance on memory, especially in societies where there is coherence among individuals and their economically productive roles. The social identities produced from familial relationships are noted in the context of how this organization of similarity and difference creates fault lines between a community of belonging and others.

The emergence of nations drawing their legitimacy from closely set bonds of belonging led to traditional networks of tribute and obligation becoming codified within the project of nation-building, exemplified in the use of cartography by elites to rationalize populations and resources, often with little reference to patterns of settlement or land usage. The appearance of elite nationalist practice in the French Revolution, characterized by the nationalizing of language and rights in formally sanctioned structures, accelerated the submersion of traditional identities and obligations through official versions of national memory intended to legitimate the present regime and provide routes for regime elites to lay claim to the past. This tendency is typified in the rise of fascism with its backwards formation of a glorious antiquity for the integral state. Drawing on this background, this chapter sketches the history of the European Union from its early iteration, as an attempt to ensure conditions so that fascism could not be repeated in Europe, to a more activist body promoting pan-European interests and identity.

This returns to the key theme: as identities are products of embedded, reflexive memory, attempts at external identity creation become detrimental to the practice and validity of memory. The argument is that in the pursuit of greater integration, a homogenization of the past takes place, so that memory becomes oppositional to an idealized Europeanism. The past exists in distinct, discrete, and localized ways—official endorsement of what is presumed to be shared puts memory in doubt, making the past a stranger. While advantage can be gained from integration, this should not be at the risk of damaging Europe's memorialized origins. Finally, this chapter also touches on the differential pressure that upheaval in global financial markets placed on European national economies in the currency union, the Eurozone. The necessity of bailing out several Eurozone members—action perceived as essential to maintain the integrity of the single currency—sparked an amount of popular debate, which, in its caricature of some nations as hard-working and others as feckless, allowed a superficial yet instructive glimpse of enduring biases beneath the mantle of union.

All identity is invented. Individuals refine their identities from the ambiguities of their situation and have identity imposed upon them through the perceptions of others. Identity is not fixed, and, as Zygmunt Bauman argues, has accelerated in fluidity—in response to shifting aspirations and increased pace of activity and change. Bauman reminds us that every choice we make about how we create ourselves in effect closes off other choices, at least for that moment.[1] When we commit to one aspect of identity, we place other potentials on hold and risk sleepless nights wondering what might have happened if we had chosen a different course of action. Identity is an investment in unknowable outcomes. We can apply general experience abstracted from life to foresee what outcomes *might* occur. But how we store and process that experience to enable us to estimate the consequences of a choice is not straightforward. The paths of action that create our identity and inform our future choices are not a simple database into which we enter a destination and let the machinery plot the easiest route. The choices we make for our future are enmeshed in how we think we understand our past.

So as not to be paralyzed by doubt, human societies have developed a range of techniques that attempt to describe the scope of choices that create individual members of a given society. With Bauman, we can recall that in much of the world, it was–for a long time–commonplace to define individuals as congruent with their economically productive role.[2] When technological change was relatively slow and social change imperceptible, it was possible to say that an individual "was" a baker, a shepherd, a king, or a fool–that these pastimes and distractions were the substance of the living organism, the function that described the person. For a very long while, Marxists held to the view that humans are defined by their labor–perhaps they still do. In a society where employment, economic productivity, and individual identity are so closely allied, the choices individuals might make are constrained by assumptions that individuals inherit along with their job. In a pastoral economy, a shepherd who is the descendent of shepherds will have access not only to his immediate knowledge of grazing and pasture, but also to accumulated knowledge–the remembered experience of grazing sheep in that place before he was born. He has an effective imprint of ancestral identity. However, in deregulated modernity, that assignment of identity to task is less plausible. There are very few people now, in most Western societies, who could be said to embody absolutely what value they produce or who continue a family trade unbroken and cumulative for generations. In rich and poor countries alike, many people work to invest in their children precisely to enable those children to choose a different productive persona to that of their parents. This privatization of identity from the socioeconomic sphere has coincided with a greater visibility of anxiety and confusion about who individuals are when they can no longer be described in relation to purpose. In the background to this is a larger anxiety of how people can form themselves and make reasoned choices when there is less certainty of experience from an accumulated past.

There are routes to identity other than economic activity, but these too are perceived to have become eroded. Perhaps the most venerable, certainly the most consuming, are familial relationships, both those we are born into and cannot avoid; and those we make by choice. A close family structure is a training ground for social interaction, for negotiation, and attempts to game the outcomes. In a family, the risk of disappointment of our objectives is never far from realization, and experiencing early inoculation from disappointment is one of childhood's most valuable lessons. Families construct exterior social identities: mother, father, daughter, son are all perceived outside the family as having certain meaning, in a similar way to the occupational constructs of old. What these familial identities mean, what duties and rights they presume becomes integrated to the clan, the tribe, some larger and recognizably distinct unit that operates at the concrete level of making claims on the world. The content of a familial role may vary from place to place, yet it seems plausible that the essentials of that role remain constant when scaled to tribal level. The father, in a patriarchy, becomes sovereign; the son becomes his subject. The individual is magnified through the family unit onto a larger landscape, and the way that unit operates is not by ad-hoc decision-making but through the preserved knowledge of previous choices filtered and shaped by experience cohesive with ancestral personalities–themselves changed and mediated through circumstance.

When this magnification grows so large as to be unavoidable, it declares itself as a national identity. That identity is not newly created: it is constructed of a people's embedded recollection of interactions with neighbors, who have undergone a comparable process of crystallization from memory to action. These interactions are crucial to the formation of national identity, as this continuum from individual to family to clan to nation can only operate at the expense of others. Every act of claiming an identity creates others who are excluded from that identity. At the point where an individual asserts that they "are" a certain thing, a division is created, fencing off others who are not that thing and making it difficult, if not impossible, for them to be so. This is the organization of populations, a stereotyping of peoples into iterations of similarity and difference. Those iterations–like the choices that made the individual–are deeply rooted in past experience, in formative choices that have become structural.

This stereotyping reaches beyond cataloguing: as Wingfield reminds us, creating notions of Other is foundational to creating notions of Enemy.[3] To identify a group as not like "us," as distinct from "us," can raise an assertion that a group's experiences make it unable to share our norms and values. Especially in times of scarcity, when access to resources is at a premium, competition and distrust can embed heightened perceptions of difference. At the extreme, we might believe those others to be capable of any monstrous deed. In the later nineteenth century, the influence of Social Darwinism on Western political thought encouraged an ethnic stereotyping that attempted to craft some absolute gauge of cultural achievement. This aimed to segment humanity into the more or less advanced races, with all manner of pseudo-scientific gradings in between.

The resulting supposed division into "leader" and "follower" nations had important, long-term effects on Europe and the world. If "memory" is presumed to be neutral in itself, there are no "leader" or "follower" nations;

each nation has developed along a path of ancestral choices determined by climate, geography, resource challenges, and other factors, with present-day identities the sum of those recollections. These identities may differ from nation to nation but none is inherently more significant if all are taken to be specific to their context. The Social Darwinist shift, crudely, is that the foundational choices of some nations—their stock of memorial knowledge—is "better" than that of others; better in the sense that a path of development that allows active and material pre-eminence over others is the most desired objective. Wingfield notes that especially in Central and Eastern Europe, different elites took up this notion of fitness, expressing their role to "civilize" other groupings. These stratifications among races and nations—mirroring the class or social positions of individuals—are taken so much as landmarks that their fiction is not always explored.

Historians of the old type used to view the submersion of local particularisms into constructed nations as symbolic of progress, arising from economic imperatives to regularize behavior. The fact that many nations are now being unpicked by their component parts is, depending on viewpoint, either a further development of the same economic processes or recognition that political nationhood is a historical aberration. Before the bourgeois revolution, when Europe presented a gilded landscape of emperors, kings, martial clergy, and petty princes, power was largely located in overlapping spheres of privilege and obligation. A prince would reside in one territory but own lands in another, or claim tribute from subordinate nobles in a third, or hold an ancient right to raise armies somewhere else entirely. He might own a mere handful of castles, yet possess holy relics regarded as among the most potent political symbols. The tribute due to rulers was not contained within territorial boundaries, but rather related to the functionality that a given ruler embodied, often derived from ancient exploits which, through official legends, became regarded as formative and definitive.

Irina Popova's fascinating study links the increasing regularization of political behavior in Europe from the eighteenth century to the spread and refinement of cartography—focused on the role of map making in expressing institutional consciousness.[4] Given the susceptibility of European thought to the significance of maps, it is worth noting Popova's analysis that maps serve to render the memorial behavior of elites into spatial terms. The measurement of a prince translates from the value of tribute owed to him or his accepted significance on a functional scale to the physical extent of territory within which he alone exerts control. Once the physical mapping of territory has been achieved, it becomes rational to chart the people, with property rights and ethnographic maps to delineate who has proper possession of any given part of the land. The map becomes proof of the elite's "spatially concrete political and cultural claims."[5] In solidifying cultural identity in relation to defined space, older assumptions and forms of knowledge become subverted. To return to the shepherd grazing his sheep, his possession in the land is ancestral knowledge of grasses, topography, weather patterns, and how these influence the behaviors of predators. The formative political map shows none of this. Map reality, in its basic iterations, is about who owns physical geography, who has the right to power in the bounded space of that geography.

The territory claimed by a group is the sphere in which it can take action and influence the actions of others.[6] Family members in the home claim their spaces to control, restrict, and shape access and activity within that space. The presumed right to do this is not created by the space nor–in this case–by mapping it but by formulation of roles in the family structure. A family unit is generally too small to deploy cartography relying, instead, on how familial relationships and economic levers delineate who has a presumed right to use space from the owner of that space. This ownership becomes cartographic when scaled beyond the family, when the oversight of the elite grows extended to the point it must be demonstrated in some transmissible way. As Popova makes clear, cartography is the property of the elite that has overview on the spaces mapped, on an assemblage of spatial units where given populations are supposed to reside. This supposition may say little or nothing about the ancestral behaviors, functions, or claimed rights of those populations. These spaces achieve territoriality when their boundaries become purposive. A boundary can originate topographically, such as the use of a mountain range or river as a limitation of territory. Mapping presents ownership interests as solidified, as though they were topographic, and this solidity of boundaries becomes disciplinary on the activities undertaken within. At its simplest, a field shown on a map is an area of delimited white space within which anything might happen. However, when the field is divided into strips and each assigned a named owner, that act both defines and demonstrates whose interests are paramount in each sliver of space. Interests are the outcome of myriad prior choices. The boundary becomes a statement of who and what does and does not belong. It actualizes the realms of nation and strangers.

Hobsbawm recalls that "nation" is foremost connected to origin–that its primary meaning is in regard to ethnic unit, while its use to denote political unit is secondary and far more recent.[7] Politicization of the term was achieved with its hyphenation to "state," a collective expression of those sharing a form of sovereignty. The substitution of people into nation and nation into state links nation to territory, so that the nation-state is a delimited sphere with disciplining boundaries within which behaviors are presumed to have shared, understood, and officially memorialized origins. This sharing of cultural norms of behavior within delimited territory is exemplified in the French revolutionary project of linguistic conformity.

The Jacobins were acutely aware that most people in France did not speak French as it was spoken in Paris and that that was a threat to the Revolution, as it made it harder to build a cohesive revolutionary consciousness against the risk that residents of Alsace or Brittany, for instance, might regard the Revolution as an alien, urban imposition. Worse, destabilization in Paris might inspire claims for local autonomy, which was certainly not the Revolutionaries' aim. The Jacobins' solution was citizenship, which is to say, a description of the shared characteristics of participants in revolutionary France. Possession of liberties and adherence to laws are central to this, as is language: not necessarily native use of French, but willingness to acquire French, to participate in the state.[8] The territorial boundaries of the Revolution became formative and disciplinary on behavior as the Jacobins imported their preferred cultural identity into provincial France. As Bauman suggests, the project of mapping, regularizing, and codifying the nation is a process of colonization, with dialect subsumed by official speech; particularist rules overturned by legal code; property-use relationships surrendered to property law; and memory dismantled in the cause of fraternity. An evolutionary sense that present choices are a product of accumulated knowledge filtered through localized experience falls beneath an onslaught of officially driven, centrally sanctioned behaviors, reflective of imposed ideals in a drive towards desired courses of action. The present ceases to be a summation of a gradualist past and becomes a launch site for future enterprise.

Western European elites in the nineteenth century focused on development of a system of nations that codified how nations related to each other in fluctuating aspects of alliance and antagonism. To specify Western Europe here is deliberate, as Western and Eastern Europe have distinct patterns of historical development within the broader context of the submission of localized knowledge to centralized norms. "Europe," as shorthand, is often intended to mean Catholic Europe– the Western sphere–where the limited politics of liberalism originated. The history of the East is different, bound to the protracted decline of the supranational empires, to the persistent fear of Russian domination, and the survival of feudal-conflictual relationships long after these had declined in the West. When the territorialization of Eastern Europe was undertaken, it was not the Eastern peoples who were asked what they wanted, but the Western powers, who established boundaries and polities to support their own interests. The rationality of nation-building was not embedded in the East until very much later.

In the West, by the mid nineteenth century, nationalism had captured the political formation of states, such that conformity of language and culture became regarded as given conditions of statehood. The symbolic grew in significance as particularism declined, with flags, anthems, and national occasions expressive of a revealed cohesion of nationhood, in the same maneuvers that caused Joseph de Maistre to lampoon the Jacobins for their attempts to invent new national holidays and traditions. Even in a small and relatively unified territory such as England, the rapid growth of industrialization and consequent spread of factory discipline swept aside particularist local holidays and localized clock time, as well as patterns of trade and land-use arrangements that derived from ancestral responses and choices no longer considered valid or useful in the age of steam. While less overtly murderous than overseas imperial adventure, this is a form of colonialism supplanting local practice by national interest.

The completion of this national interest reached its most destructive in World War I. The Versailles process of boundary adjustment that followed the war and the parceling-out of the lands of former supranational empires into national units spoke of consensus among the Western powers—the Westphalian order of nation-states was the obvious, indeed only, iteration of Europe. With nationalities grouped and territorialized, the normative construct of nation-building was ascendant. As Hobsbawm surmises, the products of this order were often not "nations" in the Western sense, but collectivities deriving unity from shared oppression, or territorialities which had been seized and defined by elites adopting a Western pose of nationalism to secure their own aims.[9] The interwar European landscape bore a less tangible scar, corrosive in shattered lives and relics of combat. A fear was immanent in the European peoples, an anxiety rooted in industrialization, in the regularization of Western culture, a fear brought to consciousness by dread of mechanized war. Roger Griffin claims it to be characteristic of human societies to manufacture myth in response to crisis. In ancient times, such myths were part of a cyclical order of decay and rebirth, so that crisis, while shocking in itself, could be held to presage renewal, as the next stage of the cycle. Griffin reminds us that in modern societies, where such faith cannot be invested in a cohesive cosmology, mythic energies seek expression through social movements and political ideologies.[10]

The geography of post–Versailles Europe was imbued with fear that Western civilization was at the point of terminal decline, that there could be no regeneration from the carnage of the trenches and the anomie that had led to war. At this point of situational crisis, many were receptive to a new voice that spoke of relieving social disintegration, of seizing the banner of the nation and turning it against those who had allowed the war to bury national glory in impotence and defeat. This voice was against those who had profited at the expense of heroic dead and displaced survivors. These voices articulated a myth of a new kind of nation–integral and indissoluble–where substitutionism was total: from individual into nation; nation into state; state into party; party into leader. The cultural pessimism of the later nineteenth century, the product of individuals alienated from ancestral memory through mechanization and the acceleration of change, became transcendent in those countries most dislocated by the conflict. This generalized paralysis was a precondition for the irruption of fascism.

Griffin carefully draws distinctions between fascism in its Italian archetype and the Nazi regime in Germany. Fascism's *irredenta* is the nation; Nazism moved beyond its *völkisch* (folk-like, of the people, but strongly suggestive of embedded organic racial memory and practice) urgings to seek *Lebensraum* (living space, suggestive of shared national entitlement or birthright) in the whole of Europe. However, what the movements share is an oddly opposing sense that ancestral feelings for the particular characteristics and history of a place can be magnified to serve a larger life, can enable recovery of the grandeur and heroic display that liberalism dismissed as outmoded, even prurient. Fascist doctrines are essentially techniques of colonization, consuming language, politics, aesthetics, memory, and every space where difference might persist. The totalizing impulse, as much as physical conquest, drives towards a utopia where fascism shapes everything and everything is fascist. This is the Jacobin legacy, where all have a duty to be what the state requires and to ensure that all others realize the true path to liberation as determined by the revolutionary state.

Following fascism's apparent defeat in World War II, utopian federalist proposals re-emerged to manage the threat that anxiety in liberal, delimited states would again find expression in totalitarian impulses. Alex Warleigh suggests that the primary goal of those who established the Union was to mitigate the anxiety which had been attendant on the Versailles settlement by devising a framework that placed security ahead of retribution.[11] As Bauman notes, the Union's nascence was not an event, there were no incendiary speeches, no slogans, little explanation of what the technical coordination of coal and steel markets might ultimately produce.[12] The Union, as exercised in technocracy, was scarcely perceptible at first and its purpose as an anticommunist cartel scarcely mentioned. Since that quiet foundation, what has emerged, in Mark Gilbert's term, is "more Europe." As Gilbert's analysis of the persistence of federalist thought shows, aspirations to integration long predate the Union's founding but, once established, its existence became essential. European integration has been used as a protective mechanism—first against the supposed economic strength of the former Soviet bloc and latterly against the rather more present threat posed by the fluctuating protectionism of the United States.[13] The economic upheavals of the early twenty-first century showed clearly how free trade rhetoric could be easily susceptible to protectionist urgings in lean times, entailing even more uncertain conditions for less influential trading blocs. Promotion of conditions where economic certainty could be realized was unexceptional in itself: it is part of the rationale of liberal states, and the initial focus of the Union on economic cooperation was sufficiently abstruse to allow distance between the Union's activities and those national sensitivities that were informed by conflict and oppression. It is the Union's shifting focus towards a role in social policy integration which has proved more problematic, opening the question of a normative pan-European civil society and bringing into view notions of a European identity conflictual both with memory created through the process of nation-building and the vestiges of older experience in localized knowledge.

The Union's keynote is promotion of liberal democracy founded on the legitimate community. Liberalism territorializes space and draws boundaries around those who are enabled to participate within the defined space. The democratic state makes selective use of nationalism to construct society by claiming a distinctiveness in space and population, such that cohesion is achieved and collective consciousness supposed, in order to drive the state towards broadly agreed objectives. Enforcement is not possible without legitimacy, and liberal democracy functions as a mirror, reflecting authority back onto a populace which is cited as source for that authority. This is the key difference between a state and a protection racket. It is the failure of these suppositions that allows totalitarianism to trade substitutionism for cohesion. The European Union cannot properly claim the liberal democratic model: its boundaries tend to shift, to enlarge without reference to shared characteristics. Despite reforms to its parliament, the European Union lacks a delimited demos accepted as source of legitimate authority. Instead, proponents of European social integration have sought to foster consensus, a sensation of shared values, constructing a pan-European order where given norms are held irreducible. This notion has some content: European peoples do have a conjoined history, which has given rise to discrete coherences of material culture. However, while this very broad sense of "European" can be accepted, it does not translate readily to ongoing consideration among diverse peoples that they share common aims and bonds. A given individual will have multiple identities that relate to that person's social and familial situation. Nevertheless, there is little evidence of increasing adoption of a European identity to augment existing roles. People may support the aspirations of the European Union, but they do not identify with it.[14]

Unsurprisingly, perhaps the market dislocations of the early twenty-first century have re-emphasized how much more deeply national interests endure, for example, in the trading of old accusations between Germany and Greece over the latter's economic difficulties. Adoption of the EURO placed the majority of Union members at the heart of each other's social, as well as fiscal, policy. Global markets demand maintenance of the Euro's integrity as marker for the credibility of the Union as an economic bloc. However, the pain of debt restructuring falls largely to those whose welfare spend is most dependent on debt, prompting disproportionate social dislocation seemingly enforced by better off states. Meanwhile, many people in those richer Eurozone countries—people who would not describe themselves as nationalist—might still find it difficult to accept in austere times that to bail out more vulnerable members of the Union protects their economy too. In these circumstances, old grievances and stereotypes resurface.

Perhaps the most dramatic manifestation of this debate is the extension of the Single European Market. The Market was generally viewed neutrally, while its focus was free trade of goods and capital. However, extension of the Market to the free movement of labor raised awkward perspectives on Europe's past. Free movement of labor cuts across the idea of boundaries as controlling access to a defined territory, clouding the foundational concept of liberal democracy—the distinction between the legitimate populace and strangers. It could also be argued that, for some, greater fluidity of populations raises ancestral fears of the malign appearance of migrants (perceived as brigands and thieves) and the disturbing statelessness of gypsies. Citizens now have to welcome incoming workers as equals, where formerly they were tolerated as sanctioned aliens. Yet, this entirely humane approach to economic migration cuts across the memorial basis of collective identity. It is a profound shift requiring renewed attempts to build shared values across the Union, if citizens are not to perceive themselves as vulnerable in their home states, a condition that contains the root anxiety of fascism.

Bauman points to the security dilemma inherent in this. National identities are a technique of order, a system to enable risk and certainty to be judged.[15] The Single European Market problematizes this order. Strangers are still strangers, in the sense that they bear an identity relationship to a different group. Shared status as citizens of the European Union and the fraternal rights which support operation of the Market, however, mean that certain individuals in given circumstances have to be viewed socially as if they were not strangers. The most obvious expression of this is being able to seek work without specific official permission: that ability means that they have come to share something of the host nation's identity. In that sharing, the host nation's identity is changed and memories are rewritten again, as a differential of identity is revoked at least officially. Enforced change in identity is a source of anxiety, the endemic fear that–in part–the Union was established to mitigate. The citizen's internal map has been redrawn by the rights attached to the newly arrived stranger. For some, this revision can be understood only in geopolitical terms, in the language of invasion. Part of the expected order has been withdrawn and consequently the world looks less certain. That individual uncertainty mirrors the impact of change at the level of the state: the territory and its boundaries still exist, but the boundaries have shifted in meaning to encompass individuals in other places possessed of specific legal rights in relation to a state other than their own. The state now owes foreign citizens the tribute of settlement and the chance to seek work. Boundaries hardened in the nineteenth century have become more permeable again.

To address the risk of resurgent fear, the Union has sought to develop a pan-national civil society to try to demonstrate that arguments over identity are not the point at issue when all citizens of all member states have a shared basis for viewing the world. This production of collective identity is a significant political and psychological challenge to the memories that underpin national and–by reversion–individual identity. Nation-building has been the task of centuries in Europe and foundational is the nation's distinction between the legitimate populace and the other. It is this past that must be recodified, if the project of a European identity is to succeed. Native memory evolved through familial and tribal experience and subsequently was formalized in nationhood, so that nationhood itself–rather than being the zenith of progress–is now susceptible to recodification. In this new construct, "the people" is the collective, supranational identity of the European. This is all-consuming, collapsing, national identity, leaving only the European and the rest of the world. A class of stranger is created by this move: that stranger is the remembered past identity that this new supranational identity supplants. Nancy Wood cites Pierre Nora's work on memory as the diverse means that communities "enact their specific relationship to the past."[16] This is not a remembrance of events fixed in time but the active and continuing administration of the past. Performative memory is constructive of the individual and the nation, or as Nora would phrase it, the memory of "the Nation." To change the terms of social identity puts the project of a pan-European social outlook in opposition to Europeans' diverse remembered pasts.

The fascists based their demands on narrative continuum of past into future, derived from imputed memories of a mythic glory purveyed as the inheritance of the Italian nation. The Jacobins had prescribed the shared characteristics of participants in revolutionary France, embedding this prescription as the central unifying memory of the Republic.[17] French national institutions continue to draw on this memory, in the state's assemblage of the populace. Moves in France to outlaw certain forms of Islamic dress, for example, may be tangentially linked to detection of terrorists, but are substantively rooted in the republican notion of secular statehood and, in particular, the transparency of the Revolution where citizens scrutinize and are scrutinized equally. This supports Nora's interpretation of the essentially oppositional character of revolutionary France: the Republic was defined by everything it was not, in relation to other polities, giving the nation-state the combative foundation necessary to carry the weight of popular sovereignty. These invented national memories function to provide causal links between the past and future, to drive the nation towards that destiny described as inherent in its history. However, the European Union's project of identity shaping seeks to sever the future from the past by interpolating an ideology of shared objectives. One manifestation of this is the postmodernist transformation of national myths into artifacts of display.[18] The cargo cult of heritage has supplanted memory by fixing a certain enactment of recollection–officially sanctioned as authentic–at a desired point in time. This solidifying of heritage is essentially reactionary, a retreat to one past and denial that pasts are many.

The translation of history into heritage and memory into display effectively detaches the past from the present, by placing the past at objectified distance in a way reminiscent of nineteenth-century exhibitions of colonial exotica. If the past becomes a permanent show of costumed acts and stylized, repetitive language, its potency is diminished and, with that loss of substance, its ability to inform the future is weakened. The Jacobins understood the value of costume, deploying studied mockery of the clothes and manners of their aristocratic enemies in order to make the *ancien régime ridicule*. The fascists co-opted ancient symbols, resurrecting and re-energizing them to exert a forcefully artificial and idealized past on the weakened present. Postmodern European societies section off the past: it is something to visit, to buy souvenirs of, a meaningless Stonehenge of observation, rather than a legacy of still-visceral pains and joys. It might be suggested that a more organic relationship still persists in parts of Eastern Europe where, in some places, the past remains active in the present, in ways that in the West, have become subsumed.

There is an important question about how the promotion of shared identity in the European polity relates to European nations' coming-to-terms with the past. To paraphrase Bauman, the task of the modern state is to manage fear.[19] Fear continually abrades the carapace of certainty, and the state has constantly to smooth away the effects of that friction. Bentham, from the midst of the French Revolution, reminds us that human beings erect political societies in the first place because they are afraid of each other's intentions and this fear of brigandage is only managed, never resolved. Fear, and the irruptions of fascism which fear enables, leaves painful memories for individuals, families, tribes and nations. For the European Union, the fear that cannot be disposed of–that informs its very existence–is the fascist era and World War II.

Students of collective memory are perpetually faced with the problem that memory does not begin. Jeffrey Olick wrote that "when historians of German memory begin their accounts in 1949, as many do, or include the period before the state in such accounts for mere contrast, they risk reproducing the basic periodizing mythologies established by the Federal Republic's first leaders."[20] This is the history writer's form of territorializing–drawing boundaries around a period as the sphere where interpretation is negotiated. What lies before in these clean slate approaches is a form of otherness glimpsed dimly through the terms of the boundaries. In Olick's argument, a writer might say: my narrative begins in 1949, and although there was a time before that, my narrative starts here with everything in place. That the human actors of these periods conveyed in themselves collective memory of indeterminate ages before, and that memory was the context for, rationale of–or release from–their actions is not reflected in boundary drawing.

Whether Italy has extirpated its fascist past remains a lively question; for Germany, and to a lesser extent Austria, very public reconciliation with the past was conditional to rehabilitation (or possibly first habilitation) as a peaceable European state. For German historians in the early years of the peace, the most urgent task was disassociation of Nazi terror from the Germany of high culture.[21] Nazism, they reasoned, could not have been a product of that culture. More than an aberration, it was an uprising of evil, an unleashing of the demonic, foreign-to-German values. The Nazis, for all their *völkisch* rhetoric, were somehow un-German. Later, conservative revisionists would return to this "entry of evil" thesis, asserting that penance was not Germany's alone to perform, but the required response to the symptomatic universality of evil. The forms of collective memory that produced these phenomena of guilt, anger, shame, and rehabilitation are, to borrow Olick's terms, a dialogue of representations. The past is never the past, but a performance, a reconstitution, and as such is purposive, continually remade to construct a required present and future. Olick's thesis focuses on the German case, but the collective representation of past events can have many modes of performance—as victims and aggressors, participants and observers, those in fear and those actively seeking conflict for their own ends—and all rehearse their accounts of past events. One might suggest that these are not the same phenomena viewed from different perspectives, but different events, rendered by distinct voices and constructive of different social identities. These events belong to those who remember: what might actually have occurred at some past point is no longer salient, and the continual re-representation of events is in response to the present situation of the specific group.

In these three very different examples—Jacobin specification of the nation, the fascist recovery of fictitious past ages, and the European Union's social integration—what is observable are external attempts to remake identity, to change from outside the interior construct of nation and stranger. The exterior momentum presents as universal: the rights of all men, the duties of blood, the shared values of a continent. The effects of the demand, however, will vary for every group that hears. As Bauman titled his book, this is a Europe of strangers, with diverse and specific locations of otherness. A European identity strives to express what nations share, but the way the message is heard by, for example, Germans and Poles cannot be identical, in the long history of otherness which is the truly shared characteristic of national identities. What we share most of all is that "we" are "us," and that others are strangers.

To rephrase a pleasing line from the short story writer Saki, nations make more history than they consume locally. Nations revise, reinterpret, and export the past, changed, magnified, or diminished. The tussles between China and Japan over how World War II is taught in schools are, in every sense, a textbook example. Still in some corners of Europe, the past is an overt weapon, a means to devalue and delegitimize others. When Europeans catalogue what they share, the Islamic tradition of Europe might scarcely be mentioned. Yet, in the Balkans, fluidity in the interactions of identity and conflict, the particular life of border places as opposed to the statist center, left a legacy of cultural symbiosis that latter day nationalist elites have sought to eliminate with murderous effect. In Kosovo, traditionally, the distinction between Christianity and Islam was often no more than a blurred expedient. Shrines and other holy sites attracted believers of both faiths, whose interest was not doctrinal, but in securing miraculous resolution from the sources perceived as most effective, a kind of marketplace of miracles. A saint's reputation for efficacy mattered more than the origin of the site's sanctification. It was the drive to destroy ambivalence in identity, to form unequivocal nations that invented the Balkan past of ceaseless centuries of ethnic strife. Conflict had always occurred, but often economically driven and interspersed with much pragmatic stability, a tradition now largely discounted. This political recasting of the past erases diversity in favor of the broader themes which suit modern purposes.[22]

Such is the risk of European identity shaping: that the fragmentary, uncertain, difficult, and troubling pasts of peoples will be treated as quarry materials from which to extract a list of self-referential statements that are, approximately, "what we share." David Lowenthal pinpointed this particular danger: that retelling the past in terms of present purposes dislocates the past from the present.[23] The memorial, experienced past grows further distant and far less pertinent than its recreated précis. A carved head in a museum case could be anything or nothing. It is whatever the curator's label says it is. Situated, in heroic aspect, on a column, it might be cajoled to say something of prestige, technique, or representation. However, without memory alive and refreshed in the people, it can say nothing about who its makers were, what formed them, what they feared, what they believed in relation to carved heads and columns, and why it mattered in context of their own collective memory. The past becomes the stranger, the segregated realm, regarded with incomprehension, disbelief, even suspicion—too alien to be real. Alongside the European Union's identity making, a parallel movement of reclaiming national pasts has gained ground. This revival of particularism, however, is equally artificial, focusing, as in the case of Kosovo, on an imagined cohesion of nationhood belied by traditional practices of ambivalence.

Study is a virulent form of reinvention, as students and their teachers make brash claims upon the past, ransacking others' texts for the words that fit the case and perhaps omitting the subordinate clause that does not have quite the right tone. This is to say that the Jacobins were not like the fascists, and the European Union's bureaucrats and politicians–though its structures might bear the Jacobin gene–are not like either. These are archetypes, used here to relate a certain story of how all attempted, in diverse ways, to section and segment the past as stranger to the present. Yesterday is always doubtful, but life without memory has little substantive meaning. The individual, the family, the tribe, the nation, all claim identities derived from memory. But, as Lowenthal suggests, modern humanity has come to doubt its stewardship of the past, its mastery of a retelling to keep the past materially present. Memory is a physical practice, or else it is nostalgia which knows only of itself.

In making the past a stranger and quarantining its oddity in the vacuum of museums, what is lost is what Nora termed the "commemorative spirit," the sense of ritual that ties identity explicitly to the succession of gone-but-cherished generations.[24] What we share now is not belonging but organization. As Nora says, control of the meaning of memory has effectively been privatized to committees and vested interests. Memory is no longer a practice but a destination.

The European Union is something of a political novelty: an object that behaves like a nation-state, but lacks the essential motive force of a populace whose culture gives it competence. It is not bound, as the old supranational empires were, by acquiescence to some *dirigiste* imperium, nor by fear of how much worse things might be outside the imperial power, as in ancient days. The Union tends to resemble a state, built from rules of harmonization, and in its own terms successful. Its guiding ethic, that the European nation-states should no longer wage war on each other, is a significant benefit. Nevertheless, the cost of this success is potentially very great. Fascist integralism is driven not by enmity but by fear; its violence derives not from some imagined past but from anxiety for the future. The fascist response is suppression of divergence in the prescribed collectivity; the fascist nation is the only reality and individuals are fractions of its power, as each soldier is a fraction of the army. Pursuit of the integration of states risks holding a mirror to integralism, where each people becomes merely a speck of the whole and the heterogeneous past, which gives the assemblage value and meaning, is quarantined as anachronistic, rather than central to how a richer future might be made after states have withered. All identity is created, all identities can change. But, each individual must own the decision of how their identity is shaped to avoid being made the stranger, in their future and their past.

Notes

1. Zygmunt Bauman, *Identity* (Cambridge, 2004), 29.
2. Ibid., 45.
3. Nancy M. Wingfield, ed., *Creating the Other: Ethnic Conflict and Nationalism in Habsburg Central Europe* (New York, 2003), 1.
4. Irina Popova, "Representing National Territory: Cartography and Nationalism in Hungary 1700-1848," in Wingfield (see note 3), 20.
5. Ibid., 22.
6. Robert David Sack, *Human Territoriality: its Theory and History* (Cambridge, 1986), 19.
7. E. J. Hobsbawm, *Nations and Nationalism Since 1780: Programme, Myth, Reality* (Cambridge, 1990), 18.
8. Ibid., 20–21.
9. Ibid., 137.
10. Roger Griffin, *The Nature of Fascism* (London, 1993), 195–196.
11. Alex Warleigh, *Democracy and the European Union: Theory, Practice and Reform* (London, 2003), 14.
12. Bauman, (see note 1), 3–4.
13. Mark Gilbert, "European Federalism: Past Resilience, Present Problems" in *Democracy and Federalism in the European Union and the United States,* ed., Sergio Fabbrini (London, 2005), 32.
14. Warleigh, (see note 11), 111.
15. Bauman, (see note 1), 7.
16. Nancy Wood, *Vectors of Memory: Legacies of Trauma in Postwar Europe* (Oxford, 1999), 17.
17. Ibid., 22.
18. Ibid., 31.
19. Zygmunt Bauman, *Europe: An Unfinished Adventure* (Cambridge, 2004), 97.
20. Jeffrey K Olick, *In the House of the Hangman: the Agonies of German Defeat 1943–1949* (Chicago, 2005), 7.
21. Ibid., 161.
22. David Lowenthal, *The Past is a Foreign Country* (Cambridge, 1985), 349.
23. Ibid., 356.
24. Pierre Nora, trans., Arthur Goldhammer, "The Era of Commemoration" in *Realms of Memory,* ed., Lawrence D Kritzman (under the direction of Pierre Nora) (New York, 1998) Vol 3: *Symbols,* 615.

Chapter 7

The Thread That Binds Together
Lidice, Oradour, Putten, and the Memory of World War II

● ● ● ● ● ● ● ● ● ● ● ● ● ● ●

Madelon de Keizer

1997 was a busy year for the committee members of The October 44 Foundation (Stichting Oktober 44). In that year, the foundation organized a lecture given by the son of a Jewish family that had gone into hiding in the small Dutch village of Putten. A commemorative stone was unveiled in memory of four Canadian soldiers who were killed during the liberation of the village in 1945, and there was also a large number of lectures given by committee members recalling the raid on Putten in October 1944, when six hundred men and boys were rounded up and deported to the labor camp Neuengamme, near Hamburg. Only forty of these returned after the war. Finally, 1997 was the year in which a choir from Neuengamme gave a performance in the Dutch Reformed Church in Putten, meant as a peace offering from the place where so many people from Putten had met their end.

The work of The October 44 Foundation, which was set up in 1982, was highly appreciated. The friends of the foundation grew in 1997 from 784 to 823 people. The chairman received a royal honor in recognition of his achievements. The activities were initiated, encouraged by, organized, and realized by a committee with eleven members. All the committee members lived in Putten, which had by this time grown into a village of twenty thousand inhabitants. One member was a German teacher and one a history teacher; the former town clerk was heavily involved, and the local government archivist was in charge of youth affairs. Other members, mostly businessmen from the village, were mainly concerned with maintaining contact with those who had returned from the German camps or with the upkeep of the memorial center devoted to the raid, which was visited by no fewer than seven thousand people during that year.

One committee member organized group trips to locations that were relevant to the history both of Putten and of World War II in general. This type of trip became increasingly common during the 1990s. People visited, individually or as part of a group, Neuengamme and other German places, such as Wöbbelin and Ludwigslust, where many of the men from Putten had been held. Trips were also arranged to Sandbostel, to celebrate the liberation of the locally situated Prisoner of War camp where a number of the deported men from Putten had been found alive in April 1945. In June, a group visited Poland, and in October, forty-five people took part in the annual remembrance of the victims of the Ladelund Concentration Camp, where many of those who had been deported during the raid on Putten had died and been buried in mass graves.

From 1945 until 1989, it was primarily the unique aspects of local history that were fostered in Putten. After the fall of the Berlin Wall, the "New Europe" became the context within which the personal and localized experiences of the raid in Putten were experienced and illuminated. In Putten, the manner in which World War II was commemorated in 1997 clearly illustrates the increasing need for a wider European context in which to place the personal suffering experienced by the people of this small community during the war. The personal, horrific fate of the inhabitants of the village that had suffered so greatly because of the war was now placed alongside that of villages, such as Oradour in France and Lidice in the Czech Republic, which had been the victims of similar repressive measures by the Germans. Both villages were visited every other year during the 1990s by a coach load of Putten residents, both old and young. One of the men who went to Oradour in 1996 wrote about his experience:

> Many wreaths are laid at the monument in the churchyard. Our group does the same. Maarten, our oldest representative (one of the survivors of the Putten raid) and Hendrik-Jan, (the youngest), each lay a wreath. Then we move on to what was once the church. The schoolchildren walk hand-in-hand, their faces serious and their eyes wide. They know what this is all about. They can feel it. This is how their little friends would have entered the church in 1944. They never came out again. This is why these children are going there to lay wreaths and flowers now, by the altar. Close to the perambulator and the bullet holes. We arrive too late to go inside with them, through the hole in the wall that used to be the entrance to the church. Standing on the path we see the children coming out again. I'm deeply moved and say aloud: "They're coming out again. Do you see that? They're coming out again!" This realization gives me a feeling of liberation. It seems as if the tension has gone from the children's faces. The light has returned to their eyes. It is over.

Remembrance of World War II has been subject to significant processes of transformation. This applies to both public and individual remembrances, which are closely intertwined. Bill Niven posits that while collective memories of war and destruction provided postwar Western Europe with a powerful impetus to push forward the European project, collective memories in the EU-27 countries are characterized more by diversity and fragmentation.[1] In this chapter, I delve deeper into the nature of the remembrance of World War II since 1989 by comparing the history of the collective memories of three places that fell victim to harsh reprisals by the Nazis in World War II. These places are Lidice (Czech Republic), Oradour (France), and Putten (the Netherlands)–three sites of horror (*Orte des Grauens*) where the Nazis committed war crimes and crimes against humanity.[2] For a few decades after 1945, remembrance of the war and occupation in these places were influenced by national remembrance policies, but after the fall of the Berlin Wall in 1989, these policies lost their regulating influence on the collective process of commemorating World War II. In turn, local remembrance was set free and, in the 1990s, began to be oriented towards people in other parts of Europe who had experienced a similar fate. The focus of this local remembrance gradually began to shift towards a new unified Europe. The events of 9/11 gave this process of remembrance a new impetus to both the global and the local.

My comparison shows that after 1989 a variety of collective remembrances occurred that, in the national context, could be experienced as fragmentation and diversity. However, this development of the local process of remembrance after 1989 involves a fundamental process of local identity formation in the context of current globalization processes, in which there is room for both cultural diversity and the expression of European values. This more or less conscious process of macro-identity culture building–which is a reaction to the modernity of the twenty-first century–should be seen as being much more than just a reflexive process. As posited by Thomas Frykman, it seems to be an ideal forum for action–for civil citizenship in a new global context.[3]

The Master Narratives

Of the three cases discussed here, Lidice and Oradour are much better known than the Dutch village of Putten, which is located not far from Utrecht, in the central part of the Netherlands. In 1944, Putten had nine thousand inhabitants. In the night of 1 October 1944, about two weeks after the unsuccessful Allied landings at the nearby city of Arnhem, the local resistance organization carried out an attack on a Wehrmacht car just inside Putten's boundaries. At four in the morning, German Wehrmacht soldiers sealed off the wider surroundings of the village and ordered the men and women to go to the center of the village to have their identity cards checked.

When the villagers arrived, the men were separated from the women. The men were then locked up in the church and the school, and the women were released. The following day, six hundred men between the ages of sixteen and fifty, mostly village residents, were deported to the Dutch transit camp (*Durchgangslager*) at Amersfoort and from there to the Neuengamme concentration camp, near Hamburg. The center of Putten was partly burnt down by a Wehrmacht unit; more than a hundred houses and other buildings—most of which were centuries-old—went up in flames. The men and boys from Putten were then deported from Neuengamme to the horrendous labor camps in northern Germany. At Ladelund camp, more than a hundred of the men died in a period of just six weeks. Only forty of the men who had been deported returned home after the war.[4]

The original village of Lidice lay twenty kilometers north of Prague. In 1942, it had 483 inhabitants, and the villagers' main activities were farming and mining. On 10 June 1942, the German occupiers razed it to the ground in reprisal for the Resistance's assassination of SS General Reinhard Heydrich, Reich Protector of Bohemia and Moravia, on 27 May 1942. This fanatical Nazi had subjected the Protectorate to a reign of terror, with policies aimed in large measure at crippling the Resistance. The inhabitants of Lidice were accused of concealing the attackers. All the male villagers between the ages of fourteen and eighty-four were shot, 191 female villagers were deported to the notorious Ravensbrück concentration camp, and the eighty-eight children were placed with German families for "re-education." The entire village was blown up and set afire, and every animal was killed. After the war, 143 of the women returned to the remains of the village, and 17 of the children were traced; two male residents (who had been living abroad) survived. In total, 340 villagers had perished.[5]

Exactly two years later, on Saturday 10 June 1944, Oradour, near Limoges in the Limousin region of central France, was surrounded by the Führer Regiment of the 2nd Waffen-SS Tank Division ("Das Reich"). It was the day on which the tobacco rations were to be distributed, and the village (population 1,574) was bustling with people. At about 2:15 that afternoon, SS soldiers proceeded to pull residents from their homes and take them to the town square. The officer of the SS, Major August Dieckmann, announced that he knew that a cache of arms and munitions was hidden in Oradour and demanded all those who possessed weapons to come forward. Nobody did so. The mayor of Oradour offered himself and his four sons as hostages, but Dieckmann declined. He had the women and children taken to the church, while the men were gathered in groups and locked up in various barns. The SS soldiers then mowed down the men and set the church and the barns on fire. The entire village was incinerated; only eight people survived the massacre.[6]

Each of these German reprisals played out in much the same way. In Ukraine, Poland, Greece, Yugoslavia, and in Italy, France, Belgium, and the Netherlands, retaliatory actions were part of the effort "to maintain order" behind the front, to wipe out the local resistance, and to serve as a general instrument of fear. It was not until after the fall of communism in 1989 and the subsequent breakdown of dominant "master narratives" that an exploration of the historiography behind these sites of horror–Lidice, Oradour, and Putten–began. After 1945, each of these places was more or less left to its respective fate. The Cold War period saw the development of a limited degree of interest, usually politically motivated, in the commemoration of specific areas. After 1989, with the East-West conflict and communist rule in Eastern Europe having come to a close, these places began to play a greater role in collective memory.[7] In the 1990s, the relevant local and national archives related to each atrocity were finally opened to the public.

It had taken fifty years for valuable interviews (dating from 1945–1947) with inhabitants of Putten to be made accessible for historical research. The revised brochure about Lidice that was published in 1992 contained a text that had been completely purged of the old communist myths explaining the cause of the village's destruction.[8] Putten was no different: historiography got off to a laborious start there in the 1980s but rapidly gained ground, such that 1998 was marked by the publication of an extensive and demystified historical monograph.[9] In the case of Oradour, in the 1990s, Sarah Farmer conducted a critical investigation into the historiography of this "Martyred Village."[10]

The new form of historiography that was being applied focused entirely on the history of memory–an approach that was greeted with great enthusiasm during the 1990s. It centered on an analysis of the constructive, identity-defining character of memory and engendered a highly demythologizing tendency.[11] Significant for the historical memories of Lidice, Oradour, and Putten is the fact that the fate of each village was linked to the history of the Resistance in each specific region. In each case, reprisals followed an act of resistance against the Germans in areas that were crucial to German strategy at that point in the war. This factor, however, would become quite problematic after 1944/45.

Pieter Lagrou demonstrates, in his comparative study of the politics of memory in France, Belgium, and the Netherlands, that these countries sought decidedly national patriotic memories after the war. "Defeat and occupation, and even liberation by allied foreign armies, constituted an unprecedented trauma for the national identities of France, Belgium, and the Netherlands. A national memory glorifying the Resistance was a precondition for postwar recovery."[12] Yet, glorification of "the" Resistance on such a national scale turned out to be extremely painful for the political memory of the villages that had suffered. In the eyes of the victims, the local resistance fighters were not heroes; on the contrary, their "ill-considered" actions had prompted terrible crimes by the German Wehrmacht. Oradour (which called itself a "village martyr") and Putten (which was known as "the village of widows") did their best to strike from memory the role of the Resistance.[13]

Since the late 1940s, national memories have been underscored even further by the construction of collective memories of the Cold War. The primarily communist-inspired resistance localized around Putten and Oradour was swept under the carpet. The memory of Lidice was largely employed in the Eastern Bloc, where the former concentration camps (Buchenwald and Sachsenhausen) were fashioned as symbols of "a truly denazified, popular-democratic Germany, whereas Auschwitz became the monument to international communist and national Polish martyrdom."[14] Heroes of the Resistance (political resistance in Lidice) were deemed worthy of commemoration. In neither the Eastern Bloc nor the West did the plight of the victims serve the aims of national reconstruction, and the construction of a postwar identity centered on the struggle for liberation. By the mid–1950s, national memory found itself at odds with local memory–an opposition of heroism (an abstracted resistance) versus martyrdom (actual victims of the war). This opposition laid the foundation for a certain degree of divergence and fragmentation that was engendered by the nationally rooted politics of memory in Europe.

Nevertheless, there are analogies to be drawn between the histories of the collective local memories of Putten, Oradour, and Lidice in the period between 1945 and 1989. Three historical phases can be distinguished: first, the initial period of mourning; second, the period during which local and national memory went their own ways; and third, the 1980s, when the threat arose that new generations would forget what had happened. The events of 1989 and 9/11 subsequently defined moments of pivotal importance in the history of the collective memory of these places–memories that came to be characterized by an ever-increasing uniformity.

Outcasts of National Memory

How did this process unfold in Putten?[15] During the initial phase of mourning, which lasted from 1945 to 1950, the Dutch village was held up as the prime example of the suffering that the German occupying forces had imposed on the Netherlands. The Dutch population empathized with Putten and contributed material aid, but historical investigation into what exactly had happened there was purposefully obstructed. Putten's role as victim was deemed useful only insofar as it provided postwar courtroom evidence for German crimes against humanity in the Netherlands. In keeping with the drive towards national unity during this period of economic and social reconstruction and the early days of the Cold War, research into the role that the Resistance had played in Putten—marked as it was by communist sentiment—was deemed anything but desirable. Heroic acts, as memorized in the statue of a dock worker in Amsterdam to commemorate the February strike of 1941, were preferred to the plight of the victims, as symbolized by the statue of the weeping woman in Putten that was erected in 1948 in memory of the victims of the German reprisal.

During the second phase in the 1950s and 1960s, Putten took its own way in seeking a dialogue with the inhabitants of Ladelund, in northern Germany. In the early 1950s, family members of the massacred villagers began to meet with residents of the villages of Ladelund and Husum, satellite camps (*Aussenlager*) of Neuengamme, where the men of Putten had died and where—near the church at Ladelund—around a hundred of them lay buried in several mass graves. The meetings were grounded in Protestant tradition and—for the Germans and the Putten residents alike—were directed towards mourning and Christian forgiveness. In these years, the national interest focused on the way the postwar community of Putten ("the village of widows") dealt with its fate and, in particular, on the role of religion and the church in coping with grief. Awareness of the massacre as a historical event faded. Putten constructed its own "resistance-free" remembrances of the war.

The third phase started in the 1980s, when Putten launched initiatives to turn the tide of dehistoricization that was serving to promote "Putten" to the status of symbol. The October 44 Foundation (*Stichting Oktober 44*) was established in 1982, and one of its declared aims is to keep history—memory—alive in a time of growing forgetfulness. According to its 1983 annual report, the foundation set itself the explicit goal of using the memory of Putten to prevent "future generations from forgetting where totalitarian rule, whether fascist or communist, can lead." The inhabitants of Putten, "more than those of many other municipalities [in the Netherlands] have... experienced what National Socialism brought." Their approach allowed Putten to claim a position of singularity and to function as an exemplar within the memory of World War II. This message was aimed especially at "the inhabitants of those German municipalities, i.e., Ladelund, Neuengamme, and Wedel, where concentration camps were established, where so many of our residents were forced to spend their war years." Residents of Putten also began travelling to other places in Germany where the men of Putten had died. Their actions were a concerted effort to reverse the process of forgetting by means of placing commemorative monuments in sites of horror.

A similar kind of periodization can be distinguished in the historical memory of Lidice.[16] After 1945, a new village was built adjacent to the old one which had been burnt to the ground. From the moment in 1942 that the Germans made their retaliatory measures against Lidice known, the world's sympathy went out to the village. Lidice became the international symbol of Nazi inhumanity. The site of the old village became a national memorial; later, a small museum was built there, and in 1955, the famous Rose Garden was planted. Yet, as we have already seen, until 1989 Lidice functioned primarily as a tool of political propaganda for the ideology of the Eastern Bloc.

Oradour was to remain the martyred village par excellence for Western Europe.[17] Farmer argues that what first brought Oradour to public attention and made it commemoratory were the facts of the massacre and the presence of material remains.[18] In Putten, on the contrary, it was decided to rebuild the village as soon as possible. But Oradour's rise to national prominence as the pre-eminent example of violated innocence was just like it was in Putten, that is, a matter of construction. "The events of the massacre had to be removed from their historical context and dramatized visually and in narrative, to be rendered suitable for telling the archetypical story of innocence and victimization."[19] The victims' association (Association des Familles des Martyrs) was zealous in ensuring that the exceptional status accorded to the village–which is tangibly memorialized in the preserved ruins of Oradour–was put to discussion at both the national and the international level.[20]

Nevertheless, in Oradour, the memory of World War II also progressed through the three phases mentioned above. Once the phase of mourning had passed, with its great show of honoring the victims of Oradour throughout the country, the paths of national and of local memory diverged. The crossroads were reached in 1953/54, when the Assemblée Nationale decided, for the sake of national unity, to grant amnesty to fourteen French men—SS members from Alsace—who had taken part in the Oradour massacre. This political decision left the village feeling deeply betrayed and, like Putten, it started its own memory and history. Henceforth, it would be a proud "outcast" of national memory.

The Europeanization of Memory

1989 saw the beginning of a new phase in the remembrance of Wehrmacht crimes in Lidice, Oradour, and Putten. In order to keep the local memory alive, both the cultural memory and the politics of history in each of these places would have to undergo a radical change: specific local memories of an extraordinary victimhood would have to be transformed into a collective European memory of shared experiences and international belonging. As the only village in the Netherlands destroyed by the Wehrmacht, Putten called on local amateur historians and interested officials—forming together a new class of "professional rememberers"—and tried to connect not only with the Germans who had been involved in Putten's wartime history, but also with other villages that had been burnt down by the Germans, in particular with Lidice and Oradour. By this point in time, they had accumulated plenty of experience in exchanging memories and in dealing with the past thanks to the network of German contacts they had built up and nurtured with such care. Here, one can trace local memory breaking through to the national and the international level.

Lidice, too, had previously taken steps to establish contact—such as on the occasion of the opening of the Rose Garden in 1955 to promote "world peace" in times of Cold War—but had come up against anticommunist sentiment in the Netherlands and elsewhere in non-communist Europe. Thus, Putten refused Lidice's request for a gift of roses. In the early 1990s, Lidice sought to make contacts abroad, especially in the United Kingdom (the Czechoslovakian government had spent the war years in exile in London, and the Czech-British Association was based there). A network of contacts now began to spread among the villages that had suffered a fate similar to that of Lidice. One particularly noteworthy facet of the international support for Lidice's memory project is that it centered, quite strongly, on protecting the ravaged region around Lidice.

Lidice, Oradour, and Putten were very willing recruits in the post-1989 (although starting before in Western Europe) Europe-wide movement towards reconciliation with Germany, which culminated in the fiftieth anniversary commemorations in 1994/95. These commemorations embodied a triumph of Western liberal values and emphasized universal rights and human rights. The characterization of Germans as "the enemy"—a characterization that until then had bound together the victims of the Third Reich—was quick to dissolve. The former sites of horror assumed a prominent position, not only during but also after these anniversary rituals, as the particular histories of the crimes committed by the Wehrmacht gained prominence within the respective national World War II histories. Putten, Oradour, and Lidice were subsequently integrated into a broad European culture of memory. After all, the anniversaries celebrated in the mid–1990s had also been driven by the notion of a unified Europe.

Of course, a certain degree of European memory and historical consciousness can be distinguished as early as 1945. Michael Harbsmeier speaks of the "Europeanization" of memory and historical consciousness "aiming at a kind of substitution of the many imagined national communities by some sort of reconstructed common European memory." However, since the late 1980s, another kind of Europeanization has emerged, one characterized by "defamiliarisation of national character combined with attempts at establishing a … European identity." The latter trend is distinct from the reconstruction of a European identity over the course of the first four postwar decades. A significant aspect of the construction of the European identity after 1990 is the "increasing number of attempts to create a more objective and uncontested, more fundamental and basic European past… at the same time adding further energy to the… defamiliarisation of national identities."[21] The warm welcome given to this Europeanization project of fashioning the new European identity was greatly stimulated by the 1992 conclusion of the Treaty of Maastricht, which established the European Union.

In order to trace how this Europeanization of memory manifested itself during the 1990s, we can turn to the example of Putten and the evolution of efforts to preserve memory there. While there was already some incidental contact with Lidice and Oradour (via a farmer who travelled to the Limousin in the 1980s to buy cows), a group of "professional rememberers"—all of them board members of the October 44 Foundation—now implemented a systematic approach. Such experts in the construction of memory also started to give structure to the memories of Lidice (under the auspices of a state-supported foundation after 1989) and of Oradour, where the Association des Familles des Martyrs continued to hold the reins.

Inspired in part by the success of what was, by now, routine trips to the German camps, the October 44 Foundation in Putten charged a new commission with the organization of more ambitious trips to its "sisters,"

Lidice and Oradour. One of the obstacles they encountered was the fact that annual commemorations in Lidice and Oradour were held around the same date, 10 June. Another was the language gap: the need to use French to communicate with Oradour was particularly problematic, and this may be why the more highly educated mayor of Putten began to assume a more significant role in their communications. Since 1990, the rule is to alternate the trip each year, that is, to travel from Putten to Oradour one year and to Lidice the next, thus resolving the date issue. Naturally, any event of special importance–such as the dedication of a memorial center (in 1992 and 1999 such centers were opened in Putten and Oradour, respectively)–are occasions on which representatives from the other villages come to show their solidarity. As such, fourteen individuals from Putten were present at the commemoration held in Oradour in 1994 to mark the fiftieth anniversary of the massacre there. The values that their efforts espoused outweighed their religious differences: Protestants from Putten felt no qualms about attending the Catholic mass given by a bishop in Oradour. However, it is worth noting that it was not until 1996 that the delegation from Putten managed to make personal contact with the powerful Association des Familles des Martyrs. In 1997, an entire bus full of people departed from Putten to participate in the commemoration of the fifty-fifth anniversary of the massacre in Lidice. Oradour and Lidice, for their part, were until recently less systematic in their communications with Putten.

The significance of the years 1994 and 1995 goes beyond simply marking the fiftieth anniversary of World War II. The presence of Queen Beatrix during commemorations in Putten in October of 1994 serves as one sign of this, marking as it did the close of Putten's special position in relation to the national memory. Now, finally, Putten was reintegrated in the national history of World War II–that most fundamental of historical episodes in terms of how it defined the Dutch identity. Putten's response to the memory of the massacre was now held up as an example for the Netherlands as a whole, where the importance of values such as tolerance and conciliation were growing apace with the increasingly multicultural society.

Putten, Lidice, and Oradour were now also granted a place in the European culture of memory. Once the ritual part of Oradour's 1994 commemoration was concluded, President François Mitterrand delivered a speech calling on all those present to be on guard against ever allowing feelings of hate to regain the upper hand, as this could culminate in another war. Among the many who gathered for the major commemoration held in Lidice in 1997 were the Czech Republic's President Vàclav Havel, several of its ministers, and the chairman of its parliament, as well as delegations from Germany, the United States, and the United Kingdom. A total of twenty-two wreaths were placed during the event and the Czech national anthem was played.

The New Regionalism

The events of 9/11 heralded the start of a phase of increasing political uncertainty. It had not taken long for shared history and memory to become a thing of the past; it was quite clear that the core values underlying them had eroded with time. This loss had occurred despite Western political efforts, during the last decade of the twentieth century, to inaugurate a new moral agenda, proceeding from Europe's (shared) role as peacekeeper in the Middle East and former Eastern Bloc countries. In 2005, when the newly drawn-up European Constitution was submitted to the European Union member states for approval, it was rejected in both France and the Netherlands. This rejection is symptomatic of the immense shift that has occurred worldwide since 9/11. In the Netherlands, the assassination of the politician Pim Fortuyn in 2002 and that of the film director and television presenter Theo van Gogh in 2004 strengthened the general perception of a world standing on the brink of a new era.

Security is the new catchword–in fact, it has become the single most important societal value. In 1999, the Canadian historian, politician, and commentator Michael Ignatieff remarked, quite rightly, that the rhetoric of universal rights tends to be a smokescreen enshrouding a fragmented world that is divided into privileged zones–where liberal values are maintained–and danger zones, where the universal moral standard simply does not have a chance. According to Ignatieff, the world picked itself up after the revolution (*Wende*) of 1989 with promises for improvement in the material and moral quality of life, but it culminated in perplexity.[22]

How are we to describe the construction of the memory and the history of the *sites of horror* now, in a time of perplexity? This is a question I should like to examine in the light of two notable developments in the culture of memory, specifically as pertaining to Putten. I argue that the recent emergence of both a specific category of *lieux de mémoire* tourism, as organized by the so-called "professional rememberers," and what I refer to as the "regionalization of memory" are expressions or forms of the construction of a new, post–9/11 identity.

Since the turn of this century, Putten has been doing its part to promote international tourism to memorial sites. Trips organized by the October

44 Foundation are no longer confined to places that are of particular relevance for Putten, but also include other famous *lieux de mémoire,* such as Auschwitz. Nor are the trips limited to a few days either side of a commemorative event; they now extend over a week or more. In 1996, a group of forty-five people travelled from Putten to Auschwitz; while in 2000, a week-long trip stopped in the Czech Republic (Lidice) and in Poland. The following year another week-long trip visited not only Oradour but also the beaches of Normandy. In 2002, thirty-two people visited both Lidice and Berlin in the course of a week.

This kind of tourism speaks for a fundamental process of identity formation in the context of modern-day globalization processes: it constitutes a kind of recognition of the self and of the other in the suffering that accompanied World War II. This recognition both acknowledges cultural diversity and gives expression to common European values. In this transnational trend of memory of World War II, "Europe" becomes a space of experience and communication. However, the more or less conscious process of macro-identity culture building—in terms of a reaction to modernity, to the insecurities of today—should, as posited by the well-known Norwegian ethnologist Jonas Frykman, be viewed as more than merely a reflexive, relatively cerebral process. It is here that the new regionalism must be brought into the picture.[23]

Over the last decade, it has become possible to speak of a veritable boom in the popularity of the national, the regional, and the local. Everything and anything connected to individual identity is popular. Rather than citizenship serving as the glue that binds national interests, nations now focus on cultural identity. This trend has its roots in the 1980s: the politics of culture carved out a sense of belonging in the context of an unpredictable world. People began to look back in time, instead of forwards to a new and shining future.

The emergence of a new regionalism is a trend that Frykman identifies as the result of macro-political processes whereby groups and individuals are inscribed into local structures. Beginning in the late 1990s, regions came to be cultivated as loci of cultural identification. The European Union injected a vital stimulus: the authorities realized that the very sense of belonging somewhere as a nation had become problematic—that the nation formed a challenge to the Union. The EU responded with a two-pronged cultural policy; intellectual traditions and events were advanced as a means of unifying the continent and giving people something with which they could all identify ("from Plato to NATO"), while the regional was advanced, with the aim of establishing political legitimacy by appealing to popular culture and opinion. This process bears a resemblance to the nineteenth century process of constructing nationality, the difference being that culture building is no longer a task for intellectuals, but one for planners, entrepreneurs, and local artists and academics. Since the regional and the local occupy a place that is separate from, or even in direct opposition to, the national, the region is better suited to transnational culture building than is the nation.

According to Frykman, the regional–rather than the national–is more in tune with the times, and is in a better position to support late modern values. The paradox facing us now is "that the national becomes particular and coercive while the provincial becomes general and optional." Although the cultural specificity of a region can be defined as being primarily a product of the central backdrop, the demotion of the nation-state is a contributing factor. While interest in formal citizenship is losing ground, people still enjoy the feeling that they are part of a common cultural identity. Nowadays, distinct identity is no longer simply imposed (examples include bourgeois culture, youth culture, immigrant culture). In fact, people actually feel that they have been freed from tradition. This freedom creates room for the individual to fashion an identity and a sense of authenticity for themselves, turning identity into "an endless interpretation process"[24]–something that is reflexive. The local has come to stand for that which is solid and deeply entrenched–precisely the qualities that contribute to security and a feeling of belonging to a larger whole.

According to Frykman, however, the need to belong and to feel safe is not only a response to life in our modern, high-risk society, but may also arise out of the need for activity. After all, the local can be considered the most rewarding arena for action. The national is overflowing with rules and regulations to the extent that it is experienced as being restrictive. The local, by contrast, signifies liberation, where "one can constitute oneself through the tasks one is able to perform." It offers "a style, a theme, a thread that binds processes, people, and memories together, what could be called–with an overused word–culture."[25]

The importance of this theory lies in the fact that it generates an understanding wherein the local is not the opposite of the global, the modern, or the world of the media, but is more of a space or an arena where things can be tested in practice, can be recreated, and made accessible. In turn, this is made possible by the fact that people already know one another and the lines of communication are short. Frykman's new regionalism offers a rich interpretive framework for the modern-day (local, regional) culture of memory in such sites of horror as Lidice, Oradour, and Putten, and that allows this culture to be analyzed as the product of a two-part process.

First, the framework has certain inherent elements of identity politics—the search for individual roots, which first got underway in the 1980s. In the Netherlands, the desire to belong was stimulated in large measure by the rapid breakdown of traditional religious and sociopolitical barriers, by secularization, and—as in Europe in general—by the threat of forgetting those central values that were linked with World War II. Second, the framework allows an understanding of the cultures of memory in Putten and other sites as being, in fact, expressions of the new regionalism that should be regarded not as reactionary, but as complementary to such macro-economic and macro-political processes as the development of the European Union in a globalizing world. The culture of memory—as centered on various core groups of survivors, their families, and the organizers of commemorative events and tourism—presents an accessible, authentic forum, a rewarding, doable, practical testing ground for the cultural transformation that has been set in motion by macro-economic and macro-political forces.

Notes

1. Bill Niven, The Dynamics of Memory in the New Europe Conference, Nottingham, United Kingdom 13–15 September 2007.
2. Gerd R. Überschär, *Orte des Grauens. Verbrechen im Zweiten Weltkrieg* (Darmstadt, 2003), xl. Überschär discusses twenty-six sites of horror, including places in Poland (Auschwitz), the Balkans (Kalavrita, Kephalonia), and Italy (Marzabotto), as well as Dresden. Putten is not included in this selection. For Putten, see Madelon de Keizer, "Kriegsverbrechen in den besetzten Niederlanden: Der Fall Putten," in *Kriegsverbrechen im 20. Jahrhundert,* eds., Wolfram Wette and Gerd R. Überschär (Darmstadt, 2001), 259–273.
3. Jonas Frykman, "Belonging in Europe. Modern Identities In Minds and Places," in *Europe: Cultural Construction and Reality,* eds., Peter Niedermüller and Bjarne Stoklund (Copenhagen, 2001), 12–23.
4. Madelon de Keizer, *Putten. De razzia en de herinnering* (Amsterdam, 1999 5. ed.); Madelon de Keizer, *Razzia in Putten. Verbrechen der Wehrmacht in einem niederländischen Dorf* (Münster, 2001); Madelon de Keizer, "The Skeleton in the Closet: The Memory of Putten, 1/2 October 1944," *History and Memory,* 3 (1995): 68–97.
5. Peter Steinkamp, "Lidice 1942," in Überschär (see note 2), 126–135; here 126–132.
6. Sarah Farmer, *Martyred Village. Commemorating the 1944 Massacre at Oradour-sur-Glane* (Berkeley, 1999); also Sarah Farmer, "Oradour-sur-Glane: Memory in a Preserved Landscape," Conference Paper, Arezzo, 1994; Ahlrich Meyer, "Oradour 1944," in Überschär (see note 2), 176–186.
7. Überschär (see note 2), xll.
8. Lidice State Center for the Preservation of Historical Relics and the Protection of Nature, District of Central Bohemia, 1982.
9. De Keizer, *Putten. De razzia en de herinnering* (see note 4).

10. Farmer, *Martyred Village* (see note 6).
11. See John R. Gillis, ed., *Commemorations. The Politics of National Identity* (Princeton, 1994); Patrick H. Hutton, *History as an Art of Memory* (Hanover, 1993); Henri Rousso, *The Vichy Syndrome. History and Memory in France since 1944* (Cambridge and London, 1991). In 1994 an international conference was held to commemorate the fiftieth anniversary of the 1944 massacres around Arezzo, which has been very stimulating for this approach. See de Keizer, "The Skeleton in the Closet" (see note 4).
12. Pieter Lagrou, "Victims of Genocide and National Memory: Belgium, France, and the Netherlands 1945–1965," *Past and Present,* 154 (1997): 185–154, here 154 and 220; see also Pieter Lagrou, *The Nationalization of Victimhood: Selective Violence and National Grief in Western Europe, 1940–1960* (Cambridge, 2003).
13. Farmer, *Martyred Village* (see note 6); de Keizer, *Putten. De razzia en de herinnering* (see note 4).
14. Lagrou, "Victims," (see note 12), 221.
15. For this section, see de Keizer, "The Skeleton in the Closet" (see note 4).
16. Steinkamp (see note 5).
17. Farmer *Martyred Village* (see note 6); Meyer (see note 6), 176–186.
18. Farmer, "Oradour-sur-Glane" (see note 6).
19. Ibid. Farmer rightfully points out in footnote 6 that the "commemoration of Oradour as a *village martyr* served to mitigate the humiliation of the defeat and French passivity during the Occupation," which was also the case in the Netherlands.
20. Farmer, *Martyred Village* (see note 6), 210.
21. Michael Harbsmeier, "Character, Identity, and the Construction of Europe," in Peter Niedermüller and Bjarne Stoklund, eds., *Europe. Cultural Construction and Reality* (Copenhagen, 2001), 5–12, here 9.
22. Cited by Martin Halliwell, *Modernism and Morality. Ethical Devices in European and American Fiction* (Houndmills, 2001), 4–5.
23. Jonas Frykman (see note 3).
24. Ibid., 19.
25. Ibid., 19–21.

Chapter 8

Memory of World War II in France
National and Transnational Dynamics

•••••••••••••••

Henning Meyer

For more than twenty years, historians, literary scholars, and social scientists have been paying more attention to the subject of collective memory, focusing particularly on memorial places as "references" that contribute greatly to the (re)formation of societal memories.[1] The vast majority of this new scholarship has analyzed and interpreted national memory dynamics, but recent years have witnessed the introduction of the idea of "European" and even "global" memorieas and memorial places. Pierre Nora, the French historian who helped to pioneer the contemporary study of collective memory through his concept of the *lieux de memoire*,[2] pointed out in the epilogue to the 2001 volume *German Memory Places*:

> There are "European" memorial places, their number is legion–such as those that have contributed to the development of the consciousness of a common European history and those that embody an idea of Europe. I am not sure whether the analysis of these places–which has already often been made–really contributes to the comprehension or the creation of a European memory, supposing, that a European memory exists, which is not imparted by the nation and does not belong to a universal heritage. Memory divides, but history unifies. In view of this insight, it seems to me, that the exact knowledge of several memory cultures makes clear what Europe has in common. It is still my opinion that the feeling of a real common affiliation can only arise from an intensified comprehension of the differences.[3]

Other authors share Nora's skepticism regarding the "globalization of remembering" or the existence of "cosmopolitan memorial places."[4] In fact, the only collective memory that almost everyone believes to have evolved in a transnational direction is memory of the Holocaust.[5] Yet, for some years, discussions have occurred about whether there are other previous national memories of World War II with a similar potential to become transnational.[6] In this chapter, I discuss the evolution of French memory culture by focusing on three memorial places: the Centre National Jean Moulin in Bordeaux, the Mémorial pour la Paix in Caen, and the Centre de la mémoire in Oradour-sur-Glane.

These examples have very different origins. The oldest of the three museums,[7] Bordeaux's Centre National Jean Moulin, was created in 1967, followed by the Mémorial pour la Paix in Caen about twenty years later in 1988, and lastly, the Centre de la mémoire in Oradour-sur-Glane in 1999. Moreover, these "concrete institutions of memory"[8] represent different foci of French World War II memory: resistance in Bordeaux, liberation in Caen, and sacrifice or victimization in Oradour. In the more than thirty years that passed between the establishment of the first and the last of these institutions, the French people's image and representations of World War II past changed considerably because of the internal evolution of French society, generational replacement, and increasing openness to European and transnational influences. I show that there is an intimate interdependence between the historical social context of a museum's creation and its representational content. The question is whether or not there are tendencies to Europeanize the memory in the context of these places, following the evolution of French collective memory.

During the postwar period in France, two dominant memories were constructed.[9] First, as Belgian historian Pieter Lagrou writes, in order to elide the deep social cleavages of the earlier twentieth century and to prevent continued civil strife, a "common remembering of the resistance" encompassing every citizen was constructed.[10] Second was the memory of victimization, suffering, and deportation. Subsequently fused with the first, the country was presented with an image of itself being "simultaneously victim, betrayed yet heroic" (*à la fois victime, trahie mais heroïque*), according to the historian Philippe Buton.[11] After a "phase of consolidation and consensus,"[12] during the later 1940s and the 1950s, the creation of the Fifth Republic and the return of Charles de Gaulle to the presidency in 1958 caused a "theatrical return to the Resistance's rhetoric."[13]

De Gaulle was legendary. He was the former leader of *France Libre* (the Resistance operating from outside of France during the years of the Nazi occupation and the Vichy collaborationist regime) and head of the provisional government immediately after the end of the war. The return of de Gaulle and the myth of the resistance that he embodied were manifested symbolically by the solemn transfer of Jean Moulin's body to the Panthéon in Paris on 18 and 19 December 1964.[14] Jean Moulin, a main figure of the Resistance operating in mainland France, had become a national hero after his death in 1943 at the hands of the Gestapo.[15] Joining the likes of Rousseau, Voltaire, Hugo, and Zola was a symbolic act of the highest significance to France's postwar memory culture.

It was in the aftermath of this event at the Panthéon and in the context of high Gaullism, that the Centre National Jean Moulin was created in Bordeaux in southwestern France in 1967. One cannot find a lot of information about this museum, either in the secondary literature or in public archives. However, the Centre's own archival holdings draw a picture of a typical French Resistance museum—one of about seventy that have been created mainly since the 1970s.[16] Being one of the first such museums makes it particularly influential and representative for this particular memory. Like the majority of Resistance museums, it was created by a group of witnesses and was supported by a well-known personality in the movement, the long-term mayor of Bordeaux (1947–1995), Jacques Chaban-Delmas,[17] who at the end of the war was de Gaulle's military representative in France.[18] His commitment to the Resistance was an important reason for his election as mayor in 1947, because Bordeaux suffered from a reputation of being especially collaborationist. Thus, Chaban-Delmas clearly sought to intensify the memory of Resistance in a town where no major Resistance event ever took place—and to which Jean Moulin had no personal connection.[19] In a way, the museum and memorial initiative was a measure to ensure his own continued legitimacy.

Unlike a lot of other Resistance museums, the Centre National Jean Moulin was not created by an association of former members, but rather a small group that included Geneviève Thieuleux, who later became the first curator of the museum. She collected objects, photos, and documents concerning the war and decided to found a museum based on these holdings. The museum, situated near Bordeaux's city hall, exhibits objects relating to Resistance, political deportation, Jean Moulin, and the *France Libre*. Like the majority of these kinds of museum, the Centre does not have substantial funding, so there is no technical, curatorial, or pedagogical support. It is really just a simple exhibition of war relics. The leading actors behind the museum are war witnesses, who have donated objects to the museum and who explain these and their historical context to visitors, mainly elementary school students. Arguably, the great variety and eclecticism of themes exhibited in the Centre can be explained by the absence of a prominent local event during the World War II period—Moulin was never active in Bordeaux. In spite of the museum's move to a larger and centrally located building in 1980/81, the Centre National Jean Moulin remains unknown nationally and internationally, but its relatively high number of visitors (about twenty thousand a year) is attributed to its central location in the city and the well-institutionalized series of school fieldtrips.

For the responsible parties, such as Mayor Chaban-Delmas, the Centre serves as a Gaullist discourse of national unity in French resistance–epitomized by the figure of Moulin–which was very typical in France in the first years of the museum's existence. Since its establishment over forty years ago and its intimate relationship to the national unity myth of the Resistance, there was no place here for memories to open up to other contexts and influences of a more transnational or even European nature. The only intention of the responsible parties and of the witnesses was to represent their idea of World War II history. Moreover, with the evolution of French collective memories over the last decades and the disappearance of witnesses–the guarantors of the Centre's discourse and its reason to be–it is losing its link to the present and its credibility. Its existence is even threatened; it now shares its curator with another local museum,[20] and during the week it only opens in the afternoons.

The social turmoil of 1968 and the death of General de Gaulle were the beginning of a new phase of national representation of the past in France, described as the "broken mirror" (*miroir brisé*)[21] by Henry Rousso, in which postwar myths were questioned and new memories gained prominence. At the beginning of the 1980s, World War II memory became a genuine "obsession,"[22] as documented by the rapidly increasing number of memory events and memory places. At this time, there was a "social need for the construction of memory,"[23] which was observed in Caen, the capital of Normandy's Calvados Department near the coast where the Allied landings took place on D-Day in 1944. In the Battle of Normandy following the landings, three-quarters of the town were destroyed. Jean-Marie Girault, long-term mayor of Caen (1970–2001) and wartime witness, identified this commemorative need and proposed the construction of a Museum of the Battle of Caen.[24] In the war, Girault was not a resistance fighter, however, he was present as a Red Cross aid when the town was bombed.[25]

During the eight years of the museum's genesis,[26] its name and concept changed several times and it even became an election issue. Many critics pointed out that there were already a lot of museums and memorial places commemorating the Allied landings and the Battle of Normandy.[27] Yet, local political advocates wanted an important project that would be able to help the weak local economy. In order to attract the essential amount of external investments and being influenced by increasing Europeanization and decades of reconciliation with the Federal Republic of Germany, as well as transnationalization of World War II memory discourses at that time (especially the rise of Holocaust consciousness across the globe), the backers decided to widen the museum's concept. Moreover, the museums project represented a second (museum-specific) "revolution": individual testimony and exhibits became less important and room was made to exhibit an attracting stenography, so the political advocates embraced innovative concepts, techniques, and museum standards. For example, the town government of Caen employed specialists, such as historians and a designer,[28] who integrated the bombings of Caen into the context of the Battle of Normandy, the Allied landings, and more generally World War II. They designed a large museum with architectural, visual, and sound effects in a stunning building that itself is allegorized by a big block of stone with a cleft in the middle.

In order to enhance the Mémorial's discourse and in search of project partners, the creators encompassed more and more people in the museum's approval. At the beginning, it was dedicated mainly to Caen's population, but later it included individuals who wanted to commemorate battles in Calvados and in Normandy, the Resistance, as well as acknowledge the crimes committed by the Nazi German occupiers. From the beginning of the project in 1981, internationalization was prioritized.[29] The first such idea was to integrate the former Allied forces by means of the commemoration of the Allied landings of 6 June 1944, even though this could be interpreted as a criticism of the conduct of the Allies, who carried out the bombings when fighting the German troops then occupying the city. Thus, the museum's backers had to find another way to capture the international dimension. Just before the ceremony marking the beginning of the construction in 1986 (and perhaps influenced by similar narratives that surrounded the fortieth anniversary of the end of the war in 1985, such as Ronald Reagan and Helmut Kohl's gesture at Bitburg), Mayor Girault explained his idea of inviting representatives of former Allied states, as well as those from Germany: "I have taken the initiative to invite to this ceremony ambassadors of all nations, which confronted each other on the sixth of June 1944, including Germany … I think that the presence of former antagonists, who once confronted each other, will be a good sign of our will to create a peaceful future."[30]

From this plan, the "universal message of peace" was born. The idea was that a common memory of all the casualties and the suffering of civilians and soldiers on both sides of the front was the only way to prevent the horrors of future wars. The message was first represented in the museum by a film entitled "Hope" (*Espérance*), which was presented at the end of the exhibition. Since 1991, they have added a gallery of the people who received Nobel Peace Prizes for their universal message of peace. Then, after the building was enlarged in 2001/02, exhibition spaces were added that concerned other military conflicts of the twentieth century, as well as spaces provided for meditation on the meaning of peace. With this overriding focus on peace, the Mémorial could link many countries to its mission. Indeed, at its inauguration, on 6 June 1988, representatives of thirteen nations in addition to those from the two German states were present,[31] all of them former World War II allies or antagonists. Later, the museum's management also invited personalities associated with pacifism and not connected to World War II, such as the Dalai Lama,[32] and organized events with world peace as their theme.[33] As a consequence of this evolution, the project eventually changed its name[34] to "Memorial of Caen–a Museum for Peace" (Mémorial de Caen–Un Musée pour la Paix). The success of the Caen initiative cannot be underestimated. Today, it is the most frequently visited museum outside of Paris and about 35 percent of the visitors are foreigners.[35]

The project for a memorial center in Oradour-sur-Glane started at the end of the 1980s and was inspired by Caen's project. But before its realization, the French World War II memory entered another new phase with President Jacque Chirac's speech at Paris's Vélodrome d'Hiver–a former cycle racing stadium near the Eiffel Tower that had been used during the war to assemble and deport French Jews to Nazi concentration and death camps. On 16 July 1995, Chirac acknowledged the responsibility of the French state for the 1942 deportations. For Philippe Buton, this was a "revolution of memory,"[36] since this was the first time the negative elements from the French past (collaboration during the Nazi German occupation and Vichy regime, as well as a longer tradition of anti-Semitism) were admitted into French collective memories, as Rousso also has pointed out.[37]

Oradour-sur-Glane is a small village near Limoges in central France. On 10 June 1944, a division of the Waffen-SS massacred the entire population (over six hundred men, women, and children) and burned the village down, apparently as a reprisal for the kidnapping and execution of an SS commander by the Resistance.[38] In 1945, de Gaulle declared Oradour to be a "symbol of the country's sacrifice,"[39] and the ruins quickly became a national pilgrimage site, with 300,000 visitors a year. In 1953, a trial took place in Bordeaux aiming to identify and to punish the perpetrators of the massacre.[40] For some of the accused–people from the French region Alsace who had been recruited into the Waffen-SS by force–the judgment was harsh; for survivors, conceptions of justice were not met. As a result, the community of those who survived, living in a new village facing the ruins since 1953, "privatized" the memory of the massacre, rejecting relations with the French state and cutting itself off in mourning. One might also add that a memory place devoted to helpless victims was not the preferred mode of remembrance during these years, given the dominion of the heroic myth of universal resistance.

This situation eventually changed thanks to the commitment of Robert Lapuelle, Mayor of Oradour (1959–1995), and his successor, Raymond Frugier. Step by step, the memory of the massacre–previously considered unique by the victims–was related more and more to the memory of National Socialist crimes committed against other villages and groups all over Europe, as well as the increasing attention devoted transnationally to victims.[41] The explicit objective was to overcome the national and international isolation of the village and its memorial place. A memorial center was planned next to the ruins to explain the history of the massacre to visitors after the survivors have passed away.[42] The exhibition was based on scientific investigation and contemporary witnesses' accounts, showing the local events in the context of World War II, as well as other war crimes. The intent is to provoke reflection.

Referring to his spectacular speech at the Vél'd'Hiv' in Paris, President Chirac participated in the inauguration of the Centre de la mémoire on 16 July 1999. In his speech there, he adapted the idea of Oradour's memory, opening it up to an even wider–and thus a European–context, "Europe has no higher meaning than opposing that which happened at Oradour, in incarnating a dream of peace and also a humanist ideal."[43] Later, on 27 January 2003, Oradour's mayor, Raymond Frugier, delivered a speech in Munich, Germany, entitled "Oradour and European Memory Work."[44] He pointed out what he thought about Oradour's place within a European memory: "World War II's memorial places, which were the theater of such tragic events, have become places which are dedicated to inner reflection of human conscience ... perhaps it is possible to jointly rewrite the premises of a truly European history, not only, what happened to each people, but in addition, what peoples want to originate by its overcoming."[45]

In his speech, the mayor also explained the role of the village and the Centre in this process: exchange and communication with other destroyed villages and victim groups, the invitation of European school classes and representatives of other European countries, the organization of European conferences, and so forth–an image of memory and reconciliation that experiences a broad European and cross-national consensus today.

In this chapter, I have tried to demonstrate–through the representative examples of three very different cases of World War II memory and their representation in museums—that certain memories, in different places and at different times, can show tendencies to a transnational memory. In Bordeaux, a center was created to distribute the Gaullist idea of unity in the idea of the Resistance. At that time, this was a common approach in France, which was strictly national and, consequently, did not allow any room for a transnational context or Europeanization. Later, after an important change in memory culture, the economic character of the project led to an opening-up of the memorial concept in Caen. The relationship between friends and enemies was reversed by representing the fact that Caen was bombed by the Allies. The way out of this dilemma was the universal message of peace, as a common lesson of suffering, destruction, and death caused by wars. Since World War II concerned the whole world, the Mémorial's approach became global. Because of the conflict-ridden history of Oradour's memory, the "national reference framework of a collective memorial construction"[46] was difficult to achieve, if not excluded. Also, the opening to a transnational context could help overcome a situation of isolation. In Oradour's case, it is almost consequently a European context because of the topic of German occupation crimes.

In the two cases of Oradour and Caen, universal messages were formulated as lessons of local tragedies, in order to place local memory within an international context. In Caen, this was the concept of a "global culture of peace and human rights,"[47] and in Oradour, it was the concept of a "globalized victim culture."[48] The national framework became less important, following a general tendency of "decentralization" of memory in France.[49]

The analysis of the way memory is represented in the three places shows the importance of local specifics, local authorities (like Mayor Chaban-Delmas in Bordeaux, Mayor Girault in Caen, Mayors Lapuelle and Frugier in Oradour), and the status of witnesses of World War II history and their testimony, but also economic reasons. On the one hand, the influence of the collective image of World War II history on the creation of a museum representing a part of this history is important. On the other hand, there are particular local memories, and each historic event has its own memory, which has an impact on the representation of a museum. The Center in Bordeaux has stayed attached to the Gaullist myth of a France united in resistance until recent days, even if French World War II memory changed substantially. In Caen and Oradour, the museums were created in the spirit of a memory opened to wider contexts and to Europeanization, but the projects were also influenced by local memories. At one moment, they even were of national relevance like the Memorial in 2004—when a common

German-French commemoration of the Allied landings took place in front of the building. Later, they have resisted new tendencies as the attempts of the political power under President Sarkozy to command World War II memory and to "re-nationalize" it (for example, by trying to revitalize the sense of national unity through an official remembering of the French Resistance).[50]

In the academic literature, some doubts have been expressed as to whether a global/European memory already exists.[51] In this chapter, I did not wish to prove the existence of a real transnational or European memory in France, but rather sought to show some of the transnational influences, trends, and their roots. Collective memory is dynamic and eclectic. I have tried to illustrate that the analysis of important museum projects representing this period could help to understand the French World War II memory and the changing of this memory.

Notes

1. "Memorial places" is the literal translation of the French "lieux de mémoire" or the German "Erinnerungsorte." For a different translation see Daniel J. Sherman, *The Construction of Memory in Interwar France* (Chicago, 1999), 3, who proposes literally "sites of memory."
2. Pierre Nora, ed., *Les Lieux de Mémoire* 7 vols. (Paris, 1984–92).
3. Pierre Nora, "Nachwort", in Etienne François and Hagen Schulze, eds., *Deutsche Erinnerungsorte III* (München: Verlag C. H. Beck, 2001), 681–686, 686 (author's own translation).
4. Hasko Zimmer, "Erinnerung im Horizont der Menschenrechte–Perspektiven der Erinnerungsarbeit im Rahmen der Globalisierung," *Jahrbuch für Pädagogik* 2003, 247–269.
5. Daniel Levy and Natan Sznaider, *Erinnerung im globalen Zeitalter: Der Holocaust* (Frankfurt/Main, 2001); Dan Diner, "Der Holocaust in den politischen Kulturen Europas: Erinnerung und Eigentum," in *Auschwitz. Sechs Essays zu Geschehen und Vergegenwärtigung*, ed., Klaus-Dietmar Henke (Dresden, 2001), 65–73. See also some receptions of this approach: Bernd Faulenbach, "Von der nationalen zur universalen Erinnerungskultur? Zu den kollektiven Gedächtnissen in der globalisierten Welt," *Jahrbuch Arbeit, Bildung, Kultur*, 19/20 (2001/02): 225–236; Zimmer (see note 4); Oliver Marchart, Vrääth Öhner, and Heidemarie Uhl, "*Holocaust* revisited–Lesarten eines Medienereignisses zwischen globaler Erinnerungskultur und nationaler Vergangenheitsbewältigung," *Tel Aviver Jahrbuch für deutsche Geschichte*, XXXI (2003), 307–334.
6. For example, see Claudia Lenz, Jens Schmidt, and Oliver von Wrochem, eds., *Erinnerungskulturen im Dialog. Europäische Perspektiven auf die NS-Vergangenheit* (Hamburg, 2002). Ute Frevert, "Geschichtsvergessenheit und Geschichtsversessenheit revisited. Der jüngste Erinnerungsboom in der Kritik," *Aus Politik und Zeitgeschichte,* B 40–41 (2003), 6–13, 13. She proposes to "Europeanize the experience of expulsion." For this, see also Dieter Bin-

gen, Wlodzimierz Borodziej and Stefan Troebst, eds., *Vertreibungen europäisch erinnern?. Historische Erfahrungen–Vergangenheitspolitik–Zukunftskonzeptionen* (Wiesbaden, 2003); Thomas Urban and Ariane Afsari, eds., *Ein Zentrum gegen Vertreibung: nationales Gedenken oder europäische Erinnerung?* (Potsdam, 2004); Jürgen Zarusky, "'Freiheitliche Erinnerung:' Vasilij Grossman und die europäische Erinnerung an Totalitarismus und Zweiten Weltkrieg," *Forum für osteuropäische Ideen- und Zeitgeschichte* 10 (2006): 81–110, here 2. Some conferences have also been held in this context, for example: Erinnerungskultur in westeuropäischer Perspektive: Niederlande, Belgien, Luxemburg und Deutschland, 22–25 May 2003, Münster, Germany; Die Zukunft der Erinnerung, 23–24 November 2006, Wolfsburg, Germany.
7. In the three cases, the notion of "museum" is strictly and deliberately avoided, because of the inactive taste of "musealization," these modern institutions interpreted as centers of active interpretation and working through. Nevertheless, for simplification, I will use this term in this article.
8. Ulrich Borsdorf and Heinrich Theodor Grütter,eds., *Orte der Erinnerung: Denkmal, Gedenkstätte, Museum* (Frankfurt/Main, 1999); Ulrich Borsdorf and Heinrich Theodor Grütter, "Einleitung", in Borsdorf and Theodor, eds., 1–10, 4.
9. Concerning France's history of the memory of World War II there is a lot of rich English, French, and German literature. Here I will note just some of the newest publications: Yves Bizeul, "Die derzeitige Umgestaltung und Umdeutung der französischen kollektiven Geschichtssammlung," in Heiner Hastedt, Christian Thies and Nikolaus Werz, eds., *Politik der Erinnerung* (Rostock, 2000), 53–74; Richard J. Golsan, *Vichy's Afterlife: History and Counterhistory in Postwar France* (Lincoln, 2000); Karin Urselmann, *Die Bedeutung des Barbie-Prozesses für die französische Vergangenheitsbewältigung* (Frankfurt/Main, 2000); Klaus Peter Walter, "Schwierige Vergangenheitsbewältigung. Die Okkupation Frankreichs (1940-1944) im Spiegel von Kinofilm und Roman," *Frankreich-Jahrbuch* (2000), 129–144; Pierre Laborie, *Les Français des années troubles. De la guerre d'Espagne à la Libération* (Paris, 2001); Henry Rousso, *Vichy : L'événement, la mémoire, l'histoire* (Paris, 2001); Robert Gildea, "Myth, memory and policy in France since 1945," in Jan-Werner Müller, ed., *Memory and Power in Post-War Europe. Studies in the Presence of the Past* (Cambridge, 2002), 59–75; Pieter Lagrou, "Frankreich," in Volkhard Knigge and Norbert Frei, eds., *Verbrechen erinnern. Die Auseinandersetzung mit Holocaust und Völkermord* (Munich, 2002), 163–175; Pieter Lagrou, *Mémoires patriotiques et Occupation nazie. Résistants, requis et déportés en Europe occidentale 1945-1965* (Brussels, 2003); Peter Carrier, *Holocaust Monuments and National Memory Cultures in France and Germany since 1989. The Origins and Political Function of the Vél d'Hiv in Paris and the Holocaust Monument in Berlin* (New York, 2005); See also for an extensive description http://www.crdp-reims.fr/memoire/enseigner/memoire_histoire/menu.htm; accessed 16 September 2011.
10. Lagrou (see note 9), 166.
11. Philippe Buton, *La joie douloureuse. La Libération de la France* (Brussels, 2004), 208.
12. Lagrou (see note 9), 170.
13. Ibid., 171.
14. Concerning this act of "phanthéonisation" see Henry Rousso, *Le syndrome de Vichy. De 1944 à nos jours,* second enlarged edition (Paris, 1990), 100–117; Maurice Agulhon, "A quoi sert le Panthéon ?," *L'Histoire,* 205 (1996): 98; Mona Ozouf, "Le Panthéon. L'école normale des morts," in Pierre Nora, ed., *Les Lieux de Mémoire* (Paris, 1997), 155–178; Maurice Agulhon, *De Gaulle, histoire, symbole, mythe* (Paris, 2000), 81–86; Patrick Garcia, "Les panthéonisations sous la Ve République: redécouverte et métamorphoses d'un ritual," in *Façonner le passé. Représentations et cultures de l'histoire XVIe- XXIe siècle,* eds., Jean-Luc Bonniol and Maryline Crivello (Aix-en-Provence, 2004), 87–106.
15. See some of the newest publications of the extensive literature relating to Jean Moulin: Alain Clinton, *Jean Moulin: 1899–1943; the French Resistance and the Republic* (Basingstoke, 2002); Michael R. D. Foot, *Six faces of courage: secret agents against Nazi tyranny* (Barnsley, 2003); Jean-Pierre Azéma, *Jean Moulin. Le politique, le rebelle, le résistant* (Paris, 2006);

Jacques Baynac, *Présumé Jean Moulin: (17 juin 1940-21 juin 1943); esquisse d'une nouvelle histoire de la Résistance* (Paris, 2007).

16. Concerning the museums of World War II in France see notably Marie-Hélène Joly and Laurent Gervereau, *Musées et collections d'Histoire en France, guide* (Paris, 1996); Marie-Hélène Joly, "Les musées de la Résistance" in *Résistants et Résistance*, ed., Jean-Yves Boursier (Paris, 1997), 173–216; Marie-Hélène Joly, "Les musées d'histoire" in *Des musées d'histoire pour l'avenir*, eds., Marie-Hélène Joly and Thomas Compère-Morel (Paris, 1998), 57–86; Sophie Wahnlich, ed., *Fictions d'Europe : la guerre au musée: Allemagne, France, Grande-Bretagne* (Paris, 2003); Christelle Neveux, *Le Mur de l'Atlantique: vers une valorisation patrimoniale?* (Paris, 2003).

17. See Henning Meyer, "Jacques Chaban-Delmas et le Centre National Jean Moulin de Bordeaux," *Revue historique de Bordeaux et du département de la Gironde* 7-8 (2005): 195–211.

18. See some more recent biographies of Chaban-Delmas: Pierre Cherruau, *Chaban de Bordeaux* (Bordeaux, 1996); Bernard Lachaise, Gilles Le Béguec and Jean-François Sirinelli eds., *Jacques Chaban-Delmas en politique: actes du colloque organisé à Bordeaux les 18, 19 et 20 mai 2006* (Paris, 2007); Dominique Lormier, *Destins d'exeption: Jacques Chaban-Delmas* (Montreuil-Bellay, 1999); Jacques Mousseau, *Chaban-Delmas* (Paris, 2000); Gilles Savary, *Chaban, Maire de Bordeaux: Anatomie d'une féodalité républicaine*, 2nd ed. (Bordeaux, 2000).

19. There is not an extensive, recent and coherent literature about the Resistance in Bordeaux. See Pierre Becamps, "L'Occupation et la Résistance" in *Bordeaux au XXème siècle*, vol. 2, ed., Joseph Lajugie (Bordeaux, 1972), 201–274; Dominique Lormier, *La Résistance dans le Sud-ouest* (Bordeaux, 1989); Dominique Lormier, *Le livre d'or de la Résistance dans le Sud-ouest* (Bordeaux, 1991); René Terrisse, *Bordeaux 1940–1944* (Paris, 1993); Guy Penaud, *Chroniques secrètes de la Résistance dans le Sud-Ouest* (Bordeaux, 1993).

20. Since 2006, its curator is also employed by the Musée d'Aquitaine, a museum of local and regional history.

21. Rousso (see note 14).

22. Ibid.

23. Denis Maréchal, "Le Mémorial de Caen entre mémoire et histoire" in Bonniol and Crivello, (see note 14), 145–158, 145.

24. "Introduction par M. le Docteur Duncombe, premier Maire-adjoint de la ville de Caen" in *Association des Amis du Musée Mémorial de la Bataille de Normandie à Caen*, Plenary assembly on 23 February 1981, Mémorial de Caen.

25. See: Serge Couasnon, *Jean-Marie Girault. Un républicain très indépendant* (Condé-sur-Noireau, 2001); Jean-Marie Girault, *Mon été 44—Les ruines de l'adolescence* (Caen, 2004).

26. The Mémorial as a modern and bigger project, for more historical documents can be found in archives other than the museum's own documentation and there are more literary and press articles. See some of the more recent articles: Benjamin Brower, "The preserving machine: the "new" museum and working through trauma–the Musée Mémorial pour la Paix of Caen," *History and Memory* 11 (1999): 77–103; Michèle Périssère, "Une histoire de la paix" in *Quel avenir pour les musées d'histoire?*, ed., Laurent Gervereau (Paris, 1999), 51–56; Claude Quétel, "Der Aufbau eines Museums für den Frieden in Caen" in *Die Zukunft der Vergangenheit: wie soll die Geschichte des Nationalsozialismus in Museen und Gedenkstätten im 21. Jahrhunderts vermittelt werden?*, ed., Museen der Stadt Nürnberg (Nuremberg, 2000), 127–136.

27. According to the former historical consultant of the Mémorial, Denis Maréchal, there were about seventeen in 1985. Maréchal (see note 23), 146.

28. Some of the historians were François Bédarida, Denis Peschanski, Etienne Fouilloux, Jean-Pierre Azéma, Henry Rousso, Robert Frank, Philippe Buton, and Dominique Veillon. The designer was Yves Devraine.

29. See *Association* (see note 24).

30. Conseil Municipal de Caen, *Séance du 12 mai 1986;* author's translation.

31. "6 juin 1988 : Inauguration du Mémorial par le Président François Mitterrand" *Mémorial de Caen*.

32. Some other visitors were: Elie Wiesel (Nobel Peace Prize 1986), Rigoberta Menchú (Nobel Peace Prize 1992), and Adolfo Pérez Esquivel (Nobel Peace Prize 1980). See *Le Journal du Mémorial* 52 (June 2005), 6.
33. These include a yearly international contest of lawyers' arguments, a competition for students about human rights, and the planting of peace's trees.
34. When the construction began on 10 September 1986, its name became Museum Memorial of the Battle of Normandy (Musée Mémorial de la Bataille de Normandie). The museum opened 6 June 1988 called Memorial of the Battle of Normandy–A Museum for Peace (Mémorial de la Bataille de Normandie–Un musée pour la Paix).
35. "Dossier de Presse" (2004), *Mémorial de Caen*.
36. Philippe Buton, *La joie douloureuse. La Libération de la France* (Brussels, 2004), 225.
37. Rousso, "Frankreich," 259.
38. Concerning the massacre of Oradour, see notably Sarah Farmer, *Martyred village: Commemorating the 1944 Massacre at Oradour-sur-Glane* (Berkeley, 1999); Jean-Jacques Fouché, *Oradour* (Paris, 2001); Ahlrich Meyer, *L'occupation allemande en France* (Toulouse: Edition Privat, 2002); Ahlrich Meyer, "Oradour 1944" in *Orte des Grauens. Verbrechen im Zweiten Weltkrieg*, ed., Gerd R. Ueberschär (Darmstadt, 2003), 176–186; Sarah Farmer, *Oradour : Arrêt sur mémoire* (Paris, 2004); Sarah Farmer and Serge Tisseron, ed., *Parlez-moi d'Oradour* (Paris, 2004). See also the contribution of Madelon de Keizer in this volume.
39. "Douloureux pèlerinage à Oradour," *Populaire du Centre,* 5 March 1945.
40. See some of the newest publications concerning the trial: Jean-Laurent Vonau, *Le Procès de Bordeaux. Les Malgré-Nous et le drame d'Oradour* (Strasbourg, 2003); Jean-Jacques Fouché, *Oradour : la politique et la justice* (Saint-Paul, 2004); Claudia Moisel, *Frankreich und die deutschen Kriegsverbrecher. Politik und Praxis der Strafverfolgung nach dem Zweiten Weltkrieg* (Göttingen, 2004); Henning Meyer, "Die französische Vergangenheitsbewältigung des Zweiten Weltkriegs durch die Rechtsprechung am Beispiel des 'Oradourprozesses'" in *Erinnern und Vergessen. Remembering and Forgetting,* eds., Oliver Brupbacher, Nadine Grotkamp et al. (Munich, 2007), 230–246.
41. Examples include Villeneuve-d'Ascq, Tulle, Lyon, Guernica, Warsaw, Rome, and Marzabotto. See Robert Lapuelle, "Cérémonies du 50ème anniversaire," *Le Radounaud. Bulletin d'information municipal,* April 1994.
42. Concerning the Memorial Center of Oradour, see Jean-Jacques Fouché, "Das 'Centre de la mémoire' in Oradour" in Museen (see note 26), 137–142; Jean-Jacques Fouché, "Le Centre de la Mémoire d'Oradour," *Vingtième Siècle. Revue d'histoire* 73 (2002): 125–137; Bettina Stuhlweißenburger, "Das Centre de la mémoire d'Oradour" in *Einsichten und Perspektiven* 3, ed., Bayerische Landeszentrale für politische Bildungsarbeit (Munich, 2005), 58–69.
43. "Discours prononcé par Monsieur Jacques Chirac, Président de la République, lors de l'inauguration du Centre de la mémoire, Oradour-sur-Glane, vendredi 16 juillet 1999;" author's translation.
44. Raymond Frugier, "Oradour und die europäische Erinnerungsarbeit," trans., 27 January 2003, at the National Archive of Munich. This speech was delivered in the context of the commemoration of the 1963 Elysée Treaty in which France and Germany agreed about their good relations.
45. Ibid., 11, 12; author's translation.
46. Zimmer (see note 4), 249.
47. Ibid., 260.
48. Ibid., 254.
49. See Rousso, "Frankreich", 257, 260.
50. See Johann Michel, *Gouverner les mémoires. Les politiques mémorielles en France* (Paris, 2010); Olivier Wieviorka, *La Mémoire désunie. Le souvenir politique des années sombres* (Paris, 2010).
51. See Faulenbach (see note 5), 225–236, 229, 234–236; Frevert (see note 6), 6–13, 13. See also Jan-Werner Müller, "Introduction: the power of memory, the memory of power and the power over memory" in Müller (see note 9), 1–35, 11. He writes: "a supranational

'European collective memory,' based on the 'Europeanisation' or even 'globalisation' of the Holocaust, might well be in the making–but this does not necessarily have the positive consequences for which one might wish. For now, European memories remain both divided and implicated in each other, which leads to the fierce contestation of historical analogies, such as 'Munich,' the 'Spanish Civil War,' and even the Holocaust, as well as a competitive telling of cautionary tales based on 'lessons from the past.'"

Chapter 9

THE FIELD OF THE BLACKBIRDS AND THE BATTLE FOR EUROPE

• • • • • • • • • • • • • • • •

Anna Di Lellio

Figure 9.1. *Turbe* of Sultan Murat in Mazgit (photo by Joan de Boer)

Historical memory is highly performative at the field of the blackbirds, a rolling Kosovo flatland six kilometers to the northwest of the capital Prishtina. At this site, in June 1389, a coalition of regional forces, led by the Serbian Prince Lazar Hrebeljanović, faced the Ottoman army of Sultan Murat I. Both leaders were killed in a battle that apparently ended with no decisive victory but led to the submission of the local nobility, shortly thereafter. The Ottomans then ruled over the Balkans until the twentieth century. Monuments marking the battlefield are placed a few kilometers apart: a memorial to the fallen Christian heroes, the *turbe* (mausoleum) of the Sultan's standard-bearer in the locality known as Gazimestan, and the Sultan's *turbe* to the west, at Mazgit. They are archeological and political signifiers of opposing camps, physical symbols of discourses and practices that "memory entrepreneurs" have adopted to plot national stories.[1] Most notable and best known among them is the Serbian narrative of the battle, constructed as a unique tale of Christian martyrdom granting Serbia historical rights over Kosovo. Less obvious plotlines built on the memorialization of the battle and its mythical protagonists are also relevant to Albanian and Turkish national discourses. In the contemporary political context, the old battlefield has become a highly resonant political symbol of European identity for all.

Facing the loss of Kosovo,[2] Serbia maintains a dominant storyline that clings to tales of Christian enmity with Albanian Muslims from 1389 up to current times. These tales confirm Serbia's, and its old province Kosovo's, primordial belonging to the "Western," "European" camp, against an alleged "Asiatic" and "jihadist" Albanian essence. Albanians, who are the overwhelming majority in modern Kosovo and seek recognition of the new state, in turn assign priority to freeing their past from a condition of "Oriental alterity" or foreignness. Folktales that represent the mythical Serb hero-assassin of the Sultan Miloš Obilić as the Albanian-Christian champion Millosh Kopiliq, signify a more "authentic" history by establishing autochthony, excising a centuries-old Ottoman past, and sharing in a broader contestation of Albanians' identification with the Ottomans and Islam. To the Turkish government, striving for membership in the European Union (EU) against the opposition of core member states, the newly restored *turbe* at Mazgit provides archeological foundations to the official narrative of a tolerant, civilizing variant of Islam that is born by Turkish history in the West.

The possibility of European belonging as historical reality–offered by the Kosovo battlefield through memory–is a crucial attribute for Serbia, Kosovo, and Turkey–all European Union applicants. In March 2012, the EU granted Serbia candidate status. The newly independent Kosovo is a NATO/EU ward, aspiring to access. Turkey, an EU candidate since 1999, has seen its bid to join the EU virtually stalled. Although their circumstances are very different, all three countries have been asked to prove not only their economic and institutional viability, but also their "Europeanness." This generally means adherence to a "modern community" that defines itself, most clearly, in opposition to the old particularisms of nation-states and national histories, while lacking in substantive coherence.[3] As a response, they have tried to bridge the apparent symbolic deficit characteristic of this understanding of community by evoking instinctive memories of earlier representations: in particular, a classic notion of Europe as a tradition of deep cultural differences vis-à-vis the Oriental Muslim "other."

By distancing themselves from the "Orient" and from Islam as its distinct signifier, the national stories rooted in Kosovo have engaged in a debate with a "thick," rather than a "thin," conception of Europe. This means that they have tried to measure up to Europe as a traditional community of values, rather than the dynamic cosmopolitan Europe of law and standards, which is officially embodied by the Union. The revival of these national memories not only anchors a particular configuration of national time and space for Serbs, Albanians, and Turks, but it also tries to configure a time and space for Europe, which the European Union, an indeterminate, deterritorialized, and ever incomplete process, denies. Outmoded and peripheral only on the surface, this dynamic of memory mirrors a concern with identity that is very present at the core of Europe, where it is frequently used as a wedge issue by populist and anti-immigrant movements in defense of an allegedly authentic and coherent European tradition. Whether the question is of individual liberties versus religious values, or multiculturalism versus assimilation, Europe's Christian character and its relationship with Islam are central themes in the effort to give positive content to the idea of Europe. The narratives outlined in this chapter both reflect and nourish the debate.

Serbian Memory and the "True West"

When, in October 2006, the excavators of an Albanian company started to dig at Gazimestan, they got dangerously near the state memorial to the fallen Serbian knights, the faux medieval tower that, since 1953, stands twenty-five meters high over the site of the 1389 battlefield.[4] The United Nations intervened to stop their work, responding to a complaint from outraged Serb leaders and Orthodox clergy, for whom the issue was not one of mere preservation. Albanians fear and loathe the site, from which Slobodan Milošević rallied large crowds to the Reconquista of Kosovo in 1989 and see in the tower another socialist-style building, void of historical value. For Serbs, authenticity cannot be an architectural concern. Gazimestan is a *campo santo,* a holy field that belongs to Serbia like all other Serbian burial grounds, because "the meadows around the tower still hide the bones of Lazar's brave knights."[5]

Figure 9.2. Serbian tower at Gazimestan (photo by Joan de Boer)

This particular designation of Gazimestan cannot be understood without considering the role of dead bodies in former Yugoslavia–the famous and the unnamed–in reorienting "people's relations to the past"[6] and establishing a nexus between nationalism and "kinship rooted in particular soils."[7] Gazimestan, the graveyard of thousands of Christian heroes, is also the place where the historical figures of Prince Lazar and the mythical knight Miloš Obilić, the assassin of the Sultan, found death, providing the main plot for a Serbian national narrative. By opting for a Heavenly Kingdom rather than submitting to the Sultan, Lazar made both a spiritual and a political choice. His "Kosovo option" reflected an unwavering loyalty to Orthodox Christianity but also included a belligerent pledge to never be defeated again; Obilić most prominently embodies the spirit of active resistance and heroic patriotism. This Serbian storyline of the battle was built on two traditions: the oral transmission of epic songs flourishing in the western Balkans in the sixteenth and seventeenth century, and the parallel myth that was uniquely institutionalized in liturgical forms by the Orthodox Church since the aftermath of the battle. Nineteenth-century poet and folklorist Vuk Karadžić wove this narrative into a literary canon of foundational national epic, constituting it as a rallying cry for national unification.[8] Although it is only one among several Serb ethnonationalist myths, the battle of Kosovo exceptionally pervades both high and low culture through its representation in popular culture, folk songs, literary texts, scholarly essays, textbooks, and political speeches.[9] It becomes a mobilizing idea when, at particular junctions of Serb history, memory entrepreneurs politically appropriate the Kosovo plot and turn it into the indispensable background for Serbia's political choices.

In the past two decades, the Kosovo myth has occupied center stage, thanks to the convergence of Belgrade intellectual elite, Church theologians, and political insurgents within the Communist nomenclature. When Slobodan Milošević came to Gazimestan on 28 June 1989 to celebrate the six-hundredth anniversary of the battle, he assumed the mantle of the avenger of Kosovo. More than one million people showed up to hear him, after rallies of thousands had marked a season of protest against the alleged Kosovo genocide of Serbs—a national populist mobilization that conferred democratic legitimacy upon his particular strand of authoritarian nationalism.[10]

At Gazimestan, Milošević used the Kosovo legacy to place Serbia squarely within Europe, but on its own terms: "Six centuries ago, Serbia heroically defended itself in the field of Kosovo, but it also defended Europe. Serbia was at that time the bastion that defended the European culture, religion, and European society in general. Therefore, today, it appears not only unjust but even unhistorical and completely absurd to talk about Serbia's belonging to Europe, Serbia is in Europe now just as much as it was in the past, of course, in its own way, but in a way that in the historical sense never deprived it of dignity."[11]

Contrary to this pro-European rhetoric, the Kosovo option translated into an anti-European choice for centralization, against party pluralism, human rights, freedom of the press, and the market economy. The rest is known, through the bloody history of the wars that accompanied the dissolution of Yugoslavia.

The anti-Muslim/anti-Albanian campaign, which was pivotal in the resurgence of Serbian nationalism, does not seem to have abated twenty years after Milošević's epochal rally. On the contrary, as Serbia lost control of Kosovo, the connection between Albanians-Muslims-Jihadists has become the staple of a wide-ranging propaganda campaign that is waged most energetically, but not only, by the Orthodox clergy.[12] Commemorations of the battle at Gazimestan are reminders that the battle continues. They are partly religious ceremonies and partly mass rallies. The highest authorities of church and state jointly preside both at Gazimestan and the monastery of Gračanica, a "tradition" that dates back only to the death of Tito and effectively took off only with Milošević.

Today, there is an evident split in the Serb political leadership between the winning pro-Western, pro-European forces and the Euroskeptics. The first camp includes the Democrats of President Tadić, the small groups of the technocratic G17 + and the Liberal Democrats, and, after the 2008 elections, Milošević's Socialists and the Progressive Party of former Radical Tomislav Nikolić. The second camp is constituted by the Serbian Democrats of Vojslav Koštunica and the Radical Party. This distinction is clearer in political terms than it is intellectually. Koštunica, the longest-lived prime minister after Milošević, has shown through his rhetoric and practice that he can be democratic and authoritarian, pro-European and against Europe.[13] The current Serb political establishment, including President Nikolić and Prime Minister Ivica Dačić, represents direct continuity with Milošević. Even while proclaiming a pro-European stand, Serb leaders maintain a defiant and uncompromising position on Kosovo and a decisive refusal to come to terms with Serbia's wartime legacy. The apprehension of indicted war criminals Radovan Karadžić and General Ratko Mladić and their delivery to The Hague occurred only to satisfy international pressure, more than a decade after the genocide of Bosnia. Both were timed to fit with the calendar of Serbian accession to the EU, a "coincidence" revealing a deeper collusion of at least part of the state with those legendary fugitives from justice.

Being better Europeans than the Europeans themselves has often been an explicit theme in intellectual, political, and clerical discourses in the post–Tito period. "Serbia never adopted an overtly hostile position to the Western Europe's civilization"–noted historian Latinka Perović–but has "determined her links to Europe in relation to a unique need: persuade Western Europe of her truth."[14] Its truth resides in Kosovo, but especially at Gazimestan. Gazimestan anchors the Serbian ethnos to a physical landscape both historically and ontologically: from this field the call originates for all Serbs to remain true to the Kosovo heroes and thus to themselves and the nation. It legitimates the ethno-nation as a repository of fundamental Christian and European values, uncorrupted by secularism and its twin, liberal democracy. Gazimestan territorializes the opposition between the cross and the crescent, where the Christian Serbian nation stands unequivocally against the Islamic Orient in its Albanian-Turk version. From this derives the homogenizing belief that renouncing the wartime legacy and compromising over Kosovo means trading Serbia's spirit for material gain. Gazimestan is constructed as a Serbian and European battlefield, where Serbia can either win or lose her sacred ground but cannot lose her soul, which is the same as the soul of Europe.

The Headless Horseman as an Albanian Christian Hero

There is no physical reminder of an Albanian presence at Gazimestan or Mazgit. Yet, in 1389, Albanians fought alongside other local forces against the Ottoman army, under the command of Prince Lazar. The memory of the battle has lived among Albanians not through monuments or literature, but in the epic oral tradition that celebrates Millosh Kopiliq as the assassin of the Sultan and as an Albanian.

Kopiliq's fantastic story—here a synopsis based on the longest variant[15]—is the geste of a Christian, Albanian warrior who decided to fight to his death, against the better judgment of cautious and ready-to-compromise unnamed leaders. No Prince Lazar partakes in this story, with the exception of a mention in one variant.[16] Kopiliq killed the Sultan, refusing to bow to his request for submission. He was subsequently decapitated by Turkish soldiers after being betrayed by an old Slav woman who revealed the secret place where he was hiding the key to his armor: his whiskers. Carrying his head under his arm, Kopiliq walked away, but died when two women saw him and caused him to drop his head.

The Albanian version of the battle of Kosovo is largely unknown because, until recently, like most Albanian epics, it has been relegated to the oral tradition and not translated.[17] The Serbian version is better known for two reasons. Widely translated, it has acquired literary fame in Europe since the nineteenth century. It has simultaneously played a central role in building Serbia's national identity providing a unifying identity for the South Slavs.[18] Elsewhere, I deal extensively with the vicissitudes of both the mythical Serb hero Obilić and the Albanian hero Kopiliq.[19] Here it will suffice to note that no historical evidence confirms the existence of either. What is important, for our purposes, is to recognize that Kopiliq, for a long time considered no more than a folk hero and a figure of local knowledge, has acquired a new life in postwar Kosovo. He found a place in official history and in the unique production and diffusion of historical memory sponsored by local intellectuals—veterans, journalists, teachers, politicians, and historians—who are engaged in re-appropriating and rewriting the past. Their goal is to produce a coherent storyline for the nation: a pan-Albanian master narrative centered on the hero's resistance unto death against foreign oppression.[20]

Kopiliq is believed to hail from a village by the same name in Drenica, a central and rural area of Kosovo, famous for its rebelliousness. He plays the role, together with historical characters from the same region, of establishing an uninterrupted genealogy of heroes through history. Not accidentally, the Kosovo Liberation Army (KLA) insurgent Adem Jashari–whose 1998 martyrdom in a massacre that killed his whole family has become a national foundational myth–is from Drenica. Jashari is the last of a long line of patriots; Kopiliq the first. As a Christian figure, Kopiliq also reinforces the formulation of a collective religious identity that downplays the Albanians' overwhelming conversion to Islam vis-à-vis their pre-Ottoman culture. He never played, or will play, the same role as Gjergj Kastrioti, also known as Skanderbeg. This fifteenth-century leader's resistance against the Ottomans, in the heart of what is now Albania, earned him the papal commendation of *Atleta Christianitatis* and remains the most eminent story in the Albanian national narrative. Kopiliq is a local Kosovo hero and a Christian, thus confirming the historical roots of Albanians in Kosovo, a place which emerged in the European consciousness of the nineteenth century and early twentieth century as "Old Serbia." Kopiliq's presence at Gazimestan proves that Albanians are autochthonous people in a land that is both Christian and European.

The emphasis that Albanians put on European identity is one strong indication of their anxieties about historical discontinuity and perceived backwardness. At different times in modern history, they have expressed these very feelings through the embrace of an "Orientalist" rejection of the Islamic East. There is no apparent contradiction between this attitude and an overwhelming Muslim identification of Albanians, especially in Kosovo. Islam is, generally and consistently, absent from the other dominant national discourses that have coexisted with the adoption of an identity as originally Christian–whether a propensity to outright discount the role of religion or the image of a tolerant and ecumenical nation.

The revival–both in Albania and in Kosovo–of a Manichean vision of Islam and the East (bad) versus Christianity and the West (good) coincides today with the possibility of European Union membership. In Kosovo, the issue already presented itself in the 1990s when Albanians started to conceptualize more decisively an independent state. A small but capable local Catholic clergy amplified the suggestion made openly in intellectual circles to convert en masse to Catholicism, "the faith of the ancestors," to correct the "error" of mass conversion to Islam.[21] Then self-styled President Ibrahim Rugova fully embraced the idea, and his legacy is the new Catholic cathedral in the center of Prishtina, the capital, where there are only a handful of Catholics. The Christian origin and identity of the Albanian nation continues to be a hot debate. In the spring of 2008, the public conversion to Catholicism by an extended family was a sensation.[22] Discussions among intellectuals–from the renowned Albanian novelist Ismail Kadare and the Kosovo writer Rexhep Qosja to bestseller writer/politician Ben Blushi—keep the issue of the "true" Christian religious identity of the nation in the spotlight.[23]

In this context, Kopiliq helps to rescue Kosovo history from the hijacking by Serbian nationalist circles in order to correct the depiction of Albanians as foreign to the land and the whole of Western civilization. The price is a rejection of the Ottoman experience. Why has an "imposing and extraordinarily important figure of the history of the Balkans and Europe," such as Kopiliq from Drenica, been confined to folklore up until now, rhetorically asks one local writer?[24] Postwar memory entrepreneurs point out that Albanians' religious affiliation, overwhelmingly—although not exclusively—Muslim, obfuscated the truth about the Christian and European origins of Albanians. Their focus is sharp and selective. It highlights Kopiliq's rebelliousness, discarding altogether the story of the saintly Ottoman Sultan who, through his assassin, occupies a central role in the epic. Fallen at Mazgit as a *shahid* (Islamic martyr) and described as *baba* (father) in the songs of rhapsodists, he has been erased from the Kosovo family album along with centuries of adaptation and integration in the Empire.

Secularization of Islamic Saints

In June 2006, the Kosovo Government received, with concerned amusement, the news that a delegation of three hundred Turkish officials, led by the Islamic Welfare Party Prime Minister Recep Tayyip Erdoğan, would arrive in Prishtina on three chartered planes. Would this be another Ottoman invasion? was the joke prompted by the announcement, where humor covered the anxiety over closer proximity to Eastern friends. The occasion of the visit was the inauguration of the newly restored *turbe* of Sultan Murat I, a monument that in modern times has been repaired twice by the Turkish Ministry of Culture and Tourism but that has never before been the object of state commemoration. The visit never happened, because Turkey subsequently canceled it, without providing detailed public explanations.

Murat's *turbe* at Mazgit is not a symbol of occupation for Turkey, but most likely the reminder of a time that is depicted as a relatively peaceful one for the Balkans, thanks to the civilizing Ottoman presence. Former Turkish Minister of Foreign Affairs, Hikmet Çetin, recounts that during a meeting on Bosnia-Herzegovina in 1992, where Milošević and Karadžić were also present, U.S. Secretary of State Lawrence Eagleburger turned to him and said: "How come you succeeded to remain in these terrible territories for 500 years?"²⁵ Conventional wisdom on the Ottoman experience in the Balkans explains this success with "Pax Ottomana" or the stability that the Ottoman supranational identity provided. The empire's tolerance of an unruly Balkan society is also a distinct idea that is propagated by official discourse and history textbooks in Turkey; it is evidence of belonging to Europe through a shared, positive past.

Yet, a common European interpretation of the Ottoman legacy has negative connotations and sees it as a rupture in the Balkans' course toward modernity. A large part of the region shares this interpretation and a feeling of resentment. For this reason, Turkey has been extremely cautious in managing both its image and its foreign policy, especially in the Balkans.²⁶ For decades, its national interest has been to gain EU membership as a modern and secular state, whose good relationship with other Muslim countries has political, not religious meanings. During the Yugoslav conflict, it worked closely with the EU and the United States; calls for solidarity with fellow Muslims in Bosnia and Kosovo stayed mostly within the confines of domestic politics. Since 1999, Turkey is back in Europe after almost a century, but only in a supporting role, with contributing forces to the NATO mission responsible for Kosovo security. In this role, Turkey found the opportunity to re-establish its Western credentials after the EU refusal, two years earlier, to consider its candidacy.

The recent interest in Sultan Murat's *turbe* is officially dictated merely by cultural heritage concerns. Renovation started in 2004, but already the NATO Turkish battalion had published a brochure for visitors in 2001, laconically explaining how the "Sultan's internal organs have been buried in the place where he was martyred," while his body lies in Bursa, Turkey. The battle naturally was important for Ottoman history, if not decisive for the conquest of the Balkans, for the simple fact that the Sultan was killed in Kosovo. Sultan Murat I is represented in early chronicles, which are the first and most exhaustive accounts of the event, as a *shaid*. However, he has never become a cult figure that amplifies the meaning of the battle; his mausoleum has been both the center of pilgrimage and the object of neglect. It is significant that Turkish visitors found it filthy and abandoned in 1660. Evliya Çelebi believed that the condition of the *turbe* was an insult and compared it unfavorably with Lazar's saintly burial place: "My Lord … the inauspicious infidel who slew this sultan lies in a monastery on yonder mountain in a fine mausoleum, lit with jewelled lamps and scented with ambergris and musk. It is supported by wealthy endowments and ministered by priests who every day and night play host to passing visitors, infidel and Moslem alike. The mausoleum of our victorious sultan, on the other hand, has no such institution or keeper to tend to it, and thus all the infidels come and treacherously deposit their excrement in it."[27]

If there is ample evidence confirming the sacredness of the place, it is more due to local popular devotion imbued with syncretism than to Muslim spirituality. For ordinary people in the Balkans, the religious affiliation of saints does not matter much, as long as they are believed to carry extraordinary powers. Equally important is the character of the site, where celebrations happen: it must be a sanctuary, a place where miracles can be delivered.[28] According to a Roma tradition, local celebrations of the Orthodox holiday of Djurdjevdan (Saint George's Day) on 6 May take place at the *turbe*. Saint George is celebrated in many Orthodox Eastern European countries, and in Kosovo, his day is a major religious holiday for "Albanians, Gypsies, and the Slavic population."[29] On 6 May 2007, the field of Mazgit was full of a celebrating crowd, very much in the spirit of a country fair. For one euro, visitors could enter the *turbe* and walk three times around Murat's coffin in the hope of having their secret wish fulfilled.

Although different from tolerance, this syncretism follows the Turkish official discourse of the Ottoman particular brand of Islam, with its capacity for respect of cultural and religious diversity.[30] Thus, the Sultan's mausoleum reminds one of the Ottoman heritage as enlightened, as well as sharing local roots. It testifies, to paraphrase former Minister of Foreign Affairs İsmail Cem, that the history and culture of Turkey, the successor to the Ottoman Empire, was molded in Kosovo and Bosnia as much as in Istanbul or Damascus: this is why "we consider ourselves both European (since seven Centuries [sic]) and Asian, and view this diversity to be an asset."[31]

The Kosovo Battlefield as a Mirror for Europe

Historical memories constructed around the Kosovo battlefield only appear to compete, because a striking commonality characterizes them. In the Serb and Albanian versions, images of the nations developed in interaction with an ideal vision of a Christian, enlightened European civilization. A constant reproach to their alleged backwardness, this imaginary world makes them feel lagging behind as heirs to the "Ottoman legacy" and does not recognize their contribution to its history. Serbs and Albanians have answered the charge by constructing national memories proving the authenticity of their European past. Both regard themselves as "guardians at the gate," a feeling based on the political mythology of *antemurale christianitatis* or outer battlement of Western European civilization. Turkey, the old enemy, also refuses its otherness, by emphasizing both Islam's contribution to human values in the practices of a tolerant Ottoman Empire and the modern Republic's secularism.

Fighting the last crusade in Kosovo, an important part of the Serb leadership would rather lose the chance to be part of the EU, the political offspring of a "soulless" continent, than give up the "cradle of Serb civilization." Keeping the focus on the intellectual tenets of such ideas, I argue that what they are engaged in is an exercise of "Occidentalism." Occidentalists oppose the two main principles on which modern Europe was founded in the seventeenth century: scientific rationality and liberal democracy.[32] Like the Jihadists, the people they mostly abhor, Serbia's memory entrepreneurs reject those principles in the name of their superior spirituality. Here, the influence of the Orthodox leadership cannot be understated.[33] It provides tireless criticism of humanism but also of Western civilization and materialism on behalf of a Pan-Slavist, intransigent, and antimodern idea of society and culture.

In Albanian intellectual and political discourse, as well as in public opinion, a mimetic Orientalism divides and labels East and West as the fundamental historical categories of backwardness and modernity. This is a recurrent and prominent trend in debates on Albanian religious identity; however, it is not the only one.[34] Poet Vasa Efendi's exhortation to unity, "the religion of Albanians is Albanianism," is very often largely presented as a factual statement that would reveal indifference to religion altogether. Another common trend is the interpretation of Albanian religious affiliations' variety as religious tolerance, in which a westernized, and therefore "civilized," version of Islam also appears. In postwar Kosovo, as well as post-communist Albania, the way to European integration is often constructed as a combination of all the above, but rests in the end on the representation of national identity as originally Christian.

In the discussion on mass conversions to Catholicism as a return to the fold, Islam becomes a historical parenthesis, secondary to the Christian–read European and modern–essence of Albanians, and identification with Europe is elaborated through the recognition of an existing "lateness" that needs to be overcome. This mode of self-representation is mimetic. It expresses the "desire for a recognizable, reformed Other, as a subject of difference that is almost the same, but not quite."[35]

There are analogies to be observed in the case of Turkey. By bracketing and repackaging its Ottoman past, Turkey has presented itself as a paradigm of modernization–an experiment in progressive Islam's ability to catch up with the West that has been lauded by outside observers. One version of this notion is that liberation from its Ottoman past makes it possible for Turkey to take its deserved place in Europe.³⁶ Its embrace of radical secularism makes a most decisive claim of European universality, and its old roots in Europe are an important historical precedent. It is also an exercise in mimicry. To paraphrase Talal Asad, it implies that once Turks are separated from their inadequate religious beliefs, they can be fully modern, thus European.³⁷

Almost one hundred years ago, mockery, a common colonial response to mimicry, was the reaction of the Victorian observer Edith Durham to the Turks' modernizing efforts that had been required by the Great Powers. While visiting Murat's *turbe,* she relentlessly denounced the failure of these efforts: the new constitution, the architectural renovation, and the clothes attempted to be modern, but looked like cheap imitations.³⁸ Rebecca West also focused not only on "the difference that is almost nothing but not quite," but also on "the difference that is almost total but not quite."³⁹ The people she met at Gazimestan were "to human beings what a ship inside a glass bottle is to a real boat."⁴⁰

Mockery is not—if it ever was—the right response to the efforts of asserting a European belonging. In fact, the joke is on the Western observers. A closer look at Serb Occidentalism, Albanian mimetic Orientalism, and Turk radical secularism reveals intransigent notions that should be incompatible with the idea of cosmopolitan Europe. On the contrary, they are debated not only outside the EU borders, but at its core. Let us take the idea of Christendom's irreconcilability with, and superiority to, "others"—whether Islam or the modern secular order—or the potentially exclusive character of a secularist universalism, which is incapable of accommodating those distinctive cultural or religious claims that often define minorities. In Europe, as a community based on human rights, respect, and protection of minorities, exclusionary modes of self-representations should not have much credence. Yet, the heightened anxiety of European Union member states with regard to its growing Muslim population, especially after 9/11 and the bombings of Madrid and London, has rendered them surprisingly relevant. In Amsterdam, director Theo van Gogh's murder in 2006, at the hands of a Moroccan immigrant professing loyalty to radical Islam, nearly destroyed a long prized tradition of multiculturalism.⁴¹ Anti-immigrant movements, represented by far Right or fringe parties, are on the rise almost everywhere. They made substantial electoral gains not only domestically, but also in recent European ballots, in the Netherlands, Austria, Denmark, Slovakia, Italy, and Finland. Nobody believes that the uphill struggle facing Turkey on its path to EU membership is only due to noncompliance with required technical standards.⁴²

While popular feelings of fear and loathing of Muslim immigrants run high, the elite intellectual and political debates are equally energized against Islam. In his very controversial 2006 Regensburg address,[43] the newly elected Pope Benedict XVI used Islam as a negative illustration of what was accomplished by Catholic Christianity: a successful synthesis of biblical faith and reason, the traditions of Jewish obedience to God, and Greek inquiry. His speech was both a declaration of the universal truth of Catholicism and a reaffirmation of its defining role of European identity. Despite repeated assertions that he intended to invite other faiths to a dialogue, he established the superiority of one religion, the only universal religion, towards which all others must converge. Benedict XVI's citation from the medieval Byzantine emperor Paleologus is not accidental–it is taken from a discussion of the emperor with his Muslim host on the rational evidence of the superiority of Christianity over Islam.[44]

Attempts to inject Christianity into political debates and institutions have been on the rise in Europe, as religion continues to face the challenges of secularization. One example is the heated discussion of the draft European Union Constitution, which in the end omitted to mention God and Europe's Christian roots, despite strong pressure from German, Italian, Polish, and Slovakian delegates among others, as well as Pope John Paul II. Nativist politicians, acclaimed intellectuals and the clergy propagate the superiority of a "Christian civilization" in crude forms and elevate ethnic discrimination to a normative defense of democracy.[45]

As the battle for Europe concerns identity and religion in Kosovo too, it might be useful to take it seriously as further reflection on the hotly contested meaning of Europeanness. Serb Occidentalism, for example, criticizes the loss of spirituality in exchange for the shallow cosmopolitanism of modern democracies but points more clearly, in its intransigence, to a dissenting tradition within Europe itself: the reaction against what Max Weber called "the disenchantment of the world."[46] If secular philosophers and politicians paid more attention to the moral and existential yearnings created by modernity, they would respond better to the resurgence of religious conservatism and exclusionary identity construction in contemporary Europe. Similarly, the failings of Turkish secularism highlight the possibility for discrimination that is embedded, for example, in the universalistic message of French *laïcité* (secularism). The French system of law, established to ensure inclusion, faces serious problems in integrating its large Muslim minority, because it is firmly grounded in cultural and political norms that are strictly French. Turkish secularism also presents itself as universal and finds its evident limitation in past and present treatment of minorities, corruption of freedom of speech, and a resurgence of religious forms of political mobilization: a purportedly inclusive Turkishness defines the outer boundaries of what the state permits one to say, think and be.

While it is right and fair to demand countries aspiring to join the EU for compliance with its cosmopolitan laws and standards, Europeans should recognize that the applicants' shortcomings and struggles are not so alien or outdated as they seem. On the contrary, by virtue of being outside its borders, they afford Europe a clearer view of its own failings: most notably the resort to essentialist nationalist identities—whether religious or secular—as a defense against the challenges of secularization and the diversity that the very rhetoric of cosmopolitanism extols.

Notes

1. "Memory entrepreneurs" are those actors who struggle over memories and "seek social recognition and political legitimacy of one (their own) interpretation or narrative of the past," Elizabeth Jelin, State Repression and the Struggles for Memory (New York, 2003), 33–34. I consistently use this term in my research on the construction of a Kosovo national narrative: see Anna Di Lellio, The Battle of Kosovo 1389. An Albanian Epic (London, 2009) and Anna Di Lellio and Stephanie Schwandner-Sievers, "The Legendary Commander: the Construction of an Albanian Master-Narrative in Post-War Kosovo," Nations and Nationalism 12, no 3 (2006): 513–529. For narrative and emplotment, I follow Hayden White's focus on "invention" and on the role of "epic emplotment" in historical works. See Hayden White, Metahistory: The Historical Imagination in Nineteenth-Century Europe (Baltimore, 1973). Among the various treatments of the distinction between narratives of the battle and its "real history" see Noel Malcolm's Kosovo: A Short History (New York, 1998), 58–80 and Di Lellio (2009), 3–48.
2. On 17 February 2008, Kosovo became independent under an arrangement providing for international supervision. The new state has been recognized so far by ninety-seven countries, but not by Serbia.
3. Marc Abélès, "Identity and Borders: An Anthropological Approach to EU Institutions," Twenty-First Century Papers: On-Line Working Papers from The Center for 21st Century Studies, no. 4 (Madison, 2004), 13.
4. "Gazimestan Monument Protected from Nearby Construction?," Koha Ditore, 8 October 2006.
5. "Digging up Gazimestan Hill, Sacrilege near the Memorial of the Kosovo Battle Knights," KiM Info Newsletter, 3 October 2006. On the occasion of the 550th anniversary of Gazimestan in 1939, the recently canonized Bishop of Orhid and Zica Nikolaj Velimirović reminded how as repository of the bodies of the Serbian knights, "Kosovo became the campo santo, the holy field." See Nikolaj Velimirović, "Kosovo 1389," in Kosovo, ed., W. Dorich (Alhambra, 1992).
6. Katherine Verdery, The Political Lives of Dead Bodies: Reburial and Postsocialist Change (New York, 1999), 112.
7. Ibid., 105.

8. An excellent critical discussion of the Kosovo myth in Serbian is Miodrag Popović, Vivodan i Casni Krst. Ogled iz Knjizevne Arheologije (Belgrade, [1974] 1998); the most comprehensive treatment of the myth in English is Thomas Emmert, Serbian Golgotha. Kosovo, 1389 (New York, 1990).
9. Ivan Čolović extensively discusses the different aspects of the myth, its diffusion and meaning in The Politics of Symbol in Serbia (London, 2002).
10. Important to notice the popular support to Milošević's authoritarianism and the opportunity given to his manipulation of this support by the socialist structure of the state. On this see N. Vladisavljević, "Serbia's Antibureaucratic Revolution. The Fall of Communism and Nationalist Mobilization in Comparative Perspective," Paper Prepared for Delivery at the Association for the Study of Nationalities (ASN) Annual World Convention, New York, 10–12 April 2008 and Jasna Dragović-Soso, 'Saviours of the Nation.' Serbia's Intellectual Opposition and the Revival of Nationalism (Montreal, 2003), 132–161.
11. Slobodan Milošević, Od Gazimestan do Sevenignena (Belgrade, 2001), 10.
12. I have dealt more extensively with this in "The Missing Revolution in Serbia: 1989–2008," International Journal of Politics, Culture and Society 22, no 3 (2009): 373–384.
13. His performative speeches are all collected in volumes. See Vojislav Koštunica, Odbrana Kosova (Belgrade, 2008) and Entre la Force et le Droit (Lausanne, 1999).
14. Latinka Perović, "Le Dos Tourné à la Modernisation," in Radiographie d'un Nationalisme. Les Racines Serbes du Conflit Yugoslave, ed. N. Popov (Paris, 1998), 123–136, 130.
15. Di Lellio (see note 1), 35–38.
16. Di Lellio (see note 1), ft. 179.
17. The first English translation of the Albanian heroic songs is by Robert Elsie and Janice Mathie-Heck, Songs of the Frontier Warriors. Këngë Kreshnikësh (Wauconda, 2004). The Kosovo epic has appeared in English only in 2009, also in Elsie's translation, in Di Lellio (see note 1).
18. In particular Obilić legitimized Serbia as the Piedmont of the South Slavs in the early twentieth century. On the use of Kosovo symbolism to generate enthusiasm and support for South Slavs unitarism, see Ivo Banac, The National Question in Yugoslavia. Origins, History, Politics (Ithaca, 1984), 202–207.
19. Di Lellio (see note 1), 18–30.
20. On the pan-Albanian master narrative and its construction see Di Lellio and Schwandner-Sievers (see note 1).
21. Dom Lush Gjergji, "Would an Independent Kosova be an Islamist State?" in The Case for Kosova. Passage to Independence, ed., A. Di Lellio (London, 2006), 159–163.
22. Anna Di Lellio, "Kosovan and Catholic," The Guardian, 21 May 2008.
23. Ismail Kadare, Identiteti Europian i Shqiptarëve (Tirana, 2006) and Pro & Kundër Blushit (Tirana, 2008).
24. Ahmet Qeriqi, Milush Kopiliqi, serb apo shqiptar? (Prishtina, 2003), 24.
25. As quoted in Can Karpat, "Kosovo Turks: Those Who Live in the Most Critical Region of Balkans," Axis Information and Analysis (AIA), Balkan Section, 15 December 2005.
26. Sylvie Gangloff explains clearly and succinctly this development in "The Impact of Ottoman Legacy on Turkish Policy in the Balkans (1991–1999)" in La Perception de l'Héritage Ottoman dans les Balkans. The Perception of the Ottoman Legacy in the Balkans, ed., S. Gangloff (Paris, 2005), 169–196.
27. Robert Dankoff and Robert Elsie, trans. and eds, Evliya Çelebi in Albania and Adjacent Regions (Kosovo, Montenegro, Ohrid) (Leiden, 2000), 21. A keeper was subsequently appointed, a man from Bukhara in modern Uzbekistan, and his family has tended the complex until now. The widow of one of his ancestors, Sanija Turbedari, a Sandjak Moslem, is the current guardian.
28. Ger Duijzings, Religion and the Politics of Identity in Kosovo (London, 2000), 79 and Frederick William Hasluck, Christianity and Islam under the Sultans, ed. M. Hasluck, (London, 1929), 68–69.

29. Duijzings (see note 28), 81. St. George is also known as Herdeljez, the combination of the names of two Moslem prophets, Hizir and Ilyas, who meet every 5 May to welcome the end of winter. The holiday has a special significance as the end of winter, and Roma sacrifice a sheep for luck in the coming year, and a record of such celebration is kept in the Kosovo Roma Oral History Project: "Roma Culture: Holidays," Who We Were, Who We Are: Kosovar Roma Oral Histories.
30. Ali Bardakoğlu, "Culture of Co-existence in Islam: The Turkish Case," 30 May 2008. Professor Ali Bardakoğlu was President of Turkish Religious Affairs of the Republic of Turkey.
31. İsmail Cem, "Turkey and Europe: Looking to the Future from a Historical Perspective," 16 September 2005.
32. Ian Buruma and Avishai Margalit, Occidentalism: the West in the Eyes of its Enemies (New York, 2004).
33. Di Lellio (see note 12); Helsinki Committee for Human Rights in Serbia, The Serbian Orthodox Church and the New Serbian Identity (Belgrade, 2006); Radmila Radić, "L' Église et la 'Question Serbe'" in Popov (see note 14), 137–177 and Dragović-Soso (see note 10), 124–125.
34. For a comprehensive discussion of the phenomenon see Enis Sulstarova, Arratisje nga Lindja. Orientalizmi Shqiptar nga Naimi te Kadareja (Chapel Hill, 2006). On the relationship between religion and national identity among Albanians, both Nathalie Clayer, Aux Origines du Nationalisme Albanais. La Naissance d'une Nation Majoritairement Musulmane en Europe (Paris, 2007) and Bashkim Iseni, La Question Nationale en Europe du Sud-Est. Genèse, Èmergence et Développement de l'Identité Nationale Albanaise au Kosovo et en Macedoine (Lausanne, 2008), offer ample material for discussion.
35. Homi Bhabha, The Location of Culture (London, 1994), 86.
36. Bernard Lewis, The Emergence of Modern Turkey (London, 1968).
37. Talal Asad, "Moslems and European Identity: Can Europe Represent Islam?" in The Idea of Europe. From Antiquity to the European Union, ed., A. Pagden (New York, 2002), 218.
38. Edith Durham, High Albania (London, [1909] 1987), 288–89.
39. Bhabha (see note 35), 91.
40. Rebecca West, Black Lamb and Grey Falcon. A Journey through Yugoslavia (London, [1940] 1994), 903.
41. Ian Buruma, Murder in Amsterdam: The Death of Theo van Gogh and the Limits of Tolerance (London, 2006).
42. An Independent Commission on Turkey, composed of diplomats, recently concluded as much in Turkey in Europe: Breaking the Vicious Circle (2009).
43. Benedict XVI, "Faith, Reason and the University. Memories and Reflections," Regensburg, 12 September 2006.
44. Manuele II Paleologo, Dialoghi con un Musulmano. VII Discussione (Bologna, 2007).
45. See the international sensation created by Oriana Fallaci's racist bestsellers, expounding on the inferiority of Islam: La Rabbia e L'Orgoglio (Milan, 2001) and La Forza della Ragione (Milan, 2004). To stay in Italy, Marcello Pera, President of the Italian Senate, made Benedict XVI's thought a manifesto for the European neo-conservatives: "Italia-Europa. Identita' Cristiana a Rischio?," Speech delivered in Bologna, 13 November 2006. The right-wing government formed in 2008 proposed to register and fingerprint all Roma residents, including minors, as a security measure. Finally, in Poland, the peculiar contemporary mix of Catholic fundamentalism populism and nationalism is discussed by Adam Michnik, "Was Pontius Pilate a Liberal Democract? Democracy between Relativism and the Absolute, (Reading Cardinal Joseph Ratzinger, Part I)." Transitional Center for Democratic Studies Bulletin 16/2 Issue 51 (2006).
46. Akeel Bilgrami, "Occidentalism, the Very Idea: An Essay on Enlightenment and Enchantment," Critical Inquiry 3 (2006): 381–411, 402.

Chapter 10

Transformation of Memory in Croatia
Removing Yugoslav Anti-Fascism

●●●●●●●●●●●●●●●

Ljiljana Radonic

Recent decades have witnessed a growth in the interdisciplinary study of collective memory, especially in relation to the Holocaust and World War II. At least in Western countries, the Holocaust has become a "negative icon,"[1] a universal imperative to respect human rights in general, and a "container" for the memory of different victims, as Daniel Levy and Natan Sznaider put it.[2] Moreover, in Europe this "universalization of the Holocaust" includes another discursive dimension—the "rupture in civilization" (*Zivilisationsbruch Auschwitz*)[3]—that has increasingly become a negative European founding myth. The unified Europe after 1945 is understood as a collective sharing a common destiny (*Schicksalsgemeinschaft*) that has learned a lesson from the Holocaust and developed shared structures in order to avoid a recurrence.

Parallel to this process of Europeanizing the Holocaust, in Eastern European countries, history has been re-narrated since 1989. The long-hegemonic historical narrative of the heroic antifascist struggle was delegitimized together with the socialist regimes, placing the trauma of the socialist crimes in the core of collective memory—often evoking symbols familiar from *Shoah* memory, such as railroad tracks and wagons. This "divided memory"[4] in the East and West has prompted representatives of post-socialist states to demand that socialist crimes be addressed to the same extent as the Holocaust. In light of the resonance of these memories, scholars have paid particular attention to the countries of Eastern Europe after 1989, focusing on both the World War II and state socialist historical periods. Nevertheless, comparative studies of Holocaust memory in post-socialist Eastern Europe have paid little attention to the countries of the former Yugoslavia.[5] For this reason, this chapter examines the case of Croatia—except Romania, the only country besides the Third Reich that ran death camps on its own during World War II.

Moreover, Croatia is a country that not only has gone through an economic and political transformation but also through a nation-building process, since the early 1990s. This nation-building process is characterized by the literal and symbolic delimitation from the old federal state of Yugoslavia. Thus, the search for national identity played a greater role than in other newly formed, post-socialist countries that did not secede from a larger entity. After a short overview of the way World War II was confronted in Yugoslavia, this chapter examines the transformation in policy regarding the past from 1990–2008, during three different historical stages: the first, following the collapse of Yugoslavia in 1990/91 and President Franjo Tuđman's rise to power; the second, after Tuđman's death and the government change in 2000; and the third, after Tuđman's "Croatian Democratic Union" won the elections again in 2003 under its new leader, Ivo Sanader. I not only analyze the content of the newly hegemonic, historical narrative with the participating and the silenced protagonists, but also the manner in which this hegemonic historical narrative has been asserted—looking at whether narrative construction has occurred democratically or in a repressive manner. Finally, I raise the question regarding how the Croatian case and its victim narrative fits into the thesis of the universalization,[6] or the Europeanization, of the Holocaust,[7] and how Croatia is adapting to the emergent European standard of dealing with World War II.

Confronting World War II in Yugoslavia

Similar to other socialist states, the rule of the Communist Party in Yugoslavia was legitimized by referring back to the partisan struggle during World War II as a legitimate means of having gained power. However, unlike Poland, Hungary, or Romania, Yugoslavia actually liberated its territory from the Nazis with almost no foreign support. Complicating matters, it was also a country that had to legitimize the existence of a Yugoslav state, following a civil war between the Ustaša (nationalist/fascist Croatian paramilitaries), Partisans (communist guerillas), and Četniks (Serbian nationalist paramilitaries). Post–1945, no specific nation/ethnic group was condemned; guilt and responsibility were externalized to the marginalized noncommunist powers. Thus, the antifascist struggle played a key role in the ideational resurrection of the Yugoslav state. The memory of the common struggle became the founding myth, and its defamation became a punishable offense.[8]

The Communist Party forbade debates about the civil war, so only one particular fragment of the past was remembered, while other sections of society found their memories marginalized. The Holocaust was treated as a minor matter, and the victims of "Fascist" atrocities were rarely subdivided into different groups, such as resistance and mass murder. During the 1960s, controversies between Serbian and Croatian historians unsettled this narrative about the "supranational" Yugoslav partisans by raising the question of the Serbian and Croatian "share" in the heroic victory, on the one hand, and in collaboration on the other.[9] Many on the Serbian side were frustrated because Serb victims were perceived to be inadequately commemorated or appreciated, and Croatians resented the latent accusation of collective guilt. As a consequence, the specific and different ways of remembering the war became an element of political mobilization in the late 1980s.[10]

Croatia from 1990–1999

The New Historical Narrative

The dissolution of Yugoslavia went together with a break with both the antifascist frame and the narrow communist dogma about how to deal with World War II. Instead of a democratic frame for historiography, each nation developed its own victim-narration according to its specific national myths. In Croatia, the Ustaša regime, whose anti-Semitism was a replica of National Socialist anti-Semitism and whose brutal mass murder of Serbs even led to protests by the Germans, was depicted as one of the most important phases in Croatia's struggle for national identity. Although antifascism was anchored formally in the new constitution, it seemed that the idea of a Croatian state was only conceivable in combination with historical revisionism concerning the character of the so-called Independent State of Croatia (Nezavisna Država Hrvatska, NDH), a Nazi puppet regime from 1941–1945.

After the breakup of Yugoslavia, Croatia was in a different position compared to most other post-socialist countries—not the least of which was because its president was a World War II historian and the chief revisionist of the country. Indeed, President Tuđman's anti-Semitic book "Wastelands of Historical Reality" (1989),[11] in which he equated the crimes committed by the Ustaša and the Partisans by minimizing the number killed in the

Ustaša concentration camp Jasenovac,[12] was the first step in establishing the frame of the historical narrative for the new state. The second step was Tuđman's idea to reconcile Ustaša and Partisans, who had, in his words, both fought for the same goal, albeit in different ways, during World War II–the Croatian cause.[13] In connection with this idea, the Jasenovac memorial area–about 100 kilometers southeast from Zagreb on the border with Bosnia–played a great symbolic role, although the site itself remained devastated after the war in the 1990s until Tuđman's death in 1999. Following the example of General Francisco Franco in Spain, Tuđman suggested bringing the bones of the Ustaša and of the soldiers of the NDH (Domobrani)–killed near Bleiburg (just over the Slovenian border in Austria) by Partisans in 1945–to a "national memorial" Jasenovac.[14] He had to change these plans,[15] as well as the anti-Semitic parts in the English version of his book, following international criticism.[16]

The tension between the two *lieux de mémoire*[17] Jasenovac and Bleiburg, which were equated by calling Bleiburg the site of the "Croatian holocaust,"[18] gives an accurate picture of national victimhood and the denial of responsibility for the Ustaša crimes during the Tuđman era. The Bleiburg commemorations under the patronage of the Croatian parliament or government always had many more visitors and were broadcast live on television–despite the Ustaša insignia present throughout the site[19]–while the Jasenovac commemorations have only been broadcast since 2003.[20] The Catholic Church dispatched bishops to the much better frequented commemorations in Bleiburg, while no Catholic priest had attended a commemoration in Jasenovac during the 1990s.[21] The only Croatian politicians Tuđman sent to attend the commemorations in Jasenovac had been Partisans in their youth, although this was hardly noticeable in their speeches at the site, since they instrumentalized the commemorations to underscore the narrative of Croatian victimhood.[22] Commemorations in Jasenovac and their instrumentalization for the Croatian nationalist cause certainly offer the best illustration of the state of the "dynamics of memory" in Croatia.

Contrary to lip service that was still paid to antifascism, most street names, which formerly commemorated the victories of the Partisan struggle and the victims of World War II, were renamed. The best known and most disputed example is the renaming of the "Square of the Victims of Fascism," the location of Ustaša police headquarter in Zagreb, into the "Square of the Croatian Heroes." Seventeen streets throughout Croatia were named after Mile Budak, a "poet" and the Ustaša Minister of Education, who was responsible for the NDH's racial laws. "Only" cafés and kindergartens were named after the leader of the Ustaša–Ante Pavelić. According to the Association of Antifascist Fighters (SAB), from the time Croatia became independent in 1991 until 1998, 2,966 memorials commemorating "victims of Fascism" or the antifascist struggle were removed or destroyed, without anyone being punished for it.[23] In 1993, a memorial plaque commemorating the "Ustaša fallen for the NDH" was placed on the building that housed the Croatian army in the town of Sinj, near Split,[24] and a memorial for the Ustaša criminal Jure Francetić–founder of the infamous "Black Legion"– was erected in Slunj in 1999.[25]

History books also reflected the revisionist approach typical of the 1990s. In Yugoslavia, half of the school books for the eighth grade of junior high school were dedicated to a discussion of World War II, but this history only encompassed the Partisan struggle for liberation.[26] After Croatia became independent, World War II was covered in only one-fifth of the new history books for the eighth grade. In these, the Independent State of Croatia was primarily discussed. The NDH was treated as Croatian history, the Croatian wish for an independent state was described, as was the structure of the regime, but its atrocities were hardly mentioned. Jasenovac was mentioned only in two lines and the term Holocaust was not mentioned at all, while Bleiburg and the crimes of the Četniks were described extensively. Shocking pictures were also included. Thus, the school books in Croatia presented an equally one-sided picture as those in former Yugoslavia had, though the slant they presented was totally different.[27]

During 1998/99, the investigation, extradition, and trial against Dinko Šakić, a former commander of the concentration camp Jasenovac who had emigrated to Argentina after the war, the intensity of the discussions about the character of the Ustaša regime and Jasenovac peaked.[28] His wife, Nada Šakić, a guard in the women's camp Stara Gradiška, was also extradited to Croatia, but was set free again, supposedly because of a lack of evidence. In the Croatian media, the Simon Wiesenthal Center in Jerusalem was harshly criticized for organizing international pressure on Croatia. In the public discourse, the extradition of the Šakićs was seen as necessary not because they had committed crimes but rather to prevent harm to Croatia's international image.[29] The few free newspapers and the international media primarily criticized the fact that Nada Šakić was freed despite the Wiesenthal Center's claim of having delivered enough evidence for her conviction. They also condemned the decision not to try Dinko Šakić for genocide but for atrocities against civilians, thereby not allowing the fundamental character of the Ustaša regime to be part of the prosecutor's agenda.[30] Also, most of the witnesses were Croatians, which suggested that most of the victims were Croatian enemies of the regime, not Serbs, Jews, and Roma.[31] The media allowed Šakić plenty of room to prove that he was still devoted to the ideals of the Ustaša and to anti-Semitism, and there were many media reports that expressed concern about the condition of his health and the quality of his food in prison.[32] In October 1999, despite political and media support, Šakić was sentenced to twenty years of prison, which was the maximum possible sentence for the crimes for which he was tried. He died incarcerated in 2008.[33]

Deficient Democracy and Deficient "History"?

After analyzing the transformation of the hegemonic historical narrative in Croatia, the question arises as to how the "memory" of the ruling elite was asserted, and which other protagonists appeared in the field of conflicting memories. My argument is that Croatia was not even a deficient democracy between 1991 and 1999 but an "authoritarian electoral regime,"[34] because democratic rules were violated in too many areas: the overwhelming authority of President Tuđman; the non-acceptance of electoral results, such as the ruling party's defeat in the Zagreb city council election of 1995; the repression of the opposition and of the free media; etc.[35] Ethnonationalist enthusiasm following independence went hand in hand with the marginalization and criminalization of differing views–especially when it came to the struggle for "the truth" about World War II. Once all daily newspapers–except *Novi list* from Rijeka–had been taken over (partly by force, as was the case for *Glas Slavonije* and *Slobodna Dalmacija*),[36] the remaining free papers were subjected to repression, to the burning of their editions,[37] and to court trials, as was the case for the weekly *Feral Tribune* after it criticized President Tuđman's idea of a "bone mix" of Ustaša and their victims in Jasenovac in 1996, allowing it to continue publishing only after an international outcry, financial support, and pressure on Croatia.[38] The monopoly of state television (HTV) remained untouched in the 1990s, and the only free radio station (Radio 101) was nearly shut down in 1996, but then began broadcasting again after heavy protests by its listeners.[39] The opposition, which had a difficult stand before the elections because of its lack of access to the media, kept silent about the HDZ's revisionism for years, because opposition to this revisionism and national victimization was viewed in the public discourse as indicating support for "the Serbs."[40] The only protest against the removal of the memorials commemorating the Partisan struggle and the renaming of streets came from the SAB, a small number of NGOs, and the few free newspapers.

In sum, what happened after Croatia gained its independence was not a "pluralization" of memory, but a total change of content from the "memory" of the Partisans to the "memory" dominated by returning Ustaša.[41] Furthermore, the violation of democratic standards corresponded with the domination of a revisionist historical narrative.

After the Tuđman Era: Democratization of Memory?

With Tuđman's death in 1999, a decade of HDZ administration ended and a coalition under the leadership of the Social Democratic Prime Minister Ivica Račan, a reformed communist, won the elections, while Stipe Mesić, also a former Communist official who first joined the HDZ, but left it again in 1994, was elected president. The authority of the presidential office was diminished soon afterwards. During the process of democratization, the manner in which the past was dealt with in Croatia also changed.

Already in 2000, a new school book appeared in which the Holocaust was mentioned and the number of victims at the Jasenovac concentration camp was given. The book claimed that 80,000 victims had perished there, which is quite an accurate figure, since current research estimate a number of 80,000–100,000 victims. Furthermore, Jasenovac was truthfully described as an extermination camp. Nevertheless, since the author of this book was Hrvoje Matković, who also wrote the previous textbook in 1998, the general tone did not change.[42] In 2003, a much more accurate school book, which discussed the Holocaust and the Nazi death camps, was published, but it was not widely accepted and only a few schools adopted it.[43]

In December 2000, the "Square of the Victims of Fascism" received its old name back, and Tuđman's reburial plans for a "national memorial" at Jasenovac were finally shelved. In contrast to the 1990s, when only representatives of different national, religious, and political organizations spoke at the commemorations in Jasenovac, Ivica Račan was the first acting prime minister to speak in 2002.[44] He balked, however, at clearly stating who had committed the crimes during the Ustaša regime. Instead, he spoke generally about the evil that happened in Jasenovac without actually naming those responsible for the atrocities. Thus, while a change of the hegemonic narrative could be observed, the former Communist Račan was nevertheless afraid of fully coming to terms with the revisionist Tuđman era. The ambivalent perspective of the Račan government was also reflected when some of its members visited Bleiburg in the same year. First, Zdravko Tomac, the Social Democratic vice-president of parliament and a former

Communist official, wanted to apologize for the killings committed by the Partisans in 1945 (despite the Ustaša iconography which dominated the commemoration year after year) but had to break off his speech because of heckling from the audience. Two days later, Račan bowed and apologized in front of the memorial in Bleiburg, which neither Tuđman nor Sanader, his successor from the HDZ, had ever visited. On the other hand, when President Stipe Mesić was asked whether he planned to visit Bleiburg in 2005, he answered: "We are not comparing Bleiburg and Jasenovac. None of the victims from Jasenovac were responsible for the people killed in the trenches and in Bleiburg, but a lot of people in Bleiburg were responsible for mass murder. They are victims, but we cannot say they are innocent. They should not have been killed and tormented, but they should have been put on trial."[45]

As president, Mesić always found clear words about the Ustaša crimes at the commemorations in Jasenovac and at other occasions. He condemned the idea of the "reconciliation of all Croats"[46] as a falsification of history and also condemned the crimes committed in the name of the Croatian state, including not only the ones in the Jasenovac death camp but also those from the more recent past, just as he supported the conviction of the old as well as of the more recent war criminals. Mesić also cooperated with the Wiesenthal Center in connection with the extradition of the Ustaša officials Milivoj Ašner (residing in Austria), who had been the chief of Ustaša police in Požega, and Ivo Rojnica (living in Argentina), the former Ustaša governor of Dubrovnik, whom Tuđman wanted to appoint as Croatia's ambassador to Argentina. This led to threats against Mesić and the "Civil committee for Human Rights," which supported the Wiesenthal Center in Zagreb.[47]

Towards European Standards: The New HDZ?

In 2003, the HDZ once again won the elections. Prime Minister Ivo Sanader was known as a Europe-oriented statesman who broke with the revisionist ideas of his predecessor. The Sanader administration removed the memorials for the Ustaša authorities Mile Budak in Sveti Rok and Jure Francetić in Slunj and started an initiative to rename the aforementioned seventeen streets throughout Croatia that carried the name of Mile Budak. During the Jasenovac commemoration in 2004, Sanader demanded: "We must not allow for the atrocities that occurred in Jasenovac and elsewhere during the Ustaša regime in the NDH to be forgotten."[48] He was the first HDZ politician in Jasenovac who broke with the tradition of mentioning the victims of

Bleiburg alongside those killed in Jasenovac and explicitly called the Ustaša regime responsible for Jasenovac[49]–while Tuđman and his followers had spoken of some kind of ontological evil that had led to the atrocities. Media critics, however, expressed their skepticism, when HDZ politicians like Andrija Hebrang and Vladimir Šeks, in diametric opposition to their prior appearances, began delivering antifascist speeches.[50] Excluding Sanader and his inner circle, the positions of the HDZ did not seem to have changed decisively, although the perspective of joining the European Union forced the party to at least officially temper its mood. Nonetheless, Ivo Zec, HDZ member of the local board in Dubrovnik, stated at one council meeting in 2004 that it would be better not to privatize local hotels than to sell them to Serbs or Jews, continuing that the latter "seen in the long run, are the greater evil."[51] Not one member of the council opposed this view and the government reacted only after a foreign investor called a press conference to indignantly raise the issue.

"The Serbs" played, and continue to play, an enormous role in the narrative of the Croatian "imagined community"[52] and today's political conflicts almost always refer to conflicting memories. In 2005, before the commemoration in Jasenovac, there was also a commemoration at the memorial site in Donja Gradina (Republika Srpska, Bosnia and Herzegovina), which used to be part of the Jasenovac memorial area. On this occasion, the President of the Republika Srpska, Dragan Cavić, stated that there is still no justice for the seven hundred thosand victims of Jasenovac. Afterwards, at the round table on "Tendencies of Historiography and Research on the Jasenovac Concentration Camp" in Banja Luka, the anthropologist Srboljub Živanović from London made the dubious statement that Croatia still had not overcome its "genocidality," although Croatian politicians, who "reduce" the figures to seventy thousand, claim the opposite.[53]

Sanader, Croatian Prime Minister until 2009, responded to the "provocation" from the commemoration at the other bank of the Sava River. He condemned "the positions of Greater Serbia in imposing the theory of the alleged genocidal tendencies of the Croatian people" and the exaggeration, but also the reduction of the number of victims. The premier emphasized contemporary Croatia's "commitment to antifascist values,"[54] but he added that the "Homeland War" (1991–1995) was also fought against one type of fascism. In 2005, he argued similarly in Yad Vashem, when he pointed out that during the war in the 1990s, the Croats were also victims of the same kind of evil as nazism and fascism, and that no one knew better than the Croats what it meant to be a victim of aggression and crime.[55] This shift away from historical revisionism, which minimized the victims of the

Ustaša state in the Tuđman era, to a new view that recognizes the Holocaust, while presenting the Croats as victims of fascism, this time of "Serbian fascism," shows the problematic nature of the "globalization of the Holocaust."[56] Thus, Levy and Sznaider are obviously right when they argue that the Holocaust is becoming more and more a "container" for the memory of different victims, but, as the aforementioned example illustrates, this development cannot be diagnosed as neutrally as the authors suggest.

Furthermore, at the end of 2005, a conflict about the purpose and the conception of the new exhibition in Jasenovac reached the Croatian public. The main problem of the new exhibition seemed to be the emphasis on the Holocaust, while the genocide against Serbs and Roma was marginalized. The director defended the exhibition by saying that it had been approved by international experts. However, these experts only came from institutions concerned with the Holocaust, who were not aware of the particular situation in Jasenovac. Critics opposed the exhibition's concept arguing that the exhibition did not show who the perpetrators were, which nation had the biggest losses, and how people were killed in Jasenovac.[57] This criticism was the reason why the exhibition opened with some delay in November 2006. As a consequence of the changes, most of the former critics of the exhibition later considered it a first step in the right direction and a work in progress, but no further improvements have been made until 2012.

In a parallel context, Reinhart Koselleck stressed that Germany cannot only commemorate the victims, but must also, or maybe first of all, remember the perpetrators.[58] In the Croatian case, there cannot be an exhibition (supported by international experts and meeting international aesthetic standards) that concentrates on the (Jewish) victims in a country and a region where "negative memory" concerning committed, not suffered crimes, is still an unmet need. The focus on the victims and a diffuse memory of the Holocaust that does not deal with the perpetrators any more is the second problem of the "Europeanization" of the Holocaust exemplified by the Croatian case.

New Victim Narratives in Accordance with European Standards

Just as the end of Yugoslavia did not lead to a quick consolidation of democracy, the manner of confronting the heritage of World War II and Yugoslavia after reaching independence had nothing to do with a "pluralization" of memory. The hegemonic narrative in Croatia changed from Partisan-dominated memory to a memory guided by the idea of a "national reconciliation" of both sides, leading to a rehabilitation of the Ustaša state. The antifascism anchored in the constitution was mere lip service, while the hegemony of Tuđman's revisionist narrative was enforced through the repression of opposing media. Tuđman's death and the new Social Democratic government led to democratization and a new "struggle for memory." The government lead by Ivica Račan initiated some steps towards breaking with the revisionism of the Tuđman era, but also feared being delegitimized if it did not accept the importance of Bleiburg for the formation of Croatian national identity. On the other hand, President Stipe Mesić was the main proponent of the shift in the official approach to the past, although his antifascist reputation suffered somewhat as it became clear that he had also promoted revisionist views during his career in the HDZ at the beginning of the 1990s.

The new HDZ leadership, under Ivo Sanader, established an official narrative in line with problematic European standards: the idea of learning from the Holocaust to avoid similar atrocities in the present and future, including the use of the Holocaust to establish one's own narrative of national victimhood after acknowledging the negative common European heritage.[59] In Sanader's case, this meant arguing that Croats were the victims of the new Serbian fascism.

After Sanader's unexpected resignation in 2009, his successor, Jadranka Kosor, continued condemning Ustaša crimes at the commemorations in Jasenovac, but this time without referring to any Serbian perpetrators. Also, the new Croatian president, Ivo Josipović, seems to follow his forerunners tradition of stressing the need to approach the past. At least this is indicated by the fact that he inaugurated a replica memorial plaque at the site of the former concentration camp Jadovno in June 2010, which had been destroyed earlier. On the other hand, Josipović was the first Croatian president who had visited Bleiburg only a few days earlier, something Mesić would never have done.

Of course, Croatia is not the only successor state of former Yugoslavia that has still not faced its "negative heritage" in an appropriate way. In Serbia and the Serbian part of Bosnia, the Holocaust usually only refers to the historical events in the Ustaša state. While Jasenovac has officially become the site of a Jewish and Serbian Holocaust, the collaboration of the Nedić government with the Nazis in Serbia has still not been reappraised.[60] Bosnian Muslims consider themselves to be "victims of the Serbian and Croatian Nazis and Fascists" in the war of 1992–1995, while the collaboration with Nazis and Fascists–for example in the "Handschar" division of the SS–is played down.⁶¹ In Slovenia, the myth of "functional collaboration" with the Nazis in order to escape from "godless Communism" is widespread, while the Holocaust of the Slovenian Jews deported from the Hungarian occupation zone is not accepted as part of Slovenia's history.⁶² Because of the strong connection between the victim narratives of the successor states of former Yugoslavia, a comparative analysis of the struggle for memory is indispensable, but still does not yet seem feasible in Zagreb, Belgrade, or Sarajevo.

This short overview shows that Croatia had to confront its past more critically than its neighbor states because of its role in World War II and the revisionist Tuđman era, in order to come closer to integration with the European memory community. However, it also shows that the "universalization" and "Europeanization" of the Holocaust enable new victim narratives compatible with these "European standards." Thus, if the often invoked "international community" would stop recycling images from World War II instead of condemning each of the crimes for what it is, this would certainly aid confronting the recent past of the wars in the 1990s.

Notes

1. Dan Diner, *Gegenläufige Gedächtnisse. Über Geltung und Wirkung des Holocaust* (Göttingen, 2007).
2. Daniel Levy and Natan Sznaider, *The Holocaust and Memory in a Global Age* (Philadelphia, 2005).
3. Dan Diner, ed., *Zivilisationsbruch. Denken nach Auschwitz* (Frankfurt/Main, 1988).
4. Stefan Troebst, "Jalta versus Stalingrad, GULag versus Holocaust. Konfligierende Erinnerungskulturen im größeren Europa," in *"Transformationen" der Erinnerungskulturen in Europa nach 1989,* eds., B. Faulenbach and F. Jelich (Essen, 2006), 23–49.
5. Jovan Byford, "When I say 'the Holocaust', I mean Jasenovac: Remembrance of the Holocaust in Contemporary Serbian Society," *East European Jewish Affairs* 37, no. 1 (2007): 51–74.
6. Levy and Sznaider (see note 2).
7. Tony Judt, *Postwar: A History of Europe Since 1945* (New York, 2005).
8. Wolfgang Höpken, "Vergangenheitspolitik im sozialistischen Vielvölkerstaat 1944–1991," in *Umkämpfte Vergangenheit. Geschichtsbilder, Erinnerung und Vergangenheitspolitik im internationalen Vergleich,* eds., P. Bock and E. Wolfrum (Gottingen, 1999), 210–243; Wolfgang Höpken, *Öl ins Feuer? Schulbücher, ethnische Stereotypen und Gewalt in Südosteuropa* (Hannover, 1996); Holm Sundhaussen, "Jugoslawien und seine Nachfolgestaaten. Konstruktion, Dekonstruktion und Neukonstruktion von 'Erinnerungen' und Mythen", in *Mythen der Nationen. 1945–Arena der Erinnerung,* ed., M. Flacke (Mainz, 2004), 375–384; Angela Richter and Barbara Beyer, ed., *Geschichte (ge-)brauchen. Literatur und Geschichtskultur im Staatssozialismus: Jugoslavien und Bulgarien* (Berlin, 2006).

9. Darko Hudelist, *Tuđman: Biografija* (Zagreb, 2004), 259.
10. Höpken "Vergangenheitspolitik" (see note 8), 224.
11. Franjo Tuđman, *Bespuća povijesne zbiljnosti* (Zagreb, 1994). For Tuđman, who stated in 1990 that he was lucky because his wife was neither Jewish nor Serbian, anti-Semitism is a historical constant (368). He argues that Jewish "anationality" (195) is the reason for their tragic fate, and equates them with their persecutors, saying that the Jews were responsible for the administration of the Jasenovac camp and that Jewish prisoners took part in the executions (316–320). Furthermore, he draws a line from Nazi fascism to "Judeo-Fascism," which is an anti-Semitic thesis well known in the West, according to which the Jews are the new Nazis. See also Radmila Milentijević, "Anti-Semitism and the Treatment of the Holocaust in Postcommunist Yugoslavia," in *Anti-Semitism and the Treatment of the Holocaust in Postcommunist Eastern Europe*, ed., R. L. Braham (New York, 1994), 225–249.
12. Serbs, Roma, Jews, and Croatian fighters against the Ustaša regime were killed in and around the five camps that constituted the Jasenovac concentration camp. 80,914 victims have currently been identified by name.
13. Mariko Čulić, *Tuđman: anatomija neprosvijećenog apsolutizma* (Split, 1999), 105–108.
14. Ibid., 109; Viktor Ivančić, *Točka na U. Slučaj Šakić* (Split, 2000), 132; *Feral Tribune*, 6 May 1996; 8 December 1997.
15. A common burial place for ten Ustaša, 100 Domobrani, and two alleged Partisans was created on a smaller scale in 1996 in Omiš, under the patronage of the (parliamentary) "Commission for the Detection of War- and Postwar-Victims"–presenting the worst example of institutional revisionism. *Feral Tribune*, 4 January 1996; 10 March 1997.
16. Čulić (see note 13), 107; *Feral Tribune*, 6 May 1996; 8 December 1997.
17. In contrast to Pierre Nora and Etienne François and Hagen Schulze in this paper the national *lieux de mémoire* are not described in an affirmative manner, but are analyzed as mythical sites of "imagined communities." Pierre Nora, *Zwischen Geschichte und Gedächtnis* (Berlin, 1990); Etienne François and Hagen Schulze, eds., *Deutsche Erinnerungsorte* (Munich, 2001).
18. John I. Prcela and Drazen Živić, *Hrvatski Holokaust. Dokumenti i svjedočanstva o poratnim pokoljima u Jugoslaviji* (Zagreb, 2001).
19. *Novi list*, 12 May 2003.
20. *Novi list*, 15 May 2006.
21. *Novi list*, 29 April 2002; For an overview of the commemorations in Bleiburg see *Slobodna Dalmacija*, 12 May 2003.
22. *Novi list*, 29 April 2002.
23. Juraj Hrženjak, *Rušenje antifašističkih spomenika u Hrvatskoj 1990-2000* (Zagreb, 2002); Ivančić (see note 14), 67.
24. *Slobodna Dalmacija*, 16 September 2004.
25. Čulić (see note 13), 106.
26. See Stanko Perazić, *Udžbenik za 8 razred osnovne škole* (Sarajevo, 1973).
27. Ivo Perić, *Povijest 8: udžbenik za 8 razred osnovne škole* (Zagreb, 1992); Hrvoje Matković, *Povijest 8: udžbenik za 8 razred osnovne škole* (Zagreb, 1998). For the whole subject see Luka Tatomir, „Hrvatski udžbenici za VIII. razred o zločinima za vrijeme drugog svjetskog rata," unpublished paper from the conference, *The State of Holocaust Studies in Southeastern Europe. Problems, Obstacles, Perspectives*, Sarajevo, 2006.
28. *Vjesnik*, 17 December 1998.
29. Ivančić (see note 14), 18, 85; *Feral Tribune*, 13 February 1999; *Vjesnik*, 3 February 1999 and 4 February 1999.
30. *Feral Tribune*, 15 March 1999; 10 April 1999; Ivančić (see note 14), 190.
31. *Feral Tribune*, 6 July 1998; 15 March 1999; 17 July 1999; 9 October 1999.
32. *Feral Tribune*, 30 January 1995; *Jutarnji list*, 6 June 1998; Ivančić (see note 14), 314.
33. Ivančić (see note 14), 294; *Feral Tribune*, 9 October 1999.
34. Steven Levitsky and Lucan A. Way, "Elections Without Democracy. The Rise of Competitive Authoritarianism," *Journal of Democracy* 13, no. 2 (2002): 51–65.

35. Mirjana Kasapović, ed., *Hrvatska politika 1990-2000* (Zagreb, 2001); Sabrina P. Ramet and Davorka Matić, eds., *Demokratska tranzicija u Hrvatskoj. Transformacija vrijednosti, obrazovanje, mediji* (Zagreb, 2006).
36. Viktor Ivančić, *Lomača za protuhrvatski blud. Ogledi o Tuđmanizmu* (Split, 2003), 198, 224.
37. Ivančić (see note 14), 41; Ivančić (see note 36), 193-198.
38. Vesna Pusić, *Demokracije i Diktature. Politička tranzicija u Hrvatskoj i jugoistočnoj Europi* (Zagreb, 1998), 194; Ivančić (see note 36), 177; *Feral Tribune*, 10 April 1999.
39. Blanka Jergović, *Odmjeravanje snaga. Novine i politika u Hrvatskoj u prvom razdoblju tranzicije* (Zagreb, 2004), 36.
40. Nikola Visković, *Sumorne Godine: Nacionalizam, Bioetika, Globalizacija* (Split, 2003), 38.
41. Paul Hockenos, *Homeland calling. Exile patriotism and the Balkan Wars* (New York, 2003), 17-102.
42. Hrvoje Matković, *Povijest 8: udžbenik za 8 razred osnovne škole* (Zagreb, 2000).
43. Mira Kolar Dimitrijević, *Povijest 8: udžbenik za 8 razred osnovne škole* (Zagreb, 2003).
44. *Novi list,* 20 April 2002.
45. *Novi list,* 23 April 2005.
46. *Novi list,* 12 May 2003.
47. *Novi list,* 18 July 2004.
48. See http://www.vlada.hr/default.asp?ru=345&gl=200403160000006&sid=&jezik=2; accessed 6 March 2007.
49. *Feral Tribune,* 18 March 2004; *Novi list,* 17 March 2004.
50. *Feral Tribune,* 29 April 2004.
51. *Novi list,* 23 June 2004; 24 June 2004.
52. Benedict Anderson, *Imagined Communities: Reflections on the Origin and Spread of Nationalism* (London, 1991).
53. *Novi list,* 18 April 2005.
54. See http://www.vlada.hr/default.asp?ru=345&gl=200505020000004&sid=&jezik=2; accessed 6 March 2007.
55. See http://www.vlada.hr/default.asp?gl=200506280000018; accessed 6 March 2007.
56. Levy and Sznaider (see note 2).
57. *Novi list,* 24 January 2006; 29 January 2006.
58. Reinhart Koselleck, "Formen und Traditionen des negativen Gedächtnisses," in *Verbrechen erinnern. Die Auseinandersetzung mit Holocaust und Völkermord*, eds., V. Knigge and N. Frei, (Munich, 2002), 21-32.
59. Knigge and Frei (see note 58).
60. Holm Sundhaussen, *Geschichte Serbiens. 19.-21. Jahrhundert* (Vienna, 2007), 421; Byford (see note 5); Jovan Byford, *Potiskivanje i poricanje antisemitizma. Sećanje na vladiku Nikolaja Velimirovića u savremenoj srpskoj pravoslavnoj kulturi* (Belgrade, 2005); David B. MacDonald, *Balkan holocausts? Serbian and Croatian victim-centred propaganda and the war in Yugoslavia* (Manchester, 2002).
61. Mustafa Imamović, *Historija Bošnjaka* (Sarajevo, 1997), 529-543.
62. Oto Luthar, "Slovenia: History between Myths and Reality", *Slovene Studies* 27, no. 1-2 (2005): 109-119; Oto Luthar and Irena Šumi, "Living in Metaphor: Jews and Anti-Semitism in Slovenia," in *Jews and Anti-Semitism in the Balkans* (Jerusalem, 2004), 29-48.

Chapter 11

GERMAN VICTIMHOOD DISCOURSE IN COMPARATIVE PERSPECTIVE

•••••••••••••••

Bill Niven

Sometimes, those who research the way today's Germany remembers its problematic past fall into the trap of imagining that it is the only country which has such a past to face. We often consider German national history to be some way "unique," as reflected, for instance, in the horrific perpetration of the Holocaust, the process of division and unification, its own particular inflection of the Cold War, and the ongoing legacy of a "double past" of National Socialism and Stalinism. However, if we consider developments in Germany's culture of memory largely in national terms, we run the risk of overlooking the fact that other European countries are also grappling with difficult pasts characterized by forms of fascism and socialism. This chapter is based on the premise that opening up the discursive framework beyond Germany's boundaries may help us to understand to what extent its present confrontation with the Nazi and communist past is typical of a wider European trend and to what extent this confrontation takes distinctive forms. In the first half of this discussion, I provide a *tour d'horizon* of recent "memory struggles," particularly in Eastern Europe, where I believe the greatest similarities to the German case can be found (I will not, however, discuss developments in the Russian Federation, which represent something of a different case). In the concluding part of the discussion, I shall ask: how different is Germany really?

The collapse of communism towards the end of the last century was accompanied throughout Eastern Europe by a wave of iconoclasm. Arguably, this iconoclasm had been anticipated by the destruction and defacement of images of Stalin or Lenin during the Hungarian and Prague uprisings of 1956 and 1968 respectively. Furthermore, in the last few years, there has been a second post-communist wave of iconoclasm in Eastern Europe.[1] The moving of the Soviet Bronze Soldier memorial in Tallinn in 2007 is the most obvious and widely publicized example.[2] Less well known, perhaps, is the fact that Lech Kaczynski, when he was the Polish President, approved legislation imposing a ban on displaying communist symbols. This was aimed not just at existing memorials or buildings; it was also designed to effectively criminalize the possession or distribution of motifs, such as the hammer and sickle. The law also applies to fascist symbols, and Kaczynski's twin brother Jaroslaw—a former prime minister and head of Poland's Law and Justice Party—had no hesitation in declaring communism a "genocidal system," whose symbols "should be compared to German Nazism."[3] A similar ban has been in place in Hungary since 2003.[4] Those tributes to communism and the Red Army that survived the first wave of destruction or removal following the breakup of the Soviet Union are unlikely to survive the second. If not destroyed or dumped, they will live on in comical memorial theme parks, such as those in Lithuania (Grutas Park) and Hungary (Szobor Park), a form of old folks' home for decrepit and unwanted stone citizens.[5]

However, it has not all been about destruction and removal. At the same time, Eastern European countries—since the end of communism—have been creating a new focus for memorialization and commemoration: the victims of communism. In the newly institutionalized historical narratives underpinning such developments, the Soviets appear not as liberators, but as the bringers of (repeated) totalitarian oppression. In December 2009, a Monument to the Victims of Communism, 1918–1989, was unveiled in Łodz, central Poland—it is dedicated, for instance, to the victims of the Soviet invasions of 1919–1920 and 1939, and to those Solidarity activists persecuted in the early 1980s.[6] In October 2009, a memorial to the victims of communism was unveiled in Trencin, in Slovakia.[7] Major memorial-cum-documentation centers commemorating either the victims of communism or both the victims of communism and National Socialism, have sprung up throughout Eastern Europe. These include the Memorial to the Victims of Communism and of the Resistance in Sighet, Romania (initiated in 1997);[8] Latvia's Museum of Occupation in Riga (since 1993);[9] Hungary's House of Terror in Budapest (since 2002);[10] and the Museum of Genocide Victims in Vilnius, Lithuania (established in 1992), which, contrary to what one might expect, is focused mainly on Lithuanian victims of Soviet persecution, not on Jewish or even non-Jewish Lithuanian victims of National Socialism.[11] It is certainly true that postcommunist Eastern Europe is increasingly constructing memorials and exhibitions to Jewish victims of the Holocaust. The website of the Holocaust Task Force—among whose members are former communist-run states, such as the Czech Republic, Estonia, Hungary, Poland, Romania, and Slovakia—provides evidence of processes of Holocaust memorialization in all member states, including the Eastern European ones.[12] Thus, Slovakia has unveiled some 100 memorials and memorial plaques to Holocaust victims since 1992, including the Central Memorial to the Holocaust of Slovakian Jews in Bratislava (1997).[13] To a degree, postwar anti-Semitism in Eastern Europe is also now memorialized. In 2006, for instance, Poland marked the sixtieth anniversary of the infamous Kielce massacre by unveiling a monument to the pogrom's victims.[14] The end of the communist era, with its anti-Semitic purges and reluctance to confront the suffering of the Holocaust, has given way to a belated attempt in Eastern Europe to acknowledge Jewish victimhood.

Nevertheless, one might question the extent of this commitment. The Holocaust Task Force's website references Latvia's Museum and Documentation Center "Jews in Latvia"; however, this was the product of a private initiative dating back to 1990 and still lacks state funding.[15] The Latvian government did support the construction of a monument (dedicated in 2007) in honor of Zanis Lipke and other Latvians who saved the lives of Jews during World War II.[16] However, there is little preparedness to confront Latvian collaboration with Nazism. During the Nazi occupation, the notorious Latvian Auxiliary Police actively participated in the murder of Jews, Roma, and mental patients. Subsequently, tens of thousands of Latvians served in Hitler's Waffen SS. How many of the latter were volunteers or participated in atrocities is still a matter of debate. Yet, in 2005, Latvian SS veterans were allowed to parade through the streets of Riga. The Latvia Foreign Ministry's website suggests that it is quite legitimate to honor Waffen SS veterans because these were "soldiers who fought against the Soviet Union in World War II."[17] Estonia's government has shown more willingness to take a stand against trends to glorify Estonians who fought in Hitler's army and the Waffen SS. A memorial to the latter, erected in Parnu, was removed by the authorities in 1992. At the time, Estonia's prime minister seemed more concerned about the memorial jeopardizing Estonia's efforts to join the EU than he was about its transformation of Estonian collaborators into anti-Soviet patriots fighting for Estonian independence and a "free Europe."[18]

Officially, Eastern European states since the fall of communism—outside of the Russian Federation—are basing their reemerging national collective memory on a narrative of victimhood at the hands of two totalitarian regimes. Thus, Latvia's Museum of Occupation in Riga seeks to provide information on what happened to Latvia and its people under two occupying totalitarian regimes from 1940 to 1991.[19] It also aims to show how the "Latvian nation was led to the brink of physical and intellectual annihilation" over the course of half a century.[20] Hungary's House of Terror, opened in 2002, likewise focuses on the two dictatorships of fascism and communism. "Having survived two terror regimes," the exhibition's website declares, "it was felt that the time had come for Hungary to erect a fitting memorial to the victims, and at the same time to present a picture of what life was like for Hungarians in those times."[21] Yet, of the two totalitarian regimes, it seems clear–to Eastern Europeans–that Soviet communism was the worse. If the Nazis practiced genocide against Jews, then the Soviets, according to the narrative, practiced it against Eastern Europeans. As already indicated, Lithuania's Museum of Genocide Victims in Vilnius, symbolically set up in a former KGB prison, is largely about Soviet persecution of Lithuanian nationals. When the Soviet deportation of Latvians from Tornakalns station in June 1941 to Siberian labor camps was commemorated in Latvia in 2004, the Latvian Ministry of Foreign Affairs declared on its website that "Communist genocide victims" had been commemorated.[22] Arguably, it is precisely this anti-Russian animus which has made the work of the "League for the Maintentance of German War Graves" (Volksbund Deutscher Kriegsgräberfürsorge, VDK) easier than might have been expected. Since 1990, the VDK has embarked upon tending and developing German soldiers' graves and cemeteries in Eastern Europe. At a military cemetery near Wrocław in 2002, the bodies of some of those German soldiers who defended Breslau against the Russian advance in 1945 were buried with the blessing of high-ranking Polish priests. Here, it seems, Germans are not remembered as occupiers, but as a determined, if ultimately unsuccessful, bulwark against Bolshevism.

Of course, there are many obvious reasons why the Soviet Union should be remembered as the key aggressor. Postwar communist rule, imposed by and maintained to varying degrees by the Soviets, dominated in Eastern Europe from 1945 through the late 1980s or early 1990s–for a far longer period than Nazi rule (and countries such as Romania and Hungary, as collaborators, long escaped the direct hand of Nazi control). The Baltic states and Poland endured Soviet control both prior to and subsequent to Nazism. Moreover, the memory of communism is far fresher in the minds of Eastern Europeans than the memory of Nazism. Confronting communist crimes–through, for instance, the Czech Republic's Office for the Documentation and Investigation of the Crimes of Communism[23]–was a very real necessity after the collapse of communism. Confronting the legacy of Nazism or fascism generally was hardly as pressing. Anti-Soviet iconoclasm and the construction of anti-Soviet national victimhood narratives also served and serve to keep Eastern European countries at a distance to post-communist Russia, while echoing longstanding anticommunist feeling in Western Europe—a way of demonstrating a desire and suitability for Western integration. Focusing more on memory of Nazi crimes, moreover, might risk alienating Germany, a key player in the EU's expansion into Eastern Europe. The rush to join the Western club is not simply driven by economic and political interests: there is still a genuine fear of Russia in some Eastern European countries, and the Soviet-critical thrust of memory expresses this fear.

However, one can be critical of this memory trend. The Russian philosopher Boris Groys, in a recent interview, points to growing nationalism in Eastern Europe. By example of Estonia and Poland, Groys argues that the communist past of Eastern European countries is being understood increasingly in terms of an "occupation," a view formulated in terms of ethnic conflict. For Groys, the motive behind this "ethnicization of communism" is mostly self-exculpation.[24] In other words: communism is projected back onto the Soviet Union, with Eastern European countries denying responsibility for it. (The more Eastern Europeans seek to disown their communist past and project communism back onto Russia, the more, of course, Russia will feel inclined to strengthen rather than critically confront the tradition of celebrating the "Great Patriotic War.")[25] Collaboration with communism is recognized in former Eastern bloc countries, but there is a tendency to single out individuals for blame, resulting in scapegoating, rather than an awareness of widespread collusion. If collusion with Nazism appears even harder to face, then it is because, for several states, this would mean accepting that they had installed their own authoritarian, fascist, or clerico-fascist regimes (one thinks of Tiso's Slovakia, Pavelic's Croatia, or Antonescu's Romania). It would also mean, for several states, accepting the part they, or groups of their citizens, had played in the Holocaust and other ethnic atrocities. One of the advantages of the totalitarian narrative, according to which Eastern Europeans were twentieth-century victims, is that it erases questions of differing levels and extents of autonomous responsibility and collaboration.

It might seem as if Eastern European countries are attempting to achieve synchronically what Western European countries achieved diachronically. There is substantial evidence that, in Northern and Western Europe, the narratives of victimhood and *Résistance,* so central to national memories in the 1950s, 1960s, 1970s, and even 1980s, are gradually shifting towards a self-critical focus on the Holocaust. This can be illustrated by the example of France. In February 2009, France's top judicial body, the Council of State, acknowledged the French government's responsibility for the deportation of thousands of Jews during World War II.[26] Throughout the first decade of the new millennium, in fact, France has made significant moves towards memorializing and commemorating the Holocaust and, specifically, the deportations–a sign, perhaps, that the "Vichy syndrome," i.e., the self-obsessed focus on the trauma of occupation is not as dominant as it was.[27] Given that memory of World War II was frozen into set formulae for decades in the former Soviet bloc–Soviets as heroes and liberators–the end of the Cold War has prompted a veritable eruption of suppressed victimhood narratives in Eastern Europe, while opening towards the West has necessitated a confrontation with the Holocaust. Denied the gradualist evolution of memory over time, a characteristic of the West, Eastern Europe has seen the simultaneous and consequently rather fraught emergence of–for want of better terms–"self-focused" and "others-focused" memory narratives. Tensions between them are currently being defused by means of the totalitarian paradigm, according to which Eastern Europeans and Jews were all victims of comparable repression and even genocide.

This is not to say that the more self-critical memory, which is evolving in the West, does not have its pitfalls. One can certainly see in the Europeanization or even globalization of Holocaust memory a well-motivated attempt to increase awareness of this genocide in order to foster a sense of historical conscience and to activate social concern in the present.[28] However, the rhetoric of acknowledgement can soon dissipate into a collection of rather vapid and formulaic assertions and avowals in which concrete acknowledgement of national responsibility for involvement in the Holocaust is either absent or watered-down. Where it is present, its actual sincerity might be questioned. It is arguably easier for nations to remember their entanglement in the destructive web of fascism, racism, and genocide, when they simultaneously claim to have learnt lessons from the past and indeed to be applying these in the present. It is also easier when memory of collaboration can be shared with other countries; the burden of memory is denationalized. "We were not the only ones, and we have moved on since" often seems to be the message.

Furthermore, it would be wrong to maintain that taking leave of well-worn myths is proving easy for all Northern or Western European countries. Having hosted a hugely significant and influential international Holocaust conference in 2000, Sweden has established itself as a pioneer of Holocaust memory in the new millennium. Yet, it was not until 2001 and 2002 that Swedish historians and journalists, such as Bosse Schön, began to seriously challenge what Schön has sarcastically called the "Pippi Langstrumpf (Longstocking) Idyll," which had long characterized Swedish memory of Sweden's role in the war.²⁹ Historian Tobias Hübinette claims that some 60,000 to 100,000 Swedes (out of a population of 6.5 million) sympathized with Nazism.³⁰ The "darker" side of Swedish society, including a degree of continuing sympathy for Nazism, has recently been explored by Swedish crime writers Henning Mankell and Stieg Larsson.³¹ Revelation of collaboration often prompts angry and indignant responses in the public realm. In 2002, Finland became embroiled in a long-running debate about the Finnish philosopher Georg Henrik von Wright after a Finnish television team discovered documents demonstrating Wright's sympathy for Nazism.³² That Finland may still need to critically examine its past was surely evidenced by the decision of a Finnish supermarket chain in 2007 to offer for sale a ring sporting a swastika as a memento to Finland's war veterans.³³ And in Italy, Mimmo Franzinelli's book on the readiness of some Italians to denounce Jews and partisans (*Delatori* [*Denouncers*], 2001) during the fascist era also prompted much debate.³⁴ Usually it has been journalists and historians who have paved the way to a more self-critical memory—but not always. The Mattéoli Report (Mission Mattéoli), for instance, published by the official Mattéoli commission in France in 2000, has done much to reveal the degree of French participation in and profit from Aryanization in wartime France.³⁵ Other pasts, too, are coming back to haunt. Spain's political establishment cannot continue to deny the sufferings of Republican forces during the Spanish Civil War, or to ensure their elision from public memory, especially as this past is literally being disinterred since 2009, prompting a flood of media debates on the subject.³⁶

And what of Germany? Like other western countries, it has been taking leave of myths in recent years: for instance, the myth of the "clean" Wehrmacht was surely shattered by the long-running exhibition "Vernichtungskrieg: Verbrechen der Wehrmacht 1941–1944" (War of Extermination: Crimes of the Wehrmacht, running 1995–1999).³⁷ The same could be said for the view that "ordinary Germans" were by and large not involved in the Nazi government's anti-Semitic ideology and praxis. This view was left in tatters after the intense media debate which accompanied the publication in Germany of Goldhagen's *Hitler's Willing Executioners*.³⁸ Germany could also be seen to have embraced memory of the Holocaust as a central element of public and political commemoration through the construction and dedication of Berlin's Memorial to the Murdered Jews of Europe (inaugurated in 2005).³⁹ However, I believe it would not be appropriate to seek to explain German memory trends only with reference to *Western* Europe. One of the main foci of public memory in Germany, certainly since 1998, is past national victimhood—as great a preoccupation, perhaps, as past national crime or levels of participation in that crime. This (from a Western perspective) reinvigoration of sentiments of national victimhood, a reinvigoration of considerable intensity, can surely best be explained by seeing it in the context of the memory trends typical of *Eastern* European countries, which I outlined above. In other words, it may have more in common with national memory trends in a country, such as Latvia or Lithuania, than it does with memory trends in France or Holland.

In some respects, of course, Germany is a unique case. Unification in 1990, while often seen as involving simply the integration and "westernization" of the former German Democratic Republic (GDR), was in fact—at least in terms of memory—a complex fusion, with resulting tensions between a country which had "grown up" with Western European postwar traditions of memory and one which had been shaped by Eastern European ones. In contrast to the situation in Eastern Europe after 1990, where a public culture of Holocaust memory needed to be developed, such a public culture—albeit still contested—existed in the Federal Republic (FRG) prior to unification with the GDR.[40] Therefore, it could be "transferred" to the new Länder. From one perspective, one might argue that the traditionally anticommunist character of West Germany smoothed the passage towards a judicial, social, and ethical confrontation with the legacies of the GDR in united Germany. From another, one could maintain that united Germany started life on a much stronger democratic base than the newly emancipated Eastern European states, and was thus more thorough, rigorous, and forceful in its process of lustration. In contrast to the situation in Western Europe, Germany after 1990 was the only western country that had to confront the fact that a significant part of its territory had been in the grip of Soviet-style socialism for half a century. It was the only country that had to find a way of mediating between two radically different memory traditions, according to which World War II was won either by socialist-inspired antifascism (the GDR view) or by Western democracy with some help from Stalin (the FRG view).

Similarities between united Germany and contemporary Eastern Europe need to be highlighted. After all, a substantial portion of Germany was part of the Eastern European bloc until 1990. The GDR was as much, indeed even more, of a Soviet satellite state than other Eastern bloc countries. The opening of the Stasi files, the removal of compromised individuals from the civil service, the trials of former border-guards, and the politicians behind the border regime—all of these measures bear a resemblance to processes of lustration and judicial proceedings against former communists in other Eastern European countries. At some of Berlin's memorial sites, the critical memorialization of the communist persecution of dissidents at the hands of the Stasi and SED parallels the critical memory of communism characteristic of contemporary eastern European countries.[41] That Germany sees itself in relation to Eastern European countries is certainly borne out by a project currently being undertaken by the Stiftung zur Aufarbeitung der DDR-Diktatur (Foundation for Working-through the GDR Dictatorship), itself comparable to the various institutions set up in Eastern Europe to examine and help to overcome the legacy of state socialism. So far, the Stiftung has largely focused on its immediate remit. In 2004, it commissioned the publication of a book charting the sites of memory of socialist dictatorship in Germany.[42] More recently, however, it has become engaged in compiling a topography of memory, which will document all European sites commemorating the victims of twentieth-century communism. According to what the Foundation calls a "cautious estimate," some 7–8,000 of these have sprung up since the fall of communism.[43]

We also need to see to understand the current reinvigoration of interest in German wartime and postwar suffering in this context. Freed, on the one hand, from the constrictions of Ostpolitik and, on the other, from the obligation to unquestioningly celebrate the historical role of the Soviet Union, many Germans feel they can now give voice to a sense of historical grievance. For the Soviets not only defeated Hitler: they raped a huge number of German women, carted off German civilians for forced labor, set up postwar internment camps in which tens of thousands of (in many cases, innocent) Germans died, played an instrumental role in the expulsion of Germans, annexed German territory and supported its annexation by Poland and Czechoslovakia, and set up a dictatorial order in eastern Germany.[44] Similar injustices, *mutatis mutandis,* were visited upon a number of Eastern European countries by the Soviets between 1939 and 1950 (and subsequently). That these countries can now recall the suffering of Polish, Czech, and Baltic states' nationals at the hands of the Soviets feeds into a discourse of self-identification as historical victim—a discourse which parallels and perhaps influenced that in Germany.

Of course, the "Germans as victims" discourse encompasses much more, in its condemnatory dimension, than criticism of the Soviets. Germans, at the end of the war, were expelled by Poles and Czechs; Germans suffered injustice, too, at the hands of other Eastern European countries, such as Romania and Yugoslavia. Thus, while Poland and Germany certainly share a critical view of the Soviets, they differ radically in their views of responsibility for expulsion. The Poles, and to a lesser extent the Czechs, take the view that the expulsions were a regrettable but nevertheless understandable response to the savage occupation of their countries by the Nazis. However, German expellees and their representatives point also to aggressive, opportunistic Polish and Czech ethnic nationalism[45] and indiscriminate brutality towards old men, women and children innocent of any role in Nazism. Germany and Poland, particularly, are locked into an ongoing saga of competitive victimhood, which current plans to build a "visible sign" to expulsions in Berlin are not doing anything to bring to an end–despite the German government's will to acknowledge the criminal role of Nazism and the suffering through expulsion of other nations.[46]

Yet, the "cross-border" bickering over historical responsibility between Poland and Germany is by no means unusual. Other Eastern European countries have been and are enmeshed in heated debates about the past and its relationship to the present. Only recently (2009), a dispute broke out between Slovakia and Hungary. The Hungarian minority in Slovakia, having constructed a memorial to Hungarian King Stephen I (c 970–1038), invited Hungarian State President Solyom to attend its unveiling; the Slovakian government responded by denying Solyom entry to the country.[47] Sensitivities deriving from the ceding of Hungarian territory to Czechoslovakia after World War I–territory which was to change hands again in 1938 and yet again in 1945, accompanied by expulsions and the creation of ethnic minorities–erupted with some vehemence.

Competitive victimhood played its part here, too: building national identity on a sense of grievance only really works if the grievances of others against you can be made to appear smaller or even unjustified. Fear of territorial revisions and the claims of renascent ethnic nationalism–unthinkable during Soviet times–also play their part. They do in the case of the tensions between Germany and Poland, too. The constant redrawing of borders in the twentieth century across Eastern Europe had deep psychological effects, whose ongoing legacy we would be wrong to play down, for all the talk of European unity.[48]

There are clear parallels between postcommunist memory trends in today's Germany and Eastern Europe; however, we must sound a note of caution. Parallels should not lead us to overlook problems of comparison or differences in approach and intention. While the self-conceptualization as historical victim in most Eastern European countries is based, for all its tendentiousness and blind spots, on the very real experience of two imposed dictatorships, for Germany to imagine itself as a victim of a "double past" would be particularly questionable, given that Germany was responsible for Nazism, the Third Reich, and World War II. Yet, there are examples of precisely such "double victimhood" constructions in recent German memorialization—most notoriously, the Neue Wache in Berlin, the memorial brainchild of Helmut Kohl, which clearly brands Germans as victims of Nazism and communism.[49] Equations between Nazism and GDR socialism are not uncommon in post–unification Germany. This serves the purpose of simultaneously playing down Nazism and exaggerating the (nevertheless considerable) severity of repression in the GDR. Some even fear that memorialization in Germany may be shifting too much towards memory of socialist crimes—at the expense of an awareness of the singular criminality of Nazism and of the particular nature of German responsibility. In 1997, the Association of Concentration Camp Memorial Sites in the Federal Republic objected to planned revisions to the Federal Strategy for Memorial Sites, not least because of the danger that the significance of National Socialism for German history would be rendered "unclear."[50] The objections of the association—and the fact that the Federal Strategy was revised in the light of these criticisms—indicate that German historians, politicians, and memorial site representatives are quick to resist attempts to shift the central focus of German memorial culture away from National Socialism. As it currently stands, the Federal Strategy for Memorial Sites explicitly points out the differences in severity between Nazism and socialism and begins with a clear acknowledgement of the inhumanity of National Socialism.[51]

In contrast to Eastern Europe, the place of Nazism in German memory arguably remains greater than that of socialism—despite developments towards focusing more on the latter, in recent years. Germans remain acutely aware of the need to remember their own crimes, another point of contrast. Furthermore, while there is an "antitotalitarian consensus" in Germany, there is less agreement on how the GDR past should be approached. Just as there are criticisms of ostensibly over-negative portrayals of the GDR, so there are objections to portrayals perceived to be too "soft." When an official commission of experts made a set of recommendations on how best to work through the past of the SED dictatorship, it was immediately accused of such a "soft" approach, because it recommended more research into the everyday life of the GDR (in addition to further research into issues of state criminality, collaboration and resistance).[52] For all the recognition that the GDR was an oppressive state, the trend of "Ostalgie"—largely without parallel elsewhere in Eastern Europe[53]—remains. While it may have a variety of roots, one is certainly the perception among some Eastern Germans that unification represents a Western-style takeover of the eastern Länder. In contrast to Eastern Europe, where Western-style liberalism was (and still is being) recreated from below, in Germany, it could be grafted onto the former GDR from the FRG, leading to charges of triumphalism where the import process was seen to be accompanied by a systematic demontage of GDR traditions (such as antifascism) and by the denigration of East Germans to second-class citizens. The West-East tensions within Germany, on top of party-political differences, mean that coming to terms with the past is, in some respects, more complex than in Eastern Europe.

In conclusion, while Germany's current interest in its own historical victimhood has many causes, one is certainly its embedment in processes triggered by the end of communism throughout Eastern Europe. While I recently argued that it was the very depoliticization of discourse surrounding German victimhood in the late 1990s, which enabled the explosion of interest in the theme in the public realm,[54] more recently, the discourse has arrived back on the political stage. Discussions surrounding the government-backed Foundation "Flucht, Vertreibung, Versöhnung" (Flight, Expulsion, Reconciliation) are clear evidence of this.[55] One view might be that Germany, by riding the waves of contemporary European memory trends, can see an opportunity to finally cast off the pariah role of European perpetrator *per se*. If the Holocaust—indeed World War II as a whole—and communism are remembered (in whatever relation) throughout Europe and as European phenomena, then such an opportunity is certainly there. But, while I believe memory trends in Germany to be participating in the international cult of self-pity, the degree and nature of its politicization within Germany remains unclear.

Without doubt, mourning the expellees, or SED victims, was not possible in the GDR, while in West Germany; as Andreas Kossert has shown, expellees and expellee themes were often treated with disdain.[56] One thing that is certainly happening is that suppressed themes are, as it were, coming up for air, which is hardly a political agenda. Moreover, the government's "visible sign" to the expulsions is surely designed to counterbalance the arguably tendentious center against the expulsions idea proposed originally by the Bund der Vertriebenen (League of Expellees).[57] We shall have to await the outcome of developments in the next years, before we will know whether Germany's participation in the international discourse of historical suffering results in a reshaping, or partial reshaping, of German national identity around concepts of victimhood.

Notes

1. See Sonja Zekri, 'Stalin als Seifenoper' (interview with Boris Groys), *Süddeutsche Zeitung*, 11 May 2007, available at http://www.sueddeutsche.de/kultur/386/406163/text/; accessed 24 February 2011. According to Zekri, "wir erleben einen zweiten postkommunistischen Bildersturz."
2. See "Tallinn's 'Bronze Soldier' Involved in a New Conflict," available at http://www.tallinn-life.com/news/news/42-Tallinn's_'Bronze_Soldier'_Involved_in_a_New_Conflict; accessed 24 February 2011.
3. See http://www.spiegel.de/international/europe/0,1518,663154,00.html; accessed 24 February 2011.
4. Ibid.
5. See Paul Williams, "The Afterlife of Communist Statuary: Hungary's Szoborpark and Lithuania's Grutas Park," Special Issue on Representations of the Past in European Memorials, ed., Bill Niven, *Forum for Modern Language Studies* 44, no. 2 (2008): 185–198.
6. See http://www.thenews.pl/national/artykul121845_monument-to-communist-victims-unveiled.html; accessed 24 February 2011.
7. See http://www.trencin.sk/en/index.php?s-cv-contentID=12288&s-cv-embeddedID=52101; accessed 24 February 2011.
8. See http://www.memorialsighet.ro/index.php?lang=ro; accessed 24 February 2011.
9. See http://www.occupationmuseum.lv/; accessed 24 February 2011.
10. See http://www.terrorhaza.hu/en/index_2.html; accessed 24 February 2011.
11. See http://www.genocid.lt/muziejus; accessed 24 February 2011.
12. See http://www.holocausttaskforce.org/memberstates.html; accessed 24 February 2011.
13. See http://www.holocausttaskforce.org/memberstates/member-slovakia.html; accessed 24 February 2011.
14. See http://kieltzer.org/memorials.html#60th; accessed 24 February 2011.
15. See http://vip.latnet.lv/LPRA/ebr_muz.htm; accessed 24 February 2011.
16. See http://www.holocausttaskforce.org/memberstates/member-latvia.html; accessed 25 February 2011.
17. See http://www.li.lv/index.php?option=content&task=view&id=139; accessed 25 February 2011.
18. See http://news.bbc.co.uk/1/hi/world/europe/2148732.stm; accessed 24 February 2011.
19. See http://www.omf.lv/gallery/JAUNAVACU_VERSIJA/HOME.htm; accessed 25 February 2011.
20. See http://www.omf.lv/gallery/OM percent20Deutsch percent202010 percent20Internet-Ausgabe.pdf; accessed 24 February 2011.
21. See http://www.terrorhaza.hu/en/museum/first_page.html; accessed 25 February 2011.
22. See http://www.am.gov.lv/en/latvia/news/archive/news/?pg=4992; accessed 25 February 2011.
23. Other examples are Poland's Institute for National Remembrance and Romania's Presidential Commission for the Study of the Communist Dictatorship in Romania.
24. See Zekri (see note 1). See also Tony Judt, *Postwar: A History of Europe since 1945,* (London, 2005), 820–31.
25. The Soviet Union, in the countries it occupied after World War II, built or encouraged the building of grand memorials to the "Great Patriotic War" as a means of legitimizing the Soviet right to implement communist regimes. Nowadays, the celebration of the Soviet victory—evident for instance in the massive extension to the memorial complex on Poklonnaya Hill in Moscow inaugurated in 1995—rather has the function of defending Russian sensitivities against anticommunist feeling in former eastern bloc countries.
26. See "French Holocaust Role Recognised," *BBC News,* available at http://news.bbc.co.uk/1/hi/7893127.stm; accessed 25 February 2011.

27. This term was coined by Henry Rousso. See Henry Rousso, *The Vichy Syndrome: History and Memory in France since 1944* (Cambridge, 1991).
28. See Daniel Levy and Natan Sznaider, *The Holocaust and Memory in the Global Age* (Philadelphia, 2005).
29. See Bosse Schön, *Hitlers svenska soldater* (Stockholm, 2005).
30. Quoted in Gerhard Fischer, "Der Mythos von Schwedens Unschuld," *Süddeutsche Zeitung*, 17/18 August 2002. See also Tobias Hübinette, *Nationalsocialismen i Sverige. Medlemmar och sympatisörer 1931–45* (Stockholm, 2002).
31. See http://www.telegraph.co.uk/culture/film/7430122/The-dark-side-of-Swedish-society.html; accessed 23 February 2011.
32. See http://www2.hs.fi/english/archive/news.asp?id=20021112IE8; accessed 24 February 2011.
33. See http://www.spiegel.de/spiegel/print/d-54683198.html; accessed 25 February 2011.
34. See Mimmo Franzinelli, *Delatori: Spie e confidente anonimi: l'arma segreta del regime fascista* (Milan, 2001). Franzinelli's work mirrors research done by Robert Gellately and Eric Johnson into levels of denunciation by "ordinary Germans" during the Third Reich. See Robert Gellately, *Backing Hitler: Consent and Coercion in Nazi Germany* (Oxford, 2001) and Eric Johnson, *Nazi Terror: Gestapo, Jews and Ordinary Germans* (London, 2000).
35. Its official French title is "Mission d'étude sur la spoliation des Juifs de France." For an online version of the report, see http://www.ladocumentationfrancaise.fr/rapports-publics/984000110/index.shtml; accessed 14 January 2010.
36. The unsuccessful efforts in 2010 to find and exhume the remains of Spanish poet Federico Garcia Lorca were particularly controversial. See http://www.telegraph.co.uk/news/worldnews/europe/spain/6826532/Lorcas-civil-war-grave-found-empty.html; accessed 25 February 2011.
37. See Hannes Heer and Klaus Naumann, eds, *Vernichtungskrieg: Verbrechen der Wehrmacht, 1941–1944* 2nd ed., (Hamburg, 1998).
38. In German translation as Daniel Jonah Goldhagen, *Hitlers Willige Vollstrecker* (Berlin, 1996).
39. For an interesting discussion of Berlin's Holocaust Memorial, see Claus Leggewie and Erik Meyer, *Ein Ort, an den man gerne geht* (Munich, 2005).
40. This is not to suggest that the German Democratic Republic had not moved towards greater acknowledgment of the Holocaust. As I have shown elsewhere, by the mid-1980s, to a degree it had. See Bill Niven, "Remembering Nazi Anti-Semitism in the GDR," in *Memorialization in Germany since 1945*, eds., Bill Niven and Chloe Paver (Basingstoke, 2010), 205–213). Without doubt, West Germany had moved much further in this regard. See Jeffrey Herf, *Divided Memory: The Nazi Past in the two Germanies* (Cambridge, 1999).
41. Such critical memorialization can be found, for instance, at the Berlin-Hohenschönhausen Memorial and the Berlin Wall Documentation Center. See http://en.stiftung-hsh.de/ and http://www.berliner-mauer-dokumentationszentrum.de/eng/index_dokz.html; accessed 24 February 2011.
42. See Anne Kaminsky, *Orte des Erinnerns. Gedenkzeichen, Gedenkstätten und Museen zur Diktatur in SBZ und DDR* (Leipzig, 2004).
43. See www.stiftung-aufarbeitung.de/downloads/pdf/conceptIGOF.pdf; accessed 24 February 2011.
44. For a highly critical view of the Soviet role at the end of the Second World War and subsequently, see Hubertus Knabe, *Tag der Befreiung? Das Kriegsende in Deutschland* (Berlin, 2005).
45. For a good discussion of the complex relationship between nationalism and communism in postwar Poland, see Michael Fleming, *Communism, Nationalism and Ethnicity in Poland, 1944–1950* (London, 2009). The biggest problem with the plans for the "visible sign" at present is the issue of the inclusion or non-inclusion on the board of directors of the head of Germany's League of Expellees, Erika Steinbach, who is regarded by the Poles

as a revisionist because of her reluctance after 1990 to recognize the Oder-Neisse line as Germany's eastern border with Poland—a reluctance she subsequently overcame.
46. See http://www.bundesregierung.de/Content/DE/Pressemitteilungen/BPA/2009/04/2 009-04-08-bkm-stiftung-flucht-vertreibung-versoehnung.html; accessed 24 February 2011.
47. See http://news.bbc.co.uk/1/hi/world/europe/8215220.stm; accessed 24 February 2011.
48. Though it would be wrong to claim that such anxieties are restricted to Eastern Europe. There have been sensitive reactions in Italy to groups in Austrian Tyrol who regularly commemorate the historical loss of parts of Tyrol to Italy by organizing processions in which crowns of thorns are held high—symbolizing South Tyrolean German "suffering" at the hands of Italy. See Michael Frank, "Freiheitsheld oder Alpen-Taliban," *Süddeutsche Zeitung,* 19/20 September 2009.
49. For a controversial perspective, see Thomas Schmidt et. al., eds, *Nationaler Totenkult. Die Neue Wache. Eine Streitschrift zur zentralen deutschen Gedenkstätte* (Berlin, 1999).
50. See Volkhard Knigge, "Stellungnahme zur *Fortschreibung der Gedenkstättenkonzeption durch den Beauftragten der Bundesregierung für Kultur und Medien vom 22. Juni 2007,*" available at http://www.gedenkstaettenforum.de/nc/gedenkstaetten-rundbrief/rundbrief/news/stel lungnahme_zur_fortschreibung_der_gedenkstaettenkonzeption_durch_den_beauftrag ten_der_bundesregie/2007/10/?tx_ttnews percent5Blimit percent5D=100&tx_ttnews percent5BbackPid percent5D=7; accessed 25 February 2011.
51. See http://www.bundesregierung.de/nsc_true/Content/DE/__Anlagen/BKM/2008-06 -18-fortschreibung-gedenkstaettenkonzepion-barrierefrei,property=publicationFile .pdf/2008-06-18-fortschreibung-gedenkstaettenkonzepion-barrierefrei; accessed 24 February 2011.
52. See Martin Sabrow et. al., eds, *Wohin treibt die DDR-Erinnerung? Dokumentation einer Debatte* (Göttingen, 2007).
53. In 2005, *Der Spiegel* reported that "Ostalgie" was not just a phenomenon of the area of the former GDR, but was also a gathering trend in Eastern Europe generally. Thus, Hungarians had developed a preference for the "good old Tisza shoes" in preference to Adidas or Puma brands, while Polish supermarkets had reintroduced "Ludwik," a washing-up liquid from socialist days. See http://www.spiegel.de/spiegel/print/d-39523462.html; accessed 25 February 2011. Nevertheless, "Ostalgie" is still associated primarily with eastern Germany. As the German Wikipedia entry at http://de.wikipedia.org/wiki/Ostalgie makes clear, "Ostalgie" refers to the longing for a particular way of life and for particular objects associated with the GDR; accessed 25 February 2011.
54. Bill Niven, "Introduction: German Victimhood at the Turn of the Millennium," in *Germans as Victims,* ed., Bill Niven (Basingstoke, 2006), 1–25.
55. See http://www.bundesregierung.de/Content/DE/Pressemitteilungen/BPA/2009/04/2 009-04-08-bkm-stiftung-flucht-vertreibung-versoehnung.html; accessed 24 February 2011.
56. Andreas Kossert, *Kalte Heimat: Die Geschichte der Deutschen Vertriebenen nach 1945* (Munich, 2008).
57. For a discussion of the League's point of view, which arguably plays down German responsibility for the processes which led to the expulsions, see Bill Niven, "Implicit Equations in Constructions of German Suffering," in *A Nation of Victims? Representations of German Wartime Suffering since 1945 to the Present,* ed., Helmut Schmitz, *German Monitor,* 67 (2007), 105–24.

Chapter 12

Shaking Off the Past?
The New Germany in the New Europe

• • • • • • • • • • • • • • •

Ruth Wittlinger

Collective memory of the Holocaust and World War II long provided the single most important factor in determining the scope of (West) Germany's foreign policy in general, as well as its European policy in particular.[1] In view of the moral, as well as material, bankruptcy of Germany in 1945 and foreign occupation in the immediate aftermath of the war, West Germany's foreign policy did not have much room for maneuver. It was also constrained by the emerging Cold War and its position as an increasingly important ally of the Western alliance system, as well as by the norms and values that had emerged as a rejection of the Nazi period. Memory of the Nazi past shaped West Germany's self-understanding, as well as the way others saw Germany and what the international community, particularly West Germany's new western allies, considered as acceptable in terms of discourse as well as policy.

First, this contribution will establish the key pillars of the Bonn Republic's relationship with Europe and illustrate how the memory of the Nazi past turned West Germany into a model European nation that was strongly committed to the European project. Then, through an examination of the changes that have taken place in terms of discourse, as well as policy, during the chancellorship of Gerhard Schröder (1998–2005) and Angela Merkel's first term in office (2005–2009), this chapter will show how the Nazi past seems to have lost its predictable grip on Germany's relationship with Europe with the result that the new Germany is a lot less reluctant to express its national interest openly and show leadership in the new Europe. This is further illustrated with an analysis of the Federal Constitutional Court's ruling on the Lisbon Treaty of June 2009 that–something unthinkable during the lifetime of the Bonn Republic–heavily emphasized the importance of

German national identity and sovereignty. In view of these developments, the chapter concludes that united Germany has shaken off its past with the result that its relationship with Europe is based on a very different foundation now and much more driven by its national interest.

The Bonn Republic: A Model European

The foreign policy consensus that emerged during the lifetime of the Bonn Republic was characterized by a clear and unambiguous commitment to Western orientation (Westbindung), especially in the early days of the new Republic, which was later complemented by a constructive policy towards the East (Ostpolitik). The new Republic's firmly anchored antimilitarism was accompanied by a strong commitment to multilateralism that was realized through membership of the key institutions of the Western alliance system, i.e., the EEC/EC/EU and NATO. There was also a consensus regarding the rejection of any kind of nationalism at home, as well as on the international stage, which made the Federal Republic an especially cooperative ally within this multilateral framework.

The key aims of West German foreign policy in the immediate postwar period were rehabilitation and—with the early emergence of the Cold War—protection from the Soviet Union. The European stage provided a suitable framework for West Germany on both accounts. In contrast to other countries that feared the loss of sovereignty through the supranationalism that the European project increasingly offered, West Germany could only benefit from this cooperation. Its rejection of unilateralism—kept alive by the memory of the Nazi past—as well as the constraints imposed on it by the Cold War made Europe a natural stage for furthering Germany's interests, even though these were hardly ever explicitly expressed. As Charlie Jeffery has noted, the emerging European institutions provided for "a displacement of responsibility (we are happy to have others govern us) and partly an insurance policy (we are not so sure we trust ourselves to govern)."[2] Furthermore, early Western integration into Europe—together with a strong commitment to its bilateral relationship with the U.S.—allowed Germany to become an important ally against the threat of communism, thus enhancing its own position. In addition, European integration gave momentum (and expanding markets) to West Germany's economic recovery and increasing prosperity.

Accordingly, West German political elites, as well as society at large, developed increasingly positive attitudes towards European integration. The idea of Europe also provided West Germany with a kind of ersatz identity.

From the 1950s onwards, West Germans increasingly preferred European integration over the concept of the nation-state,[3] with a European identity suggesting a forward looking approach that made identification with the discredited German nation seemingly redundant.

Increasing prosperity allowed West Germany to be a model European, even if this meant financial sacrifices. As long as it contributed to a furthering of the European project at large, neither political elites nor public opinion seemed to mind that West Germany became the "paymaster" of Europe. At the same time as its political elites avoided pursuing West Germany's national interest openly, they steered clear of showing leadership, unless it was in tandem with France.[4] The "lessons learnt from the past" thus resulted in what has been termed West Germany's "European imperative"[5] or "reflexive Europeanism"[6] and together with its "leadership avoidance reflex"[7] became the trademarks of the European policy of the Bonn Republic. Europe became a central part of West German identity and the raison d'état of the Federal Republic.[8] In contrast to other European nations like Britain and France, Germany also managed to maintain a balance between its commitment to Europe and transatlantic relations. European integration provided advantages for Germany's allies, since it offered what has been described as "double containment."[9] A strong, anticommunist Western Europe was seen not only to provide a strong defense against Soviet influence but was also able to "tame the Germans."[10]

As it turned out, the European project also provided a solution, when the prospect of German unification arose in autumn 1989. Even though enthusiasm for German unification was mute amongst Germany's European neighbors and–in the case of Britain–there was considerable vocal opposition from Margaret Thatcher, France, in particular, saw the key to solving "the German problem" in furthering the European project. Provided that a united Germany would be closely tied into a European framework, France agreed not to object to unification.

In particular, Helmut Kohl's rhetoric reminded Germans, their European neighbors, and the international community at large that even a united Germany would not renege on its commitment to Europe. Drawing on collective memory of World War II, Kohl described German and European unity not only as "two sides of the same coin" but also more dramatically, as a "question of war and peace." In line with this, he also accorded Europe a central place in his Ten Point Program for Policy on Germany of 28 November 1989, which provided a kind of blueprint for German unification.

A few years later, the Maastricht Treaty–aimed at creating an ever closer union that would tie united Germany irrevocably into Europe–probably provided the turning point in Germany's European policy, since it marked the end of Germany's Europeanism by default.[11] Even staunch Europeans, like Kohl, had to respond to an emerging, more critical stance in public opinion towards the European project with the result that already towards the end of Kohl's chancellorship, Germany's European policy became less committed and proactive[12] or, as then Foreign Office State Secretary Hans Friedrich von Ploetz described it, "more British."[13]

Europeans by Choice, not Necessity?

A new emphasis on costs and benefits thus emerged in the 1990s, intensifying during the period of the Red-Green coalition under Schröder.[14] By and large, this government consisted of a new generation of political leaders who had no living memory of the period between 1933 and 1945, and, even though collective memory of the Holocaust and World War II continued to be employed, these references had lost their predictability and did not necessarily result in a pro-European consensus as it had done under previous governments. As Timothy Garton Ash pointed out in 1994, it could not be taken for granted that the Euro-idealism of subsequent generations in Germany would be as widespread or intensive as that of the immediate postwar generation.[15] Schröder was clearly much less reluctant to express Germany's national interest more explicitly, which was largely based on the different approach towards Germany's Nazi past that Schröder adopted.

There is no question that at least in terms of rhetoric—even though the sincerity of this was questioned on a number of occasions[16]—the Red-Green coalition placed the collective memory of World War II and the Holocaust at the very heart of German national identity. In contrast to previous attempts that were aimed at "drawing a final line under the past," Schröder made it clear on numerous occasions that in his view the period between 1933 and 1945 was a key part of Germany's self-understanding. For instance, he stated that: "the past can neither be undone nor can it be overcome. But one can learn from history and that is what we Germans have done … Memory of the National Socialist period, of war, genocide, and crime has become part of our national identity."[17] Rather than this unambiguous acknowledgment of German culpability resulting in an inability to identify with the German nation or a kind of "negative nationalism," Schröder's approach seemed to achieve the opposite and resulted in a new national confidence. Rather than acting as a constraint on the German chancellor and his perception of Germany, it seemed to empower him. During a talk show in November

1998, he described the Germany that he was planning to represent as "less inhibited" and–even more remarkably–"in a positive sense maybe even more German."[18] With this, Schröder created a novel approach to Germany's Nazi past. Until then and as the *Historikerstreit* (Historians' Dispute) in 1986/87 had made abundantly clear, positive expressions of German national identity had either been promoted by the political Right and were based on attempts "to draw a line" under the past or had been impossible, as the political Left traditionally had argued, because of the centrality of Auschwitz. Schröder, however, spoke of the "self-confidence of a grown-up nation" that did not need to feel inferior or superior towards others but rather a nation that "faces history and its responsibilities, but that–in spite of all its readiness to engage with it–looks ahead to the future."[19]

Unsurprisingly, Schröder's assertive rhetoric also became apparent regarding Europe. At a party conference only a few months before becoming chancellor, Schröder set out his view of the differences between his approach towards Europe and that of the previous generation. Asserting that for his and particularly for the younger generation, Europe was a normal part of life, he argued that the euro was not a price that had to be paid for German history or a question of war and peace, as his predecessor had made out. In his view, Germany did not want the euro to overcome the past but as an option for the future.[20] According to Schröder, in contrast to previous generations of political leaders, European integration became a matter of choice rather than duty. In his first government declaration in November 1998, Schröder claimed that today Germans were democrats and Europeans not because they had to be but because they really wanted to be.[21]

Rather than using German history to legitimize a modest and integration-friendly approach, Schröder used references to the past to argue in favor of more assertiveness for Germany on the international stage. In his view, it was always the "dangerous imbalances in the national confidence" which caused extremism and problems.[22] In contrast to Kohl, whose European rhetoric had made extensive use of Germany's historical memory to legitimize his European policy,[23] Schröder was not afraid to be more critical of the European project. Already during his time in opposition, he had described the euro as a "premature birth" (*Frühgeburt*), and at the beginning of his chancellorship, he repeatedly complained about the way Brussels was wasting German taxpayers' money, announcing an end to the use of the German checkbook to facilitate further European integration. During the run-up to the German EU Presidency in a speech to the Bundestag on 10 December 1998, Schröder announced that the country was unable, as well as unwilling, to continue "to buy the goodwill" of its neighbors with payments which turned into "an intolerable burden on the budget at home."[24] While Kohl, at least rhetorically, often had made no distinction between German and European interests, Schröder "did away with this fiction of the European interest being the same as the German interest. You can talk of the German national interest in a much more relaxed way today. The time was ripe for this and he acknowledged it."[25]

This new approach was not restricted to Schröder, according to Charlie Jeffery and William Paterson, but part of a "value shift, a changed normative sense of how it is that Germany should engage with Europe."[26] This also appears to be reflected in attitudes towards Europe in society at large, with the "permissive consensus" or "tacit approval" of the European project of the 1970s and 1980s declining from the mid 1990s onwards. Although in May/June 2005, 50 percent of respondents were still in favor of European integration, 43 percent felt that it created more disadvantages than advantages.[27]

However, this is not to say that German collective memory was not used anymore. Foreign Minister and Green leader Joschka Fischer ensured that the German past would continue to be present in the discourse on Europe, for example, when he described the German government's support for Eastern enlargement as not only necessary for stability in Europe but also a historical moral duty.[28] Indeed, Germany's policy on the EU's Eastern enlargement illustrates the new approach very well. Even though Germany supported the widening efforts, the chancellor fought hard to ensure that a transitional period would protect the labor market from sudden and intensive inward migration as a result of the accession of eastern and central European states.

The Return of Leadership and Germany's National Interest

Fundamental discussions about the place of Germany's Nazi past in German national identity that had accompanied Schröder's advent to power in 1998 were noticeably absent when Angela Merkel came to office in 2005. Merkel continued Schröder's approach, insofar as she acknowledged German culpability without any ifs and buts—particularly apparent in Germany's relationship with Israel. However, at the same time, Merkel's government set out to complement the institutionalization of Holocaust centered memory—as manifested in the completion of the Memorial to the Murdered Jews of Europe in Berlin under Schröder—with the institutionalization of the memory of German victimhood. The coalition agreement between the

CDU/CSU and the SPD of 2005 committed the government to pursuing the establishment of a "visible sign" in Berlin to commemorate forced migration, flight, and expulsion. In spite of this initiative, Merkel never left any doubt that she considered the causal relationship between Hitler's aggressive expansionism and the expulsions of Germans from the East to be of vital importance when acknowledging German victimhood.[29]

Similar to Schröder's approach, an acknowledgement of German culpability did not result in a lack of assertiveness in the way Merkel represented Germany. Quite to the contrary, due to Germany's totalitarian experience, as chancellor, Merkel seemed to consider herself properly qualified to comment on contemporary human rights abuses in other countries. The way she criticized Presidents George W. Bush and Vladimir Putin, as well as China, over human rights violations testifies to this. Merkel attempted to enrich German collective memory by adding some positive aspects. The success story of the Bonn Republic and the struggle for freedom in the German Democratic Republic in 1989 have been key motifs in her speeches.

Moreover, when Merkel came to office in 2005, the EU–in particular in its attempt to constitutionalize itself–had reached a deadlock in the wake of the failed referenda in France and the Netherlands. Most striking was the fact that unlike what happened in Germany's previous European presidencies, Europe was looking towards German leadership to find a way out of the crisis,[30] and Merkel dutifully provided it.

In some ways, Merkel seemed to return to Kohl's rhetoric by claiming that European unity continued to be a question of "war and peace," since peace and democracy "should never be taken for granted," even though the EU had made peace in Europe a "familiar normality."[31] In her government declaration on 14 December 2006, Merkel asserted that Europe was the key concept for peace in the twentieth century and would remain the key concept for the twenty-first century.[32] She also made it clear, however, that securing peace was no longer sufficient as a raison d'être for current generations and added that it was common values, such as freedom, justice, democracy, the rule of law, and a respect for human rights, that held Europe together internally.[33]

However, in contrast to Helmut Kohl, whose rhetoric largely referred to World War II and who had emphasized reconciliation with former enemies, Merkel–in view of her biography hardly surprising–linked the rationale for the European project to the division of Europe and the freedom that had been achieved for all of Europe. Referring explicitly to her own experience, she pointed out that as a citizen of the GDR, she used to live in Europe but not the European Union. She described it as good fortune for the peoples of Europe to have achieved integration, which ensured freedom and made affluence possible. Depicting the EU as a house that she had only seen from the outside until 1990, she described it as even nicer from the inside and said that she would never want to leave it again.[34]

Merkel was the key architect of the so-called Berlin Declaration, which was to commemorate the fiftieth anniversary of the signing of the Treaties of Rome in 2007. Trying to spell out the rationale for European integration fifty years on, the Declaration draws on collective memory of war as well as the continent's division by stating: "Thanks to the yearning for freedom of the peoples of Central and Eastern Europe the unnatural division of Europe is now consigned to the past. European integration shows that we have learnt the painful lessons of a history marked by bloody conflict." However, at the same time, the Berlin Declaration makes clear that history and the notion of war are not enough to bind Europe together, but that it is the common values of the present that provide the basis: "We are striving for peace and freedom, for democracy and the rule of law, for mutual respect and shared responsibility, for prosperity and security, for tolerance and participation, for justice and solidarity."[35]

In spite of her pro-integrationist rhetoric, her attempts to provide European integration with a new rationale and her occasional preparedness to return Germany to its role as the EU's "paymaster,"[36] Merkel has also not shied away from pursuing Germany's national interest, even if that isolated Germany in the short term. For example, at the summit in December 2008, she protected Germany's heavy industry even though this meant a revision of her original position in the climate deal. She prioritized the protection of German jobs over environmental concerns and the EU's efforts to pass a package of emission regulations. The media reacted with surprise with one headline in the Guardian reporting "EU Giant isolated as Merkel puts Germany first."[37] As Garton Ash has pointed out in this context "[i]t's nothing new that France and Britain are behaving like France and Britain.... What's new is that Germany is now behaving like France and Britain."[38] Angela Merkel's conduct during the eurozone debt crisis provides ample evidence for the new and much more assertive approach, which is guided by Germany's national interest.

Most importantly, however, Merkel has shown no reluctance at all to providing leadership in the European Union, and, in spite of significant problems, she managed to lead the EU out of the impasse over the constitution and negotiated the Lisbon Treaty–signed by the member states in December 2007–during Germany's EU Presidency. Expectations towards Germany to show leadership in Europe have also become increasingly accepted domestically. At the end of 2008, Fischer—usually quite sensitive to Germany's historical legacy and its implications—accused Germany under Angela Merkel "of failing as a leading power in Europe,"[39] and in his Berlin Address in 2009, Federal President Horst Köhler asserted that "Germany as the largest economy in the European Union has a leadership role to play."[40]

Asserting National Sovereignty: The Federal Constitutional Court Ruling on the Lisbon Treaty

Even though within the first two decades after unification the past appears to have lost its predictable grip on Germany's behavior in Europe, with political elites having lost their reluctance to show leadership and express Germany's national interest explicitly, the most serious challenge to Germany's continued Europeanism came not from German governments but from the German Federal Constitutional Court. A number of people—including Peter Gauweiler from the CSU and the parliamentary party of the Left Party (Die Linke), represented by their chairmen Gregor Gysi and Oskar Lafontaine—brought forward a complaint which argued that the Lisbon Treaty was not compatible with the German Basic Law (constitution). The complainants claimed that the Lisbon Treaty made the democratic deficit of the European Union worse and that the Treaty further eroded German national sovereignty by transferring more powers to Brussels. The Lisbon Treaty was said to undermine the power of the German parliament and thus violated the principles of representative democracy. The constitutional court judges in Karlsruhe—having the final say on the constitutionality of legislation—ruled in June 2009 that the Treaty was compatible with the Basic Law but demanded that the role of the German parliament had to be strengthened, in order to ensure that the democratically elected representatives of the German people would continue to play a major role in all decision-making. The Court demanded that the Act Extending and Strengthening the Rights of the Bundestag and the Bundesrat in European Union Matters had to be amended before ratification could take place.

 Rather than the decision itself, it was the over seventy page-long ruling that accompanied it that made the preservation of German constitutional and national identity, and its sovereignty, the core issues that was truly remarkable and constitutes a milestone in Germany's relationship with Europe. In general terms, the Court emphasized that European unification was not to be realized in a way that would infringe the ability of member states to shape the economic, cultural, and social conditions of the lives of their citizens. It even specified particular policy areas that it considered vital to remain within the jurisdiction of a sovereign state (e.g. criminal law, the use of force, fiscal decisions on public revenue and expenditure, welfare provisions, and decisions that are of a particular cultural importance).[41] The Court also interpreted the provisions of the Treaty to mean that member states' constitutional and political identities would be preserved and that member states continued to be responsible for the fundamental direction of the politics and policies of the Union. In a prescriptive rather than descriptive manner, the ruling left no doubt that it did not consider the Treaty to violate German national sovereignty in any way: "Germany will remain a sovereign state and therefore legal actor of international law."[42]

As one commentator pointed out, sovereignty is a notion that is neither used in the Basic Law nor in the EU Treaties, and in spite of its extensive use, the Court did not define its meaning.[43] Nevertheless, the root *souverän* appeared forty-nine times in the Lisbon decision, a highly inflationary use when compared to previous rulings, such as Solange I and II in which it did not appear at all or the Maastricht ruling in which it figured only eight times.[44] Similarly, German identity featured strongly in the ruling, and in spite of a lack of discussion regarding what that actually was and how it would be infringed upon, according to one commentator, it was mentioned thirty-six times.[45]

This emphasis on German national identity and sovereignty as laid down in the Court ruling is something quite new in the German discourse on European integration. As Jo Eric Murkens has pointed out, traditionally, "being a member of the European Union was not experienced as a loss of sovereignty but understood as an extension of Germany's ability to act and acceptance in an equal partnership."[46]

The reactions to the ruling have been mixed and have ranged from assessments that suggested that it meant "the end of European integration as we know it" to suggestions that the ruling might "sabotage the engine a bit."[47] According to Fischer, the way the Court ruling evoked the specter of a European federal state reminded one of the British Conservative Party's traditional Euroskepticism.[48]

In any case, the ruling of the Federal Constitutional Court of 30 June 2009 provides the first binding document of a key player of the German political system to set out a very critical attitude towards further European integration, at the same time as celebrating the German nation-state, its democracy, identity, and sovereignty. Therefore, it clearly articulates a novel approach to Germany's relationship with Europe and is very likely to further erode what used to be Germany's "reflexive Europeanism" or "European imperative." The ruling clearly came down in favor of the nation-state at the expense of potential further integration. Most importantly, in the context of this chapter, instead of emphasizing Germany's historical and constitutional commitment to further European integration, it celebrated the sovereignty and identity of the German nation-state.

The New Germany in the New Europe

Under Schröder especially, Germany developed a new approach that accommodated its Nazi past more comfortably within the wider framework of its national identity. Positive expressions of German national identity became possible, in spite of a clear and unambiguous acknowledgement of German culpability; this continued under Merkel's first term in office. Increasing confidence at home also has resulted in a much more assertive stance in the Berlin Republic's approach to Europe.[49] Even though Germany still does not have institutionalized Euroskepticism as, for example, Britain, its European policy has become less predictable and more driven by cost/benefit analyses. As Paterson has pointed out, whereas what he calls Germany's European vocation "came to be seen as the defining feature of the Bonn Republic, it has been subject to pressure and erosion in the Berlin Republic and is increasingly contingent, contested and circumscribed."[50]

The Berlin Republic's relationship with Europe thus differs from that of the Bonn Republic, in a number of ways. The Bonn Republic's emphasis on multilateralism and reluctance to express its national interest have given way to rather confident articulations of Germany's own interest and its former "reflexive Europeanism" cannot be taken for granted any more. In addition, Germany has shed its former "leadership avoidance reflex" and is prepared to show leadership much more openly and in a much less inhibited way. It now also clearly distinguishes between Germany's national interest and the interest of the European Union, even though it has resumed its role as "paymaster" at times. However, in view of united Germany's economic problems, German political elites have to be much more sensitive towards the possibility of anti-European sentiments developing if they display too much readiness to finance compromises in the EU. Germany's increasing assertiveness as a nation also means that the European dimension is increasingly losing its importance as a kind of *ersatz* identity.

Nevertheless, even though there has been an overall decline, support for European integration in society at large continues to be quite high, particularly when compared to other member states. According to a Eurobarometer Report published in 2009, 60 percent of respondents declared themselves to be in favor of membership compared to a European average of only 53 percent. Similarly, 47 percent of Germans continued to have a positive image of the European Union.[51] At the same time, at least comparatively speaking, German political elites are likely to continue to be largely integration-friendly, even if the previous automatism has disappeared. However, in future, it is quite possible that they might at times hide behind the Lisbon ruling of the Federal Constitutional Court and argue that it prevents them from agreeing to particular initiatives.

While the collective memory of World War II has lost its predictable grip on Germany's relationship with Europe, something similar appears to have happened on the European stage. Following the most successful period of European integration in the aftermath of the collapse of communism, which saw the EU expand to a membership of twenty-seven with many more waiting to be admitted, particularly the long and cumbersome process that was supposed to lead to a constitution for Europe and ended up with a watered down compromise in the shape of the Reform or Lisbon Treaty, showed just how difficult it is to find a new resonant rationale for European integration. Fischer articulated this in his Humboldt speech in 2000 when he claimed that the "problems of the twenty-first century cannot be solved with the fears and the formulae of the nineteenth and twentieth centuries."[52] In contrast to expectations, the European project has not resulted in the emergence of a European identity. Quite to the contrary, European Union member states assert their national interests more than ever and the diversification of memory trends that has happened in Europe since the fall of communism, makes it doubtful that a common identity will emerge in the near future. As one commentator described it, "[t]oday's European Union is twenty-seven states in search of a story"[53]—and one might add, of an identity and memory.

Notes

1. See also Ruth Wittlinger, *German National Identity in the Twenty-First Century: A New Republic After All?* (Basingstoke, 2010), chapters 4 and 5.
2. Quoted in William E. Paterson, "Does Germany Still Have a European Vocation?" *German Politics* 19, no.1 (2010): 41–52, 43.

3. Manuela Glaab, "Einstellungen zur deutschen Einheit" in *Handbuch zur deutschen Einheit 1949-1989-1999,* eds. Werner Weidenfeld and Karl-Rudolf Korte (Frankfurt/Main, 1999), 306-316, 310.
4. William E. Paterson, "Germany and Europe" in *Developments in German Politics,* eds. Stephen Padgett, William E. Paterson, and Gordon Smith (Basingstoke, 2003), 206-226, 207.
5. Frank Brunssen, *Das neue Selbstverständnis der Berliner Republik* (Würzburg, 2005), 27.
6. Paterson (see note 2), 13.
7. Paterson (see note 4), 211.
8. Miriam Karama quoted in Gisela Müller-Brandeck-Bocquet, "Die Europapolitik des vereinten Deutschland" in *Neue deutsche Außenpolitik,* ed., Wichard Woyke (Schwalbach, 2003), 47-73, 47.
9. Wilfried Loth, "Die doppelte Eindämmung. Überlegungen zur Genesis des Kalten Krieges 1945-1947," *Historische Zeitschrift* 238 (1984): 611-631.
10. Gregor Schöllgen, *Der Auftritt* (Berlin, 2004), 35.
11. Christian Schweiger, *Britain, Germany and the European Union* (Basingstoke, 2007), 62.
12. Müller-Brandeck-Bocquet (see note 8), 54.
13. Quoted in Werner Link "Alternativen deutscher Aussenpolitik," *Zeitschrift für Politik* 46, no. 2 (1999): 125-143, 128.
14. Charlie Jeffery and William E. Paterson, "Germany and European Integration: The Shifting of Tectonic Plates," *West European Politics* 26, no. 4 (2003): 59-75, 68.
15. Timothy Garton Ash, "Germany's Choice," *Foreign Affairs* 73, no. 4 (1994), 65-81, 74.
16. See for example, Karl Wilds, "Identity Creation and the Culture of Contrition: Recasting 'Normality' in the Berlin Republic," *German Politics* 9, no. 1 (2000): 83-102; Michael Jeismann, *Auf Wiedersehen Gestern. Die deutsche Vergangenheit und die Politik von morgen* (Munich, 2001); Bill Niven, "Introduction" in *Germans as Victims,* ed. Bill Niven (Basingstoke, 2006), 1-25, 10.
17. Gerhard Schröder, "Gedenken an den 8. Mai 1945: 'Wir stehen erst jetzt am Ende einer langen Nachkriegszeit,'" *Süddeutsche Zeitung,* 6 May 2005.
18. Quoted in Marcel Tambarin, "Vom Dritten Reich zur 'Berliner Republik:' Deutschlands Suche nach der Normalität," in *Alte und neue Identitätsbilder im heutigen Deutschland,* eds. Anne Saint Sauveur-Henn and Marc Muylaert, (Leipzig, 1999), 97-106, 102.
19. Presse- und Informationsamt der Bundesregierung, *Bulletin 2005* (Berlin 2006).
20. Gerhard Schröder, Speech at the SPD Party Conference, 17 April 1998.
21. Gerhard Schröder, Regierungserklärung, 10 November 1998.
22. Ibid.
23. Thomas Banchoff, "German Policy Toward the European Union: The Effects of Historical Memory," *German Politics* 6, no.1 (1997): 60-76.
24. Gerhard Schröder, Speech to the Bundestag, 10 December 1998.
25. Kurt Biedenkopf quoted in Regina Karp, "The New German Foreign Policy Consensus," *The Washington Quarterly* 29, no.1 (2006): 61-82, 76.
26. Jeffery and Paterson (see note 14), 70.
27. Wilhelm Knelangen, "Die neue deutsche Europapolitik für eine andere EU?" *Aus Politik und Zeitgeschichte.* Beilage zur Wochenzeitung Das Parlament, 38-39 (2005): 24-30, 26.
28. Joschka Fischer, Speech to the European Parliament in Strasbourg, 12 January 1999.
29. For more details, see Ruth Wittlinger, "The Merkel Government's Politics of the Past," *German Politics and Society* 26, no.4 (2008): 9-27.
30. *Europäische Rundschau,* 2, 2007.
31. Interview with Chancellor Angela Merkel, *Bild-Zeitung,* 23 March 2007.
32. Angela Merkel, Regierungserklärung, 14 December 2006.
33. Speech by Chancellor Angela Merkel to the *Deutsche Gesellschaft für Auswärtige Politik,* 8 November 2006.
34. Speech by Angela Merkel to the European Parliament during Germany's EU Presidency, 17 January 2007.

35. The Berlin Declaration is available at http://www.eu2007.de/de/News/download_docs/Maerz/0324-RAA/English.pdf; accessed 15 September 2011.
36. Sven Bernhard Gareis, *Deutschlands Außen- und Sicherheitspolitik* (Opladen, 2005), 98.
37. *The Guardian*, 12 December 2008.
38. Timothy Garton Ash, "One Great Power Will Be Absent from the London G20 Summit," *The Guardian*, 26 March 2009.
39. Joschka Fischer "Deutschland versagt als Führungsmacht," *Spiegel Online*, 19 December 2008.
40. President Horst Köhler's Berlin Address, 24 March 2009.
41. Paragraph 252 of the ruling, available at http://www.bundesverfassungsgericht.de/entscheidungen/es20090630_2bve000208.html; accessed 15 September 2011.
42. Ibid.
43. Roland Bieber, "An Association of Sovereign States," *European Constitutional Law Review* 5 (2009): 391–406, 398.
44. Jo Eric Khushal Murkens, "Identity trumps Integration: The Lisbon Treaty in the German Federal Constitutional Court," *Der Staat* 48, no.4 (2009): 517–534, 520.
45. Jan-Herman Reestman, "The Franco-German Constitutional Divide: Reflections on National and Constitutional Identity," *European Constitutional Law Review*, 5 (2009): 374–390, 375.
46. Murkens (see note 44), 522.
47. "The World from Berlin: Brussels is no longer just a side dish," *Spiegel Online*, 1 July 2009.
48. Joschka Fischer, "Ein nationaler Riegel," *Die Zeit Online*, 10 July 2009.
49. See also Eric Langenbacher, "Still the Unmasterable Past? The Impact of History and Memory in the Federal Republic of Germany," *German Politics* 19, no.1 (2010): 24–40 who argues that the phase of intensive memory work might be coming to an end.
50. Paterson (see note 2), 41.
51. Eurobarometer 72, *Nationaler Bericht Deutschland,* Autumn 2009.
52. Joschka Fischer "From Confederacy to Federation: Thoughts on the Finality of European Integration," Speech at Humboldt University, Berlin, 12 May 2000.
53. Timothy Garton-Ash, "Today's European Union is 27 states in search of a story," *The Guardian*, 4 January 2007.

Conclusion

A Plea for an "Intergovernmental" European Memory

•••••••••••••••

Eric Langenbacher

The contributors to this volume have examined many of the most important theoretical and empirical dynamics affecting collective memories in early twenty-first-century Europe.* The innovative, conceptual approaches include the emphasis placed on "hinge" generations in East and West, the necessity of explicitly gender-based analytics, the "memory-market dictum," dynamics of family memory, and the distinction between nationalized memory discourses and meta-narrativity. Several chapters delve into intellectual history, looking at the early twentieth-century genesis and post–World War II evolution of the European idea, and the nexus between collective identity, the nation-state, and memory as they pertain to the construction of European identity. Empirical case studies from all corners of Europe encompass countries with well-established memory traditions, such as France, Norway, and Germany, and other cases—mainly in Central and Eastern Europe like Croatia, Poland, and Serbia—where liberalized collective memory discourses are (necessarily) barely twenty-years-old and where a "double memory" of Nazi-era and communist crimes creates heightened complexity. Moreover, many of the contributions have abjured in-depth single or paired case studies (however fruitful methodologically) and look more briefly at a much broader set of comparative cases, such as Italy, Spain, Russia, the Czech Republic, Austria, the Netherlands, and Estonia.

Despite the diversity of the contributions, several common themes have emerged from this volume, each of which deserves some additional reflection. First, most of the cases examined are still dominated by what Claus Leggewie has called the "First Circle [of European memory]: The Holocaust as Europe's Negative Founding Myth."[1] The resilience of this memory speaks not only to the sheer magnitude of the existential events on which it is based—and the continued necessity of working through aspects of the trauma, especially in Central Europe—but also to the relative absence of any other galvanizing postwar or European event that has the power to compete with World War II-era memories. Indeed, the last several decades have witnessed the diffusion of hegemonic Holocaust-centered "cosmopolitan" memories,[2] i.e., the memory of massive human rights abuses perpetrated by Nazi Germans in the 1930s and 1940s. Commemoration of Holocaust victims has proliferated across the continent—from the Memorial to the Murdered Jews of Europe in the center of Berlin to memorials erected on the former Nazi Party grounds in Nuremberg, near where the Vel' d'hiv was located in Paris and on the Judenplatz in Vienna. Several supranational/European initiatives also characterize this process: the Stockholm International Forum on the Holocaust in 2000 (which led to even more countries mandating treatment of this historical tragedy in school curricula); the censure of Austria in 2000 after the electoral success of the xenophobic Freedom Party of Jörg Haider; the projection of these normatized memories onto the period of imperialism and colonialism with Europeans as perpetrators. This hegemonic memory also has diffused into Central and Eastern Europe—perhaps most notably in Poland. Despite earlier controversies, such as the dispute over a convent and cross at Auschwitz or the debate unleashed by Jan Gross's scholarship about the massacre of Jews by Poles at Jedwabne, the construction of the Museum of the History of Polish Jews in Warsaw (opening in 2013) epitomizes the pan-European acceptance of the Holocaust-centered memory.[3]

This memory regime began its rise to prominence after the 1960s, as the earliest postwar memory discourses of heroic national resistance ebbed. However, just as the hegemony of this memory had been established, its contents began to shift. The triad—perpetrator, bystander and victim[4]—has long been at the core of this memory, and the resulting experiential or behavioral types have long been codified. Originally, there were Nazi and then Nazi German (an important semantic and moral-political shift) perpetrators, the vast majority of the European populace were bystanders, and victims were conceived predominantly as Jewish. Yet, as Timothy Snyder and others have pointed out, this was a particular Western European conception generated by specific and necessarily partial experiences (given the discursive iron curtain across the continent) and evidence based on the popularity of Anne Frank and conceptions of concentration camps like Dachau, and, a little later, Auschwitz (as a concentration and death camp, as well as an industrial entity), rather than extermination camps, such as Treblinka, mass shootings (Babi Yar), and the willful starvation of millions.[5]

Conclusion

Over the last twenty years, each of these types has evolved. Regarding victims, Sinti/Roma, homosexuals, the disabled, and Slavic civilians have been added. An amorphous category of "political opponents"–most other victims of the Nazis were leftists and especially communists–although always present in some form and in some countries (the near adulation of Christian and conservative opponents of Hitler in Adenauer-era Germany) had withered after the 1960s, but more recently has regained attention. In some contexts, certain "nationalists" and heroic "resistors" are also included in this expanded victim category. As a consequence, Jewish victims are being relativized–in the benign sense of the word, as the inclusion of other victims has not (usually) been due to anti-Semitic motivations. These shifts may indicate that "Holocaust" memory is increasingly a misnomer and that a more general memory of the "World War II" era or "Nazi crimes" may be emerging or, more appropriately, returning–as a more expansive memory was typical of earlier postwar decades. That said, this emerging third phase of World War II memory is not a mere recycling of the conceptions of the 1950s, because many of the victim groups now discussed (e.g., Sinti and Roma) were previously excluded.

The understanding of "bystanders" has slowly shifted from an exonerating to an incriminating category, especially in Germany. Today, there are frequent imputations of collective guilt, which are now widely accepted (at least publically) in contrast to earlier years where this was rather defensively rejected as an inappropriate provocation. When Martin Hohmann, a right-wing, Christian, Democratic, Bundestag deputy delivered an inflammatory speech in which he argued that treating Germans as a collectively guilty people (*Tätervolk*) is as inappropriate as holding Jews responsible for Bolshevism, given the early prominence of Jewish leaders before and after the 1917 revolution; he was roundly condemned, expelled from the CDU's parliamentary group, and eventually kicked out of the party.[6] Elsewhere in Europe, these collective guilt discourses were also increasingly heard after 1990. The debate about the Évian Conference of 1938, the Allies' failure to bomb Auschwitz (although already mentioned in the 1980s), Swiss/Swedish processing of Nazi gold and other financial instruments, and the dishonoring of Nazi era insurance policies on technicalities are examples here.

Finally, the conception of perpetrators has expanded. In Germany, big business, average soldiers, and many of the professions are now placed in this category. Many of the postwar myths have been shattered–in the 1990s regarding the "clean" Wehrmacht and, more recently, the supposed lack of complicity in the German Foreign Office, after the 2010 publication of the results of a five-year study into the history of this ministry and its diplomats during the Third Reich.⁷ There has also been increasing attention devoted to non-German perpetrators—Scandinavian, Dutch, Belgian, and French SS volunteers; Finns during the Winter War and beyond; the disproportionate number of Austrians in the Nazi machinery of death; and Eastern Europeans from places like Latvia, Lithuania, or Hungary.⁸ Moreover, there is also much more attention devoted to those who benefitted materially from the expropriation of Jewish property and professionally from the career and business opportunities that opened up, because of the oppressed, expelled, and murdered Jewish (and other) victims of the Nazi regime throughout Europe.⁹

In Western Europe, the typology has also been deconstructed. Indeed, the long hegemonic fourth experiential/behavioral type—the heroic member of the resistance—is largely part of the veritable "dustbin of history." Particularly noteworthy is France, with the shattering of the "Vichy Syndrome," including a bursting of the Gaullist "everyone was in the Resistance" myth and a recognition of the degree of complicity many French citizens and state institutions had in collaborating with the Nazi machinery of murder—as exemplified by the 2011 apology from the French national railroad.¹⁰ One might also understand recent memory discourses in Italy and especially Spain in such terms. The categories of victims, perpetrators, and bystanders are extremely convoluted in the memory of the Spanish Civil War, where atrocities were committed on both Republican and Nationalist sides (so that no one emerges as unequivocally heroic) and where most people simply stood by allowing the atrocities to occur through passive acquiescence. More generally, there is an acknowledgment that European societies in the 1930s and 1940s were characterized by deep socioeconomic and cultural cleavages, civil-war like conditions, and rather widespread support for fascist and Nazi movements and policies.¹¹

Second, European countries are still in a kind of memory flux—as the consequences of 1989 are worked through, the generation of witnesses passes from the historical stage, and cultural memories for the *longue durée* are constructed. As important as all of these processes are across the continent, perhaps developments in Germany are of the most significance. Indeed, Germany has been and remains the "hinge" country—not only economically (the engine of the European economy), but also when it comes to collective memories. The hegemonic Holocaust-centered memory regime was originally and still predominantly colored by the German case—representing a possible example of the uploading of nationally specific memory discourses to a European level—and its sustenance and diffusion has been possible only because of German agency, stemming from its laboriously

Conclusion

constructed "culture of contrition" in the quintessential "sorry state."[12] Too often, analysts of the German case describe a rather homogenous post-unification period, but it is increasingly clear that the 1990s witnessed a particularly intensive confrontation with the Third Reich that was the culmination of several decades of memory work. That decade was characterized by seemingly continuous debates about various aspects of Nazism and, more importantly, about Germans' failings to come clean and make appropriate amends in the earlier postwar years as well as about proper forms of commemoration.[13]

Memory discourses have begun to shift in this key actor, since around the time that the capital returned to Berlin in 1999. Competing memories of the East German dictatorship (2009 witnessed the twentieth anniversary of the fall of the Berlin Wall; 2011 marked the fiftieth anniversary of its construction)[14]–not even to mention the recent wave of interest in the German Resistance–Stauffenberg, Sophie Scholl, the Rosenstrasse protest in Berlin[15]–are rising in importance. The return of the memory of German suffering (hegemonic in the early postwar years) has been an epochal change with consequences that are still playing out for both domestic and international memory dynamics.[16] With the rise of these complicating memories, the slow but steady decline in the salience of the World War II period–now over sixty-five years in the past–not to mention the increasing diversity of the country's population (with immigrants and their descendants not feeling the same responsibility for the Nazi legacy), and the intrusion of current economic events like never before in the postwar period (Euro, financial and economic crises), will that country remain the European leader of contrition-based memory and a corresponding political culture? Will the third and fourth post–Nazi generations continue to accept their role as transhistorical villain? Will the ever-present desire to be a "normal" country pursuing self-interested policies and exerting power finally relativize Holocaust memory, which previously has inhibited such behavior?

Moreover, as several of the authors in this volume have noted, there is a clear downside to the diffusion of "cosmopolitan," de-nationalized, and Europeanized Holocaust memory. The historical facts of the unique suffering and murder of European Jews by Nazi German perpetrators must be maintained in memory. As important as it is for individual countries to come-to-terms with their degree of complicity and, in many cases, support for the Nazi project, ultimate German agency cannot be elided. The war of extermination was a Nazi German and not a European project (despite the Nazis' own rhetoric at times). In this context, one can understand the sensitivities in Poland generated by erroneous, unselfconscious references to "Polish" death camps in various international media and the resulting successful effort to officially rename Auschwitz, the "Former Nazi German Concentration Camp Auschwitz-Birkenau."[17]

Third, out of this mnemonic fluidity has emerged a more specific Central and East European memory regime. Many of the victims in the World War II era were Slavic—gentile Polish, Ukrainian, Belarusian, and Russian civilians, and Soviet prisoners of war (three million starved to death by the Wehrmacht). During the Cold War, these victim groups were rarely included in conceptions of Nazi victims—especially in the dominant Western memory regime, but also in the countries themselves (even in the most "national" of the communist systems like Poland or Yugoslavia). Either these victims were subsumed into the category of "antifascists" or they were ignored (for example, dead Red Army prisoners conveyed weakness in the eyes of the communist elite). The fact that representatives of these victimized groups have found voice and attention is a major new dynamic—which has also slowly (and often controversially) led to a reassessment of the nature of the Nazi worldview and war—no longer understood to be motivated specifically by anti-Semitism, but rather by a more general racism.

These groups of victims have been added to the victims of communism in general, and Stalinism in particular—including crimes like the 1940 massacre of more than 20,000 Polish soldiers (many in the forest of Katyn), police, and intellectuals that the Soviets blamed on the Nazis until 1990. These developments have precipitated intense debates about the interaction and comparability of the two twentieth-century European totalitarian regimes—and the status and place of each victimized group in more general remembrance. At times, there is even an unseemly competition among various groups for validation of "ultimate" victim status.[18] In addition, after decades of artificial "freezing" under communism, the memory of ethnic nationalism and strife—from the World War II era, but also before—has returned. This is particularly clear in the Balkans and Baltic lands, but the resurgence of the memory of German suffering (as well as the earlier history of ethnic antagonisms in Central Europe)[19] and its reception in places like Poland and the Czech Republic can also be understood in this context. Finally, there is an emergent and hugely controversial memory discourse surrounding the collaboration of Eastern European regimes and citizens with the Nazis, in places like Slovakia, Croatia, and Hungary.[20]

On a similar note, several other regional collective memory clusters may be appearing. In addition to the Central/East European memory regime, including (to an extent) Germany and to which Finland and Greece could be added, there are many commonalities between France, the Benelux countries, Denmark, Norway, and even Italy, creating a West European memory type; Germany would also fit partially here. Germany's placement in both of these memory clusters is a twenty-first century version of its *Mittellage,* a bridge or hinge between various sub-European cultural and memory constellations. The amoral neutrality of Switzerland and Sweden is another type—Portugal and Spain may also fit here, but Spain, with its legacy of Civil War and long authoritarian regime, probably necessitates its own category.[21] Only the victorious United Kingdom and Soviet Union/Russia are sufficiently distinctive from these continental types (and from each other) to stand outside of these commonalities. Interestingly, these clusters loosely correspond to different informal groupings in the European Union—the more "*communautaire*" original member states (core Europe), a Central and East European bloc, and a group of more Euroskeptical "outliers," such as Sweden, Switzerland, and the United Kingdom.

Fourth, this volume intimates the "unity in diversity" of the continent today—that there are unique dynamics in each national case, but that each is part of an increasingly connected and integrating common space in which some kind of standardization or Europeanization is occurring. Despite substantial scholarship on "Europe" and "Europeanization," there is still a lack of consensus regarding an actual definition. One of the issues is that there are weak and strong understandings of "Europeanization." The weak version merely asserts that different places on the European continent are becoming more alike in a minimal sense thanks to a diffusion of standardized norms and practices. Indeed, regime variability has decreased, as virtually every country west of Russia and Belarus has adopted a form of liberal democracy (usually parliamentary); socioeconomic structures are converging as the agricultural and industrial sectors shrink and as populations age (albeit at different rates). Moreover, English has emerged as a resilient and non-controversial (usually) *lingua franca* across the continent.

The stronger version of the Europeanization concept states that there are certain distinctive core conceptions at the heart of what it means to be "Europe" or European—as opposed to the national, liberal, or Western. These tenets are novel and usually created and disseminated by transnational (EU) institutions. As Johan Olsen notes, "Europeanization, here, includes both the strengthening of an organizational capacity for collective action and development of common ideas, such as new norms and collective understandings"[22] Alternately, he speaks of a pattern of "mutual adaptation among co-evolving institutions."[23]

This stronger version of the thesis is highly problematic to operationalize and substantiate in any meaningful sense. No one has even convincingly defined what "Europe" is—geographically (Turkey? Georgia? Russia, all the way to Vladivostok? And what about immediately adjacent countries, such as Morocco or Israel?)—or conceptually—as evidenced by debates about the inclusion and eventual lack of any reference to Christianity or a (Judeo-) Christian heritage in the preamble to the aborted EU Constitution in 2003–2005.[24] Given the sensitivities regarding Christianity in the widely secularized (with a growing Muslim minority) continent today, Europe usually defines itself based on abstract (social) democratic and Enlightenment values (human and social rights, self-determination, negative and positive freedoms). These values, of course, are hardly monopolized by Europe making them problematic components of a sound definition. In light of these difficulties, most authors resort to metaphysical and often-tautological alternatives. Exemplary is Gerard Delanty who writes that Europe is an "invention … a historically fabricated reality of ever-changing forms and dynamics … the emblem and central organizing metaphor of a complex civilization. But Europe is more than a region and polity, it is also an idea and an identity."[25] Thus, it appears productive to conceptualize Europeanization only in the weaker sense—diffusion of norms, institutions and practices in both more passive and more active inter-state or inter-societal senses.

What does all of this mean for concerns about Europeanization of collective memory? Not to sound too Euroskeptical (although this certainly resonates with the current Zeitgeist) but a truly "strong" European memory really does not seem to exist in any meaningful sense. Perhaps a collective memory of the "European project" will emerge—certainly there are some EU actors that are assiduously attempting to foster this. Examples include the festivities in 2007 in conjunction with the fiftieth anniversary of the Treaty of Rome[26] or elite-led attempts to reframe history in a "European" context—World Wars I and II as a European civil war—as exemplified by various Erasmus and European Commission (particularly the Education and Culture Directorate General) initiatives such as CLIOH.[27] However, there is next to no resonance among European publics for these ambitious constructs—i.e., there is a dearth of evidence that this is affecting anyone's identity or memory. Memories, like politics, are still overwhelmingly national, if not increasingly so.[28]

Additionally, there appears to be a tendency for negative, traumatic events—or ones that involved regime upheaval (demise of communism) or communal sacrifice (Britain's victory in World War II)—to overwhelm and squeeze out the more positive triumphs or benign achievements. The resonance in Germany of 9 November—when the Wall fell, as well as the anniversary of the *Kristallnacht* pogrom of 1938—is illustrative, as opposed to 3 October–Kohl's arbitrary choice for the Day of German Unity. Few even noticed the celebrations in conjunction with the fiftieth anniversary of the Treaty of Rome (25 March 2007). Fewer know that "Europe Day" is 9 May–perhaps overshadowed by 8 May, the anniversary of the end of World War II in Europe–or 5 May if one prefers the Council of Europe to the European Union. Ironically, the lack of negative, traumatic events associated with the European project and the benign, piecemeal nature of European integration, create serious impediments to the creation of a "strong" European memory.

Nevertheless, as argued throughout this volume, a degree of convergence–Europeanization in the weak sense–and the emergence of a "weak" European memory are discernible. Of course, it is contestable that this kind of convergence is more salient today than during the Enlightenment or "long" nineteenth century. One obvious difference is that such influences have moved beyond elites today to a degree unthinkable in 1890. The Eurovision song contest, European soccer competitions, and mass tourism to places like Mallorca, Euro Disney, or Mikonos are germane in this context. But these infrequent events hardly constitute a common European culture–television and film-viewing habits (except for Hollywood blockbusters) are still overwhelmingly national.

Such a "weak" understanding of Europeanization will no doubt disappoint the legions of Euro-cheerleading intellectuals. Many argue in a functionalist manner for the necessity of creating or "imagining" a new identity, a new solidarity that fits with the empowered supranational European level. As Klaus Eder puts it: "no other society is more based on abstract modes of communication than European society. It lacks more than any other social formation, the prerequisites for a 'naturalist' or 'groupist' collective identity. Europe is farthest from the hordes of primates, which is why it needs a strong collective identity."[29] To put it pithily, in the absence of such solidarity, how will Germans accept the necessity of bailing out the Greeks, or the Irish, or the Italians? No doubt, we will see the return of scaremongering tactics, epitomized by Helmut Kohl's original justification for European Monetary Union, recently reiterated in his remarks to Angela Merkel to "save" the Euro and stand by Greece. In calling for continued German support for European integration and another bailout for Greece, he opined: "We Germans perpetrated terrible crimes. We have abused our name. We have sworn never to do this again."[30]

Maybe it is time for these elites to re-think these positions. In this context, I sometimes think that the most problematic book published in the last generation was Benedict Anderson's *Imagined Communities*,[31] because his complex and nuanced argument about the construction of collective identities by nation-builders has been interpreted to mean that all identity constructs are "artificial" elite products that can also be deconstructed, replaced with another (preferable) alternative, and foisted upon mass publics given sufficient motivation, energy, and funding. This partial understanding of Anderson's argument overlooks the "raw materials" and the often-ancient "tribal" solidarities on which such identities are based.[32] Ernest Renan's insight about nations—and more generally, any evocative collective identity—being "daily plebiscites" still applies. Collective identities are not created out of elites' wishful thinking, well-intentioned exhortations, celebrations of "Europe Day" (one or both), newspaper op/eds, and European Commission fiats alone.

Moreover, as Norbert Elias, Michel Foucault, and Eugen Weber (among many others) have emphasized,[33] there is always an element of power—usually with a healthy dose of coercion—involved in the construction of any culture and collective identity. This factor that has not be sufficiently addressed by advocates of "strong" Europeanization. European norms and regulations are either generated internally and undemocratically by the sizable European technocracy (and then imposed often through the European Court of Justice) or represent a national norm that is adopted by the European level and imposed on others, i.e., the replication of the Bundesbank's mandate in the European Central Bank. Whatever the case, such impositions are almost always resented and resisted—with increasing frequency as the "bite" of European integration and standardization increase, or as recently manifested in the imposition of German economic preferences on other Euro members such as Greece. Whatever one thinks about the specific policies, the point is that power is being wielded, and the exercise of such is always resented by those who are being compelled to do something that they would not otherwise do. This is equally true for any "European" memory discourse—exemplified by the resistance in many countries to adopting a more standardized memory of World War II and the Holocaust in which the guilt of collaboration, co-perpetration, or having stood by is expected to be accepted, internalized and apologized for. Moreover, an essential element of any collective memory or identity—as Renan also observed long ago in conjunction with the establishment of national identities—is also a degree of forgetting and those whose experiences are thereby sidelined in this exercise of discursive power are understandably displaced.

Another power-related factor that has been neglected is the necessity of "creative destruction." By this I mean that for a European memory or identity to truly emerge, it needs to supersede currently hegemonic memories and identities, which are located predominantly at the national level (not even to mention the continued and even renewed salience of subnational identities). For the European level to have real resonance, these pre-existing forms must be destroyed (just as nation builders had to destroy feudal and aristocratic modes of organization and identity) or, at a minimum, substantially weakened and relativized. Today, there is a buffet of identities from which citizens can pick and choose, but it is also true that most individuals prioritize identities and many constructs are squeezed into insignificance or latency, as a result. Twenty years ago, there was more evidence that this relativization of national identities was happening–exemplified by the discourse about "postnationality" or Jürgen Habermas's constitutional patriotism (*Verfassungspatriotismus*).[34] But, recent scholarship shows that such concepts and related concerns, such as "cosmopolitanism," have lost their élan even amongst the elite intellectuals who tried to "imagine" them in the first place–and never resonated with mass publics in any case.[35] Even twenty-first-century Germans–the least patriotic of nations worldwide after 1945–are much prouder and self-assured than at any other point in the last sixty years.

Thus, the elite and intellectual project to "build Europe" with a strong European identity and memory is extremely fraught. Before even more energy is expended towards this end, at a minimum, the right questions ought to be posed and debated. Is "unity in diversity" sustainable (or even definable)? Do actors really want willfully to destroy all of the local color that has made Europe what it has always been on the altar of some nebulous conception of "Europe?" Why should "Europeanization"–as the homogenizing analogue to the much-derided concept of "Americanization"–be something to celebrate, especially when it could very well destroy what has made Europe what it is? This is to say that Europe is Europe because of its cultural diversity–its unprecedented multiplicity of languages, ethnicities, national and subnational memories and identities.[36]

Perhaps Europeanization at its best means the establishment of institutionalized forums for communication, dissemination, and assessment of collective memories and identities. These would be places where differences can be discussed, understood, or translated; where conflicts can be mediated, and hopefully resolved; where interactive discourses are highlighted and not destroyed by some one-size-fits-all, technocratic diktat. If this would emerge, European actors would simply be administrators of such discursive spaces–referees and disseminators of the debates. In this manner, diversity of memory and identity can be maintained and negotiated, as opposed to elided–Europe can remain European. Come to think of it, this is akin to the inter-governmental and not the federalist approach to European integration.

Notes

* Many of the contributions included in this volume were presented at the "Dynamics of Memory in the New Europe" conference held from September 13–15, 2007 at Nottingham Trent University, UK. The organizers of the conference, Bill Niven and Ruth Wittlinger, are grateful for the generous support of Nottingham Tent University and the University of Durham.
1. Claus Leggewie, "Seven Circles of European Memory," *Eurozine,* 20 December 2010.
2. Daniel Levy and Natan Snzaider, *The Holocaust and Memory in the Global Age* (Philadelphia, 2006).
3. Antony Polonsky and Joanna B. Michlic, eds., *The Neighbors Respond: The Controversy over the Jedwabne Massacre in Poland* (Princeton, 2004). Robert Cherry and Annamaria Orla-Bukowska, eds., *Rethinking Poles and Jews: Troubled Past, Brighter Future* (Lanham, 2007); See also http://www.jewishmuseum.org.pl/en/cms/home-page/; accessed 19 August 2011.
4. Raul Hilberg, *Perpetrators, Victims, Bystanders: The Jewish Catastrophe, 1933–1945* (New York, 1992).
5. Timothy Snyder, *Bloodlands: Europe between Hitler and Stalin* (New York, 2010).
6. "Germany's far right: Raus," *The Economist,* 13 November 2003.
7. Hannes Heer, *Vernichtungskrieg: Verbrechen der Wehrmacht 1941–1944* (Hamburg, 1995); Eckart Conze, Norbert Frei, Peter Hayes and, Moshe Zimmermann, *Das Amt und die Vergangenheit: Deutsche Diplomaten im Dritten Reich und in der Bundesrepublik* (Munich, 2010). It should be noted that the latter book has been criticized heavily. See Rainer Blasius, "'Das Amt und die Vergangenheit:' Ein Kommissionsproblem," *Frankfurter Allgemeine Zeitung,* 27 November 2010, available at http://www.faz.net/artikel/C30923/das-amt-und-die-vergangenheit-ein-kommissionsproblem-30319135.html; accessed 26 August 2011.
8. "Die Komplizen: Hitlers europäische Helfer beim Judenmord," *Der Spiegel,* 21 (2009). See also Tony Judt, *Postwar: A History of Europe since 1945* (New York, 2005); Christopher Hale, *Hitler's Foreign Executioners: Europe's Dirty Secret* (New York, 2009).
9. See, for example, Richard J. Evans, *The Third Reich in Power: 1933–1939* (New York, 2006); Martin Dean, Constantin Goschler and Philipp Ther, *Robbery and Restitution: The Conflict over Jewish Property in Europe* (New York, 2007).
10. See, Maïa de la Baume, "French Railway Formally Apologizes to Holocaust Victims," *The New York Times,* 25 January 2011. See also, Henry Rousso, *The Vichy Syndrome: History and Memory in France since 1944,* trans. Arthur Goldhammer (Cambridge, 1991).
11. See Judt (see note 8).
12. David Art, *The Politics of the Nazi Past in Germany and Austria* (Cambridge, 2006); Jennifer J. Lind, *Sorry States: Apologies in International Affairs* (Ithaca, 2009).
13. See Eric Langenbacher "From an Unmasterable to a Mastered Past: The Impact of History and Memory in the Federal Republic of Germany," Special Issue: The Federal Republic at 60, *German Politics* 19, no. 1 (2010): 24–40.
14. See Hope Harrison, ed. "Special Issue: The Berlin Wall after Fifty Years; 1961–2011," *German Politics and Society,* 29, no. 2 (2011).

15. Importantly, each of these moments of resistance has been immortalized in mass market films.
16. Bill Niven, ed., *Germans as Victims: Remembering the Past in Contemporary Germany* (Houndsmills, 2006); Helmut Schmitz, ed., *A Nation of Victims? Representations of German Wartime Suffering from 1945 to the Present* (Amsterdam, 2007).
17. Mark Tran, "Poles claim victory in battle to rename Auschwitz," *The Guardian*, 27 June 2007.
18. Tony Judt, "From the House of the Dead: On Modern European Memory," *The New York Review of Books*, 6 October, 2005.
19. See, for example, Jeremy King, *Budweisers into Czechs and Germans: A Local History of Bohemian Politics, 1848–1948* (Princeton, 2002).
20. See "Die Komplizen, as well Judt and Hale (see note 8).
21. Turkey and Ireland were the other neutral countries that leaned heavily towards the Allied side. Over 30,000 Irish fought with the Allies, and Turkey entered the war on the Allied side in late February 1945, as well as earlier being a safe haven for Jews and conduit to Palestine for Jewish refugees.
22. Johan P, Olsen, "The Many Faces of Europeanization," *Journal of Common Market Studies*, 40, no. 5 (2002), 929.
23. Ibid., 941.
24. Philip Schlesinger and François Foret, "Political Roof and Sacred Canopy? Religion and the EU Constitution," *European Journal of Social Theory* 9, no. 1 (2006): 59–81.
25. Gerard Delanty, *Inventing Europe: Idea, Identity, Reality* (New York, 1995), 3.
26. See, for example, Hannes Hansen-Magnusson and Jenny Wustenberg, "Forging a European Memory: The Treaties of Rome as a Common Tradition in the Making?," Paper presented at the 18th International Conference of Europeanists, Barcelona, Spain, 20–22 June 2011.
27. See http://www.cliohworld.net/; accessed on 27 August 2011. There are also EU-funded professional networks such as Euro–Clio for history educators. See http://www.euroclio.eu/new/index.php; accessed on 27 August 2011.
28. Jürgen Habermas, *Europe: The Faltering Project* (Cambridge, 2009); see also Alan Milward, *The European Rescue of the Nation-State* (Berkeley, 1992).
29. Klaus Eder and Willfried Spohn, eds., *Collective Memory and European Identity: The Effects of Integration and Enlargement* (Aldershot, 2005), 218.
30. Judy Dempsey, "Kohl Makes Plea for European Unity," *The New York Times*, 17 May 2011. See also Berthold Kohler, "Die CDU und Europa: In Sorge um das Erbe," *Frankfurter Allgemeine Zeitung*, 25 August 2011 available at http://www.faz.net/artikel/C30100/die-cdu-und-europa-in-sorge-um-das-erbe-30491456.html; accessed 26 August 2011.
31. Benedict Anderson, *Imagined Communities: Reflections on the Origin and Spread of Nationalism* (New York, 1991).
32. See, for example, John A. Armstrong, *Nations before Nationalism* (Chapel Hill, 1982).
33. Norbert Elias, *The Civilizing Process* (New York, 1978); Michel Foucault, *Discipline and Punish: The Birth of the Modern Prison* (New York, 1977); Eugen Weber, *Peasants into Frenchmen: the Modernization of Rural France, 1870–1914* (Stanford, 1976).
34. Jürgen Habermas, *The Postnational Constellation: Political Essays* (Cambridge, 2001).
35. See Claire Sutherland, ed., "Special Issue: Cosmopolitanism and the Study of German Politics," *German Politics and Society* 29, no. 3 (2011).
36. Indeed, there is a well-established literature that always has defined Europe in contrast to other civilizations (Islamic, Chinese) precisely by its ethnic, linguistic and cultural diversity. See, for example, Jared Diamond, *Guns, Germs, and Steel: The Fates of Human Societies* (New York, 1997).

Notes on Contributors

●●●●●●●●●●●●●●●

Helle Bjerg, senior lecturer, PhD, works with teacher education and research at University College Capital, Copenhagen, Denmark. She teaches history and history didactics and does research within the field of school leadership and development, teacher education, poststructuralist educational studies, and history didactics. She has published on the issue of history didactics and memory culture on WWII and the Holocaust.

Christian Gudehus is managing director of the Center for Interdisciplinary Memory Research and responsible for the research cluster Transformation Research within the Norbert Elias Center for Transformation Design and Research at the University of Flensburg, Germany. His main fields of research are memory studies and reception studies (focusing on film, exhibitions, and memorials), as well as the social psychology of collective violence. Among other books, he edited *Remembrance and Memory: An Interdisciplinary Handbook* (in German) in collaboration with Ariane Eichenberg and Harald Welzer, and *Violence: An Interdisciplinary Handbook* (in German, 2013) with Michaela Christ.

Hans-Joachim Hahn is Emeritus Professor at Oxford Brookes University. He specializes in German literature and thought, mostly focusing on the nineteenth century, especially on the Romantic era and the German "Vormärz." He has recently published on Gottfried Keller, Hermann Hesse, and Gottfried Benn and is currently working on Walter Mehring and German Dadaism. Recent publications include: *The 1848/49 Revolutions in German-speaking Europe* (2001), and edited with Uwe Seja, *Gottfried Keller, Die Leute von Seldwyla. Kritische Studien–Critical Essays* (2007).

Madelon de Keizer (PhD, Leiden University, 1991) is senior researcher at the NIOD Institute for War, Holocaust, and Genocide Studies in Amsterdam. In the academic year 2005–2006, De Keizer spent a semester at Harvard University as an Erasmus Scholar. As a spin-off of the three public lectures that she held there, she wrote *De dochter van een gazan. Carry van*

Bruggen en de Nederlandse samenleving 1900–1930/ The Gazzen's Daughter, Carry van Bruggen and Dutch Society (2006). In recent years, she has specialized in memory and history, publishing a book on memory and World War II in the Netherlands after 1989, entitled *An Open Wound* (2011). In spring 2012 she published a biography of the journalist, resistance member, and Cold War politician Frans J. Goedhart (1904–1990).

Eric Langenbacher is visiting assistant professor and director of Honors and Special Programs in the Department of Government, Georgetown University where he received his PhD in 2002. He was awarded a Fulbright grant in 1999–2000 and was voted faculty member of the year by the graduating seniors of Georgetown's School of Foreign Service in 2009. Recent publications include with Yossi Shain *Power and the Past: Collective Memory and International Relations* (2010); with Jeffrey Anderson, *From the Bonn to the Berlin Republic: Germany at the Twentieth Anniversary of Unification* (2010); and *Between Left and Right: The 2009 Bundestag Elections and the Transformation of the German Party System* (2010).

Claudia Lenz is the research coordinator at the European Wergeland Centre on Education for Intercultural Understanding, Human Rights, and Democratic Citizenship in Oslo, Norway. She studied at the University of Hamburg, completing her PhD in 2002. Publications include *Haushaltspflicht und Widerstand: Erzählungen norwegischer Frauen über die deutsche Besatzung 1940–1945 im Lichte nationaler Vergangenheitskonstruktionen* (2003).

Anna di Lellio is a sociologist and policy analyst with interests ranging from American culture and politics, to security and nationalism in the Balkans. She has consulted with international organizations in Kosovo, including positions with OSCE and the United Nations. She currently lectures at The New School for Public Engagement and at New York University in New York City. Professor Di Lellio has published widely on affairs in the region, and is the author of *The Battle of Kosovo 1389. An Albanian Epic* (2009) and the editor of *The Case for Kosova. A Passage to Independence* (2006).

Henning Meyer completed his PhD in Contemporary History (2006) from Bordeaux 3, France, and Augsburg, Germany. The title of his thesis is "The Evolution of French 'Memory Culture' of World War II Based on Three Examples of 'Memory Places': Bordeaux, Caen, and Oradour-sur-Glane." Since July 2011, he has been a project manager at Datawords, Saint-Ouen, France. Previously, he was editorial and publishing manager at WAO, Heidelberg,

Germany (2008 to 2011); assistant to editor-in-chief of the magazine *Paris-Berlin,* Paris; and a language teacher (2007 and 2008). Since 2008, he has been a member of the Editorial Council of EuroJournal Pro-Management. He has published scholarly articles in areas related to French memory of World War II, resistance, liberation, and victimhood, as well as journalistic articles about French-German relations, European politics, and memory.

Bill Niven is professor of Contemporary German History at Nottingham Trent University in the UK. His publications include *Facing the Nazi Past: United Germany and the Legacy of the Third Reich* (2001); *The Buchenwald Child: Truth, Fiction, and Propaganda* (2007; German edition, 2009); and the edited volumes *Germans as Victims: Remembering the Past in Contemporary Germany* (2006); and, co-edited with Chloe Paver *Memorialization in Germany since 1945* (2010). He is currently writing a book on cultural representations of the flight and expulsion of Germans from central-eastern Europe.

Ljiljana Radonic teaches on European memory conflicts after 1989 at the Department of Political Science and coordinates the interdisciplinary doctoral program "Austrian Galicia and its Multicultural Heritage" at the University of Vienna, Austria. She studied political science, philosophy, and translation and wrote her doctoral thesis on "The War on Memory–Croatian Politics of the Past between Revisionism and European Standards" (2010) within the interdisciplinary doctoral program "Cultures of Difference: Transformation Processes in Central Europe" at the University of Vienna. Recent publications include "Der erste postsozialistische Prozess gegen einen Kriegsverbrecher aus dem Zweiten Weltkrieg–Kroatien als Beispiel vorbildlicher Aufarbeitung?" (*Österreichische Zeitschrift für Politikwissenschaft,* 2012) and "Standards of Evasion–Croatia and the 'Europeanization of Memory'" (*Eurozine,* 2012).

Mark Wagstaff studied social and political theory at Birkbeck College, University of London, achieving his master's with a thesis on Benthamite political society. He currently works in social policy in London and retains an aspiration to continue his studies in political science. Mark is also a novelist and short story writer, with publications in the U.K. and U.S.

Ruth Wittlinger is senior lecturer in the School of Government and International Affairs at the University of Durham, U.K. She has published on postunifcation Germany, European integration, British perceptions of Germany and the Germans, and politics and literature. Her latest monograph is

German National Identity in the Twenty-First Century: A Different Republic After All? (2010).

Mark A. Wolfgram is associate professor of Political Science at Oklahoma State University-Stillwater. His first book is *"Getting History Right": East and West German Collective Memories of the Holocaust and War* (2011). His work has also appeared in *Political Science Quarterly, Holocaust and Genocide Studies,* and the *European Journal of Communication* among others. He studies the process of collective memory formation from a comparative perspective and is currently working on a project focused on the postunification period in Eastern and Western Germany. He also is conducting similar research in the region of the former Yugoslavia.

Harald Wydra is a fellow of St Catharine's College at the University of Cambridge. He holds a PhD in Social and Political Sciences from the European University Institute in Florence. Before coming to Cambridge in 2003 he taught Political Science at the University of Regensburg. He held visiting fellowships at the *École des Hautes Etudes en Sciences Sociales* in Paris and the Australian National University in Canberra and was a Visiting Professor at the Université *Paris Ouest Nanterre La Défense.* He is a founding editor of the academic journal *International Political Anthropology* (http://www.politicalanthropology.org). His books include *Communism and the Emergence of Democracy* (2007) and *Democracy and Myth in Russia and Eastern Europe* (co-editor) (2008). He is currently completing a book manuscript entitled *Politics and the Sacred* and also editing a volume (together with Agnes Horvath and Bjørn Thomassen) on *Breaking Boundaries: Varieties of Liminality* (forthcoming). He has research interests in European Politics, comparative democratisation, political anthropology, and interpretive methods in the social sciences.

IBLIOGRAPHY

Adler, Nanci. "The Future of the Soviet Past Remains Unpredictable. The Resurrection of Stalinist Symbols amidst the Exhumation of Mass Graves," *Europe-Asia Studies,* 57, no. 8 (2005): 1093–1119.
Agulhon, Maurice. *De Gaulle, Histoire, Symbole, Mythe* (Paris, 2000).
Alexander, Jeffrey C. *The Meanings of Social Life: A Cultural Sociology* (Oxford, 2003).
Alexander, Jeffrey C., Ron Eyerman, Bernard Giesen, Neil J. Smelser, and Piotr Sztompka. *Cultural Trauma and Collective Identity* (Berkeley, 2001).
Art, David. *The Politics of the Nazi Past in Germany and Austria* (Cambridge, 2006).
Asad, Talal. "Muslims and European Identity: Can Europe Represent Islam?" in *The Idea of Europe. From Antiquity to the European Union,* ed., A. Pagden (New York, 2002).
Assmann, Aleida. *Der lange Schatten der Vergangenheit: Erinnerungskultur und Geschichtspolitik* (Munich, 2006).
Assmann, Aledia, and Ute Frevert. *Geschichtsvergessenheit, Geschichtsversessenheit. Vom Umgang mit deutschen Vergangenheiten nach 1945* (Stuttgart, 1999).
Assmann, Jan. "Collective Memory and Cultural Identity," *New German Critique* 65 (1995): 125–133
———. *Religion and Cultural Memory* (Stanford, 2000).
Banchoff, Thomas. "German Policy Toward the European Union: The Effects of Historical Memory," *German Politics* 6, no.1 (1997): 60–76.
Bal, Mieke, Jonathan Crewe, and Leo Spitzer, eds. *Acts of Memory: Cultural Recall in the Present* (Hanover, 1999).
Banac, Ivo. *The National Question in Yugoslavia. Origins, History, Politics* (Ithaca, 1984).
Bauman, Zygmunt. *Europe: An Unfinished Adventure* (Cambridge, 2004).
Becker, Wolfgang, and Norbert Schöll. *In jenen Tagen… Wie der deutsche Nachkriegsfilm die Vergangenheit bewältigte* (Opladen, 1995).
Bell, Duncan. *Memory, Trauma, and World Politics* (Basingstoke, 2006).
Bhabha, Homi. *The Location of Culture* (London, 1994).
Bilgrami, Akeel. "Occidentalism, the Very Idea: An Essay on Enlightenment and Enchantment," *Critical Inquiry* 3 (2006): 381–411.
Bingen, Dieter, Wlodzimierz Borodziej, and Stefan Troebst, eds. *Vertreibungen Europäisch Erinnern? Historische Erfahrungen–Vergangenheitspolitik–Zukunftskonzeptionen* (Wiesbaden, 2003).
Bizeul, Yves, "Die derzeitige Umgestaltung und Umdeutung der Französischen Kollektiven Geschichtssammlung," in Heiner Hastedt, Christian Thies and Nikolaus Werz, eds., *Politik der Erinnerung* (Rostock, 2000).

Bjerg, Helle, Erik Thorstensen, and Claudia Lenz, eds. *Historicizing the Uses of the Past. Scandinavian Perspectives on History Culture, Historical Consciousness, and Didactics of History Related to World War II* (Bielefeld, 2011).
Borsdorf, Ulrich, and Heinrich Theodor Grütter, eds. *Orte der Erinnerung: Denkmal, Gedenkstätte, Museum* (Frankfurt/Main, 1999).
Brower, Benjamin. "The Preserving Machine: the "New" Museum and Working through Trauma–the Musée Mémorial pour la Paix of Caen," *History and Memory* 11 (1999): 77–103.
Brubaker, Rogers, and Margit Feischmidt. "1848 in 1998: The Politics of Commemoration in Hungary, Romania, and Slovakia," *Comparative Studies in Society and History*, 44, no. 4 (2002): 700–744.
Buruma, Ian. *Murder in Amsterdam: The Death of Theo Van Gogh and the Limits of Tolerance* (London, 2006).
Buruma, Ian, and Avishai Margalit. *Occidentalism: the West in the Eyes of its Enemies* (New York, 2004).
Byford, Jovan, *Potiskivanje i poricanje antisemitizma. Sećanje na vladiku Nikolaja Velimirovića u savremenoj srpskoj pravoslavnoj kulturi* (Belgrade, 2005).
———. "When I say 'the Holocaust', I mean Jasenovac: Remembrance of the Holocaust in Contemporary Serbian Society," *East European Jewish Affairs* 37, no. 1 (2007): 51–74.
Carrier, Peter. *Holocaust Monuments and National Memory Cultures in France and Germany since 1989. The Origins and Political Function of the Véld'Hiv in Paris and the Holocaust Monument in Berlin* (New York, 2005).
Cherry, Robert, and Annamaria Orla-Bukowska, eds. *Rethinking Poles and Jews: Troubled Past, Brighter Future* (Lanham, 2007).
Clayer, Nathalie. *Aux Origines du Nationalisme Albanais. La Naissance d'une Nation Majoritairement Musulmane en Europe* (Paris, 2007).
Čolović, Ivan. *The Politics of Symbol in Serbia* (London, 2002).
Connerton, Paul. *How Societies Remember* (Cambridge, 1989).
Conze, Eckart, Norbert Frei, Peter Hayes, and Moshe Zimmermann. *Das Amt und die Vergangenheit: Deutsche Diplomaten im Dritten Reich und in der Bundesrepublik* (Munich, 2010).
Coudenhove-Kalergi, Richard. *Europe Must Unite,* trans. Sir Andrew McFadyean (Glarus, 1939).
———. *From War to Peace,* transl. by Constantine Fitgibbon (London, 1959).
———. *Kampf um Europa* (Zurich, 1949).
Davies, Douglas J. *A Short History of Death* (Oxford, 2005).
Dean, Martin, Constantin Goschler, and Philip Ther. *Robbery and Restitution: The Conflict over Jewish Property in Europe* (New York, 2007).
De Keizer, Madelon. "Kriegsverbrechen in den besetzten Niederlanden: Der Fall Putten," in *Kriegsverbrechen im 20. Jahrhundert,* eds., W. Wette and G. Überschär (Darmstadt, 2001).
———. *Razzia in Putten. Verbrechen der Wehrmacht in einem niederländischen Dorf* (Münster, 2001).

———. "The Skeleton in the Closet: The Memory of Putten, 1/2 October 1944," *History and Memory* 3 (1995): 68–97.
Delanty, Gerard. *Inventing Europe: Idea, Identity, Reality* (New York, 1995).
Desfor Edles, Laura. *Symbol and Ritual in the New Spain* (Cambridge, 1998).
Di Lellio, Anna. *The Battle of Kosovo 1389. An Albanian Epic* (London, 2009).
———. "The Missing Revolution in Serbia: 1989–2008," *International Journal of Politics, Culture and Society* 22, no 3 (2009): 373–384.
Di Lellio, Anna, and Stephanie Schwandner-Sievers. "The Legendary Commander: the Construction of an Albanian Master-Narrative in Post-War Kosovo," *Nations and Nationalism* 12, no. 3 (2006): 513–529.
Diner, Dan. *Gegenläufige Gedächtnisse. Über Geltung und Wirkung des Holocaust* (Göttingen, 2007).
———, ed. *Zivilisationsbruch. Denken nach Auschwitz* (Frankfurt/Main, 1988).
Douglas, Mary. *Natural Symbols: Explorations in Cosmology* (London, 1996).
Dragović-Soso, Jasna. *"Saviours of the Nation." Serbia's Intellectual Opposition and the Revival of Nationalism* (Montreal, 2003).
Duijzings, Ger. *Religion and the Politics of Identity in Kosovo* (London, 2000).
Edelman, Murray. *From Art to Politics: How Artistic Creations Shape Political Conceptions* (Chicago, 1995).
Eder, Klaus, and Willfried Spohn, eds. *Collective Memory and European Identity: The Effects of Integration and Enlargement* (Aldershot, 2005).
Elias, Norbert. *The Germans* (New York, 1996).
Eliot, Thomas Stearn. "The Unity of European Culture," in *Notes Towards the Definition of Culture* (London, 1962).
Elsie, Robert, and Janice Mathie-Heck. *Songs of the Frontier Warriors. Këngë Kreshnikësh* (Wauconda, 2004).
Emmert, Thomas. *Serbian Golgotha. Kosovo, 1389* (New York, 1990).
Enzensberger, Hans-Magnus. *Ach Europa! Wahrnemungen aus sieben Ländern. Mit einem Epilog Aus dem Jahre 2006* (Frankfurt/Main, 1987).
Farmer, Sarah. *Martyred Village. Commemorating the 1944 Massacre at Oradour-sur-Glane* (Berkeley, 1999).
Faulenbach, Bernd. "Von der nationalen zur universalen Erinnerungskultur? Zu den kollektiven Gedächtnissen in der globalisierten Welt," *Jahrbuch Arbeit, Bildung, Kultur,* 19/20 (2001/02): 225–236.
Feldmann, Jackie. "Marking the Boundaries of the Enclave: Defining the Israeli Collective through the Poland 'Experience," *Israel Studies* 7, no. 2 (2002): 84–114.
Fernández, Paloma Aguilar. *Memory and Amnesia: The Role of the Spanish Civil War in the Transition to Democracy* (Oxford, 2002).
Figes, Orlando. *The Whisperers: Private Life in Stalin's Russia* (London, 2007).
Fivush, Robyn. "Remembering and Reminiscing: How Individual Lives Are Constructed in Family Narratives," *Memory Studies* 1, no. 1 (2008): 51–52.
Fleming, Michael. *Communism, Nationalism and Ethnicity in Poland, 1944–1950* (London, 2009).
Fouché, Jean-Jacques. "Le Centre de la Mémoire d'Oradour," *Vingtième Siècle. Revue d'histoire* 73 (2002): 125–137.

———. *Oradour* (Paris, 2001).
———. *Oradour: La Politique et la Justice* (Saint-Paul, 2004).
François, Etienne, and Hagen Schulze, eds. *Deutsche Erinnerungsorte* (Munich, 2001).
Franzinelli, Mimmo. *Delatori: Spie e Confidenteanonimi: L'armasegretadel Regime Fascista* (Milan, 2001).
Frevert, Ute. "Geschichtsvergessenheit und Geschichtsversessenheit revisited. Der jüngste Erinnerungsboom in der Kritik," *Aus Politik und Zeitgeschichte,* B 40–41 (2003) : 6–13.
Friedrich Naumann Foundation. *Gemeinsame Vergangenheit und die Gegenwart. Polnisch-russisch-deutscher Trialog der Historiker und Journalisten* (Moscow, 2008).
Frykman, Jonas. "Belonging in Europe. Modern Identities In Minds and Places," in *Europe: Cultural Construction and Reality,* eds., P. Niedermüller and B. Stoklund (Copenhagen, 2001).
Gadamer, Hans-Georg. *Wahrheit und Methode. Grundzüge einer philosophischen Hermeneutik,* (Tübingen, 1990).
Gangloff, Sylvie. "The Impact of Ottoman Legacy on Turkish Policy in the Balkans (1991–1999)" in *La Perception de l'Héritage Ottoman dans les Balkans. The Perception of the Ottoman Legacy in the Balkans,* ed., S. Gangloff (Paris, 2005).
Gellately, Robert. *Backing Hitler: Consent and Coercion in Nazi Germany* (Oxford, 2001).
Gilbert, Mark. "European Federalism: Past Resilience, Present Problems" in *Democracy and Federalism in the European Union and the United States,* ed., S. Fabbrini (London, 2005).
Gillis, John R., ed. *Commemorations: The Politics of National Identity* (Princeton, 1994).
Golsan, Richard J. *Vichy's Afterlife: History and Counterhistory in Postwar France* (Lincoln, 2000).
Gross, Jan T. *Fear: Anti-Semitism in Poland after Auschwitz* (New York, 2006).
Gudehus, Christian. "Germany's Meta-discursive Memory Culture: Skeptical Narratives and Minotaurs," *German Politics and Society* 6, no. 4 (2008): 99–112.
Habermas, Jürgen. "Europas zweite Chance," *Vergangenheit als Zukunft* (Zürich, 1990).
———. "Europa: Vision und Votum," *Blätter für deutsche und internationale Politik* 52, no. 5 (2007): 517–520.
———. *Europe: The Faltering Project* (Cambridge, 2009).
———. *The Postnational Constellation: Political Essays* (Cambridge, 2001).
Halbwachs, Maurice. *The Collective Memory,* trans. Francis J. Ditter Jr. and Vida Yazdi Ditter (New York, 1980).
Hale, Christopher. *Hitler's Foreign Executioners: Europe's Dirty Secret* (New York, 2009).
Harrison, Hope, ed. "Special Issue: The Berlin Wall after Fifty Years; 1961–2011," *German Politics and Society,* 29, no. 2 (2011).
Heer, Hannes. *Vernichtungskrieg: Verbrechen der Wehrmacht 1941–1944* (Hamburg, 1995).
Heinlein, Michael. *Die Erfindung der Erinnerung. Deutsche Kriegskindheiten im Gedächtnis der Gegenwart* (Bielefeld, 2010).

Herf, Jeffrey. *Divided Memory: The Nazi Past in the two Germanies* (Cambridge, 1999).
Hesse, Hermann. "Die Brüder Karamasow oder der Untergang Europas," in *Sämtliche Werke*, ed., V. Michels, vol. 18 (Frankfurt/Main, 2002).
Hilberg, Raul. *Perpetrators, Victims, Bystanders: The Jewish Catastrophe, 1933-1945* (New York, 1992).
Hockenos, Paul. *Homeland Calling. Exile Patriotism and the Balkan Wars* (New York, 2003).
Hoffman, Eva. *After such Knowledge: Memory, History, and the Legacy of the Holocaust* (New York: 2004).
Höpken, Wolfgang. "Vergangenheitspolitik im sozialistischen Vielvölkerstaat 1944–1991" in *Umkämpfte Vergangenheit. Geschichtsbilder, Erinnerung und Vergangenheitspolitik im internationalen Vergleich*, eds., P. Bock and E. Wolfrum (Göttingen, 1999).
Hübinette, Tobias. *Nationalsocialismen i Sverige. Medlemmar och sympatisörer 1931-45* (Stockholm, 2002).
Hutton, Patrick H. *History as an Art of Memory* (Hanover, 1993).
Iseni, Bashkim, *La Question Nationale en Europe du Sud-Est. Genèse, Èmergence et Développement de l'Identité Nationale Albanaise au Kosovo et en Macedoine* (Lausanne, 2008).
Jeffery, Charlie, and William E. Paterson. "Germany and European Integration: The Shifting of Tectonic Plates," *West European Politics* 26, no. 4 (2003): 59-75.
Jeismann, Michael. *Auf Wiedersehen Gestern. Die deutsche Vergangenheit und die Politik von morgen* (Munich, 2001).
Jensen, Olaf. *Geschichte machen. Strukturmerkmale des Intergenerationellen Sprechens über die NS-Vergangenheit in Deutschen Familien* (Tübingen, 2004).
Johnson, Eric. *Nazi Terror: Gestapo, Jews and Ordinary Germans* (London, 2000).
Joly, Marie-Hélène. "Les musées de la Résistance" in *Résistants et Résistance*, ed., J.-Y. Boursier (Paris, 1997).
Joly, Marie-Hélène, and Laurent Gervereau. *Musées et Collections d'Histoire en France, Guide* (Paris, 1996).
Judt, Tony. *Postwar. A History of Europe Since 1945* (London, 2005).
Kadare, Ismail. *Identiteti Europian i Shqiptarëve* (Tiranë, 2006).
Kaminsky, Anne. *Orte des Erinnerns. Gedenkzeichen, Gedenkstätten und Museen zur Diktatur in SBZ und DDR* (Leipzig, 2004).
Kansteiner, Wulf. "Finding Meaning in Memory: A Methodological Critique of Collective Memory Studies," *History and Theory* 41 (2002): 179-197.
———. *In Pursuit of German Memory: History, Television, and Politics After Auschwitz* (Athens, 2006).
Kertzer, David I. *Ritual, Politics, and Power* (New Haven, 1988).
Knabe, Hubertus. *Tag der Befreiung? Das Kriegsende in Deutschland* (Berlin, 2005).
Knelangen, Wilhelm. "Die neue deutsche Europapolitik für eine andere EU?" *Aus Politik und Zeitgeschichte*. Beilage zur Wochenzeitung *Das Parlament*, 38-39 (2005): 24-30.
König, Helmut, Julia Schmidt and Manfred Sicking, eds. *Europas Gedächtnis. Das neue Europa zwischen nationalen Erinnerungen und gemeinsamer Identität* (Bielefeld, 2008).

Körber, Andreas, Waltraud Schreiber, and Alexander Schöner, eds. *Kompetenzen Historischen Denkens. Ein Strukturmodellals Beitragzur Kompetenzorientierung in der Geschichtsdidaktik* (Neuried, 2007).
Koselleck, Reinhart "Formen und Traditionen des negativen Gedächtnisses" in *Verbrechenerinnern. Die Auseinandersetzung mit Holocaust und Völkermord*, eds., V. Knigge and N. Frei, (Munich, 2002).
Kossert, Andreas. *Kalte Heimat: Die Geschichte der Deutschen Vertriebenen nach 1945* (Munich, 2008).
Koštunica, Vojislav. *Odbrana Kosova* (Belgrade, 2008).
Laborie, Pierre. *Les Français des Années Troubles. De la Guerre d'Espagne à la Libération* (Paris, 2001).
Lachaise, Bernard, Gilles Le Béguec, and Jean-François Sirinelli, eds. *Jacques Chaban-Delmas en Politique: Actes du Colloque organisé à Bordeaux les 18, 19 et 20 Mai 2006* (Paris, 2007).
Lagrou, Pieter. "Frankreich" in Volkhard Knigge and Norbert Frei, eds. *Verbrechen Erinnern. Die Auseinandersetzung mit Holocaust und Völkermord* (Munich, 2002).
Lagrou, Pieter. *Mémoires patriotiques et Occupation nazie. Résistants, Requis et Déportés en Europe occidentale 1945–1965* (Brussels, 2003).
———. *The Nationalization of Victimhood: Selective Violence and National Grief in Western Europe, 1940–1960* (Cambridge, 2003).
———. "Victims of Genocide and National Memory: Belgium, France and the Netherlands 1945–1965," *Past and Present,* 154 (1997): 185–154.
Langenbacher, Eric. "Still the Unmasterable Past? The Impact of History and Memory in the Federal Republic of Germany," *German Politics* 19, no. 1 (2010): 24–40.
———. "The Mastered Past? Collective Memory Trends in Germany since Unification," *German Politics and Society* 28, no. 1 (2010): 42–68.
———. "Twenty-first Century Memory Regimes in Germany and Poland: An Analysis of Elite Discourses and Public Opinion," *German Politics and Society* 26, no. 4 (2008): 50–81.
Langenbacher, Eric, and Yossi Shain, eds. *Power and the Past: Collective Memory and International Relations* (Washington, 2010).
Lebow, Richard Ned. *A Cultural Theory of International Relations* (Cambridge, 2008).
Lebow, Richard Ned, Wulf Kansteiner, and Claudio Fogu, eds. *The Politics of Memory in Postwar Europe* (Durham, 2006).
Leggewie, Claus. "Seven Circles of European Memory," *Eurozine,* 20 December 2010.
Leggewie, Claus, and Erik Meyer. *Ein Ort, an den man gerne geht* (Munich, 2005).
Lenz, Claudia. *Haushaltspflicht und Widerstand. Erzählungen norwegischer Frauen über die deutsche Besatzung 1940–45 im Lichte nationaler Vergangenheitskonstruktionen* (Tübingen, 2003).
Lenz, Claudia, Jens Schmidt, and Oliver Von Wrochem, eds. *Erinnerungskulturen im Dialog. Europäische Perspektiven auf die NS-Vergangenheit* (Hamburg, 2002).
Levy, Daniel, and Natan Sznaider. *The Holocaust and Memory in the Global Age* (Philadelphia, 2005).

Lind, Jennifer J. *Sorry States: Apologies in International Affairs* (Ithaca, 2009).
Loraux, Nicole. *The Divided City: Forgetting in the Memory of Athens* (New York, 2002).
Lowenthal, David. *The Past is a Foreign Country* (Cambridge, 1985).
Luthar, Oto. "Slovenia: History between Myths and Reality," *Slovene Studies* 27, no. 1–2 (2005): 109–119.
Luthar Oto, and Irena Šumi. "Living in Metaphor: Jews and Anti-Semitism in Slovenia," in *Jews and Anti-Semitism in the Balkans* (Jerusalem, 2004).
MacDonald, David B. *Balkan Holocausts? Serbian and Croatian Victim-centred Propaganda and the War in Yugoslavia* (Manchester, 2002).
Mann, Heinrich. *Essays,* ed., A. Kantorowicz, vol. 2 (Berlin, 1956).
Mann, Klaus. *Auf der Suche nach einem Weg* (Berlin, 1931).
———. "Die Heimsuchung des europäischen Geistes" in Klaus Mann, *Auf verlorenem Posten, Aufsätze, Reden, Kritiken 1942–1949* (Reinbek, 1994).
Mann, Thomas. "Achtung Europa!" in *"Achtung Europa!," Essays 1933–1938,* eds., H. Kurzke and S. Stachorski (Frankfurt/Main, 1995).
Marchart, Oliver, Vrääth Öhner, and Heidemarie Uhl,. "Holocaust revisited–Lesarten eines Medienereignisses Zwischen Globaler Erinnerungskultur und nationaler Vergangenheitsbewältigung," *Tel Aviver Jahrbuch für deutsche Geschichte,* XXXI (2003): 307–334.
Merelman, Richard M. *Partial Visions: Culture and Politics in Britain, Canada, and the United States* (Madison, 1991).
Meyer, Henning. "Die französische Vergangenheitsbewältigung des Zweiten Weltkriegs durch die Rechtsprechung am Beispiel des 'Oradourprozesses'" in *Erinnern und Vergessen. Remembering and Forgetting,* eds., O. Brupbacher, N. Grotkamp, et al. (Munich, 2007).
———. "Jacques Chaban-Delmas et le Centre National Jean Moulin de Bordeaux," *Revue Historique de Bordeaux et du Département de la Gironde* 7-8 (2005): 195–211.
Michel, Johann. *Gouverner les Mémoires. Les Politiques Mémorielles en France* (Paris, 2010).
Milentijević, Radmila. "Anti-Semitism and the Treatment of the Holocaust in Postcommunist Yugoslavia" in *Anti-Semitism and the Treatment of the Holocaust in Postcommunist Eastern Europe,* ed., R. L. Braham (New York, 1994).
Milošević, Slobodan. *Od Gazimestan do Sevenignena* (Belgrade, 2001).
Milward, Alan. *The European Rescue of the Nation-State* (Berkeley, 1992).
Müller, Jan-Werner, ed. *Memory and Power in Post-War Europe: Studies in the Presence of the Past* (Cambridge, 2002).
Moisel, Claudia. *Frankreich und die Deutschen Kriegsverbrecher. Politik und Praxis der Strafverfolgung nach dem Zweiten Weltkrieg* (Göttingen, 2004).
Musil, Robert. *Der Mann ohne Eigenschaften,* ed., Adolf Frisé (Hamburg, 1952).
Neveux, Christelle. *Le Mur de l'Atlantique: Vers une Valorisation Patrimoniale?* (Paris, 2003).
Niethammer, Lutz. *Lebenserfahrung und Kollektives Gedächtnis. Die Praxis der "Oral History"* (Frankfurt/Main, 1980).
Niven, Bill, ed. *Germans as Victims: Remembering the Past in Contemporary Germany* (Basingstoke, 2006).

———, ed. "Special Issue on Representations of the Past in European Memorials," *Forum for Modern Language Studies* 44, no. 2 (2008): 185–198.
Nora, Pierre, ed. *Les Lieux de Mémoire* 7 vols. (Paris, 1984–1992).
Olick, Jeffrey K. *In the House of the Hangman: the Agonies of German Defeat 1943–1949* (Chicago, 2005).
Olick, Jeffrey. *States of Memory: Continuities, Conflicts, and Transformations in National Retrospection* (Durham, 2003).
———. *The Politics of Regret* (London, 2007).
Olsen, Johan P. "The Many Faces of Europeanization," *Journal of Common Market Studies*, 40, no. 5 (2002): 921–952.
Ortega y Gasset, José. *The Revolt of the Masses* (New York, 1993).
Paletschek, Sylvia, and Sylvia Schraut, eds. *The Gender of Memory Cultures of Remembrance in Nineteenth- and Twentieth-Century Europe* (New York, 2008).
Palmberger, Monika. "Distancing Personal Experiences from the Collective: Discursive Tactics among Youth in Post-War Mostar," *L'Europe en Formation*, 357 (2010): 107–124.
Paris, Erna. *Long Shadows: Truth, Lies, and History* (New York, 2002).
Paterson, William E. "Does Germany Still Have a European Vocation?" *German Politics* 19, no. 1 (2010): 41–52.
Penaud, Guy. *Chroniques Secrètes de la Résistance dans le Sud-Ouest* (Bordeaux, 1993).
Périssère, Michèle. "Une histoire de la paix" in *Quel Avenir pour les Musées d'Histoire?*, ed., L. Gervereau (Paris, 1999).
Perović, Latinka. "Le Dos Tourné à la Modernisation," in *Radiographie d'un Nationalisme. Les Racines Serbes du Conflit Yugoslave*, ed. N. Popov (Paris, 1998).
Petrusewicz, Marta. "A Nazione Mancata: The Construction of the Mezzogiorno after 1848" in *Myth and Memory in the Construction of Community*, ed., B. Strath (Zürich, 2000).
Polonsky, Antony, and Joanna B. Michlic, eds. *The Neighbors Respond: The Controversy over the Jedwabne Massacre in Poland* (Princeton, 2004).
Prcela John I., and Drazen Živić. *Hrvatski Holokaust. Dokumenti i svjedočanstva o poratnim pokoljima u Jugoslaviji* (Zagreb, 2001).
Pusić, Vesna. *Demokracije i Diktature. Politička tranzicija u Hrvatskoj i jugoistočnoj Europi* (Zagreb, 1998).
Quétel, Claude. "Der Aufbau eines Museums für den Frieden in Caen" in *Die Zukunft der Vergangenheit: Wie soll die Geschichte des Nationalsozialismus in Museen und Gedenkstättenim 21. Jahrhunderts vermittelt werden?*, ed., Museen der Stadt Nürnberg (Nuremberg, 2000): 127–136.
Reestman, Jan-Herman. "The Franco-German Constitutional Divide: Reflections on National and Constitutional Identity," *European Constitutional Law Review*, 5 (2009): 374–390.
Rosenzweigand, Roy, and David Thelen. *The Presence of the Past: Popular Uses of History in American Life* (New York, 1998).
Ross, Marc Howard. *Cultural Contestation in Ethnic Conflict* (Cambridge, 2007).
Rousso, Henry. *The Vichy Syndrome: History and Memory in France Since 1944* (Cambridge, 1991).

———. *Vichy: L'événement, la Mémoire, l'Histoire* (Paris, 2001).
Sabrow, Martin, ed. *Wohin treibt die DDR-Erinnerung? Dokumentation einer Debatte* (Göttingen, 2007).
Sack, Robert David. *Human Territoriality: its Theory and History* (Cambridge, 1986).
Schatz, Edward, ed. *Political Ethnography: What Immersion Contributes to the Study of Power* (Chicago, 2009).
Scherbakova, Irina. "Landkarte der Erinnerung. Jugendliche berichten über den Krieg," *Osteuropa*, nos. 4-6, (2005): 419–433.
Sherman, Daniel J. *The Construction of Memory in Interwar France* (Chicago, 1999).
Schmidt, Thomas, Friedrich Dieckman, and Jerzy Kanal. *Nationaler Totenkult. Die Neue Wache. Eine Streitschrift zur Zentralen Deutschen Gedenkstätte* (Berlin, 1999).
Schmitz, Helmut, ed. *A Nation of Victims? Representations of German Wartime Suffering from 1945 to the Present* (Amsterdam, 2007).
Schudson, Michael. *Watergate in American Memory: How We Remember, Forget, and Reconstruct the Past* (New York, 1992).
Schweiger, Christian. *Britain, German and the European Union* (Basingstoke, 2007).
Sewell, William H. *Logics of History* (Chicago, 2005).
Smith, Dennis, and Sue Wright, eds. *Whose Europe? The Turn towards Democracy* (Oxford, 1999).
Snyder, Timothy. *Bloodlands: Europe between Hitler and Stalin* (New York, 2010).
Strath, Bo, ed. *Myth and Memory in the Construction of Community* (Zürich, 2000).
Stuhlweißenburger, Bettina. "Das Centre de la mémoire d'Oradour" in *Einsichten und Perspektiven* 3, ed., Bayerische Landeszentrale für Politische Bildungsarbeit (Munich, 2005).
Sulstarova, Enis. *Arratisjenga Lindja. Orientalizmi Shqiptarnga Naimite Kadareja* (Chapel Hill, 2006).
Sundhaussen, Holm. "Jugoslawien und seine Nachfolgestaaten. Konstruktion, Dekonstruktion und Neukonstruktion von 'Erinnerungen' und Mythen" *Mythen der Nationen. 1945–Arena der Erinnerung*, ed., M. Flacke (Mainz, 2004).
Sutherland, Claire, ed. "Special Issue: Cosmopolitanism and the Study of German Politics," *German Politics and Society* 29, no. 3 (2011).
Tambarin, Marcel. "Vom Dritten Reich zur 'Berliner Republik:' Deutschlands Suche nach der Normalität" in *Alte und neue Identitätsbilder im heutigen Deutschland*, eds., A. Saint Sauveur-Henn and M. Muylaert, (Leipzig, 1999).
Troebst, Stefan. "Jalta versus Stalingrad, GULag versus Holocaust. Konfligierende Erinnerungskulturen im größeren Europa," *Transformationen derErinnerungskulturen in Europa nach 1989*, eds., B. Faulenbach and F. Jelich (Essen, 2006).
Überschär, Gerd R. *Orte des Grauens. Verbrechen im Zweiten Weltkrieg* (Darmstadt, 2003).
Urban, Thomas, and Ariane Afsari, eds. *Ein Zentrum gegen Vertreibung: nationales Gedenken oder europäische Erinnerung?* (Potsdam, 2004).
Urselmann, Karin. *Die Bedeutung des Barbie-Prozesses für die Französische Vergangenheitsbewältigung* (Frankfurt/Main, 2000).
Verdery, Katherine. *The Political Lives of Dead Bodies: Reburial and Postsocialist Change* (New York, 1999).

Vonau, Jean-Laurent. *Le Procès de Bordeaux. Les Malgré-Nous et le Drame d'Oradour* (Strasbourg, 2003).
Von Hofmannsthal, Hugo. "Blick auf den geistigen Zustand Europas," *Gesammelte Werke in Einzelausgaben,* ed., H. Steiner, *Prosa IV* (Frankfurt/Main, 1955).
Wahnlich, Sophie, ed. *Fictions d'Europe : la Guerre au Musée: Allemagne, France, Grande-Bretagne* (Paris, 2003).
Walter, Klaus Peter. "Schwierige Vergangenheitsbewältigung. Die Okkupation Frankreichs (1940–1944) im Spiegel von Kinofilm und Roman," in *Frankreich-Jahrbuch* (2000), *Politik, Wirtschaft, Gesellschaft, Geschichte, Kultur* (Opladen, 2000).
Warleigh, Alex. *Democracy and the European Union: Theory, Practice and Reform* (London, 2003).
Welzer, Harald, ed. *Der Krieg der Erinnerung. Holocaust, Kollaboration und Widerstand im europäischen Gedächtnis* (Frankfurt/Main, 2007).
Welzer, Harald, Sabine Moller, and Karoline Tschuggnall. *Familiengedächtnis. Über die Weitergaber der Deutschen Vergangenheit im Gespräch Zwischen den Generationen* (Frankfurt/Main, 2002).
———. *Opa war kein Nazi: Nationalsozialismus und Holocaust im Familiengedächtnis* (Frankfurt/Main, 2002).
Wertsch, James. *Voices of Collective Remembering* (Cambridge, 2002).
West, Rebecca. *Black Lamb and Grey Falcon. A Journey through Yugoslavia* (London, 1994).
Wieviorka, Olivier. *La Mémoire Désunie. Le Souvenir Politique des Années Sombres* (Paris, 2010).
Wilds, Karl. "Identity Creation and the Culture of Contrition: Recasting 'Normality' in the Berlin Republic," *German Politics* 9, no.1 (2000): 83–102.
Wingfield, Nancy M., ed. *Creating the Other: Ethnic Conflict and Nationalism in Habsburg Central Europe* (New York, 2003).
Williams, Paul. "The Afterlife of Communist Statuary: Hungary's Szoborpark and Lithuania's Schön, Bosse, *Hitlers svenska soldater* (Stockholm, 2005).
Winter, Jay. *Sites of Memory, Sites of Mourning: The Great War in European Cultural History,* New Edition (Cambridge, 1998).
Winter, Jay, and Emmanuel Sivan, eds. *War and Rememberance in the Twentieth Century* (Cambridge, 1999).
Wittlinger, Ruth. *German National Identity in the Twenty-First Century: A New Republic After All?* (Basingstoke, 2010).
———. "The Merkel Government's Politics of the Past," *German Politics and Society* 26, no. 4 (2008): 9–27.
Wolfgram, Mark A. "The Process of Collective Memory Research: Methodological Solutions for Research Challenges," *German Politics and Society* 25, no. 1 (2007): 102–113.
———. *"Getting History Right": East and West German Collective Memories of the Holocaust and War* (Lewisburg, 2011).
Wolfrum, Edgar. *Geschichtspolitik in der Bundesrepublik Deutschland: der Weg zur bundesrepublikanischen Erinnerung 1948–1990* (Darmstadt, 1999).

Wöll, Andreas, and Harald Wydra, eds. *Democracy and Myth in Russia and Eastern Europe* (London, 2008).
Wood, Nancy. *Vectors of Memory: Legacies of Trauma in Postwar Europe* (Oxford, 1999).
Wróbel, Piotr. "Double Memory: Poles and Jews after the Holocaust," *East European Politics and Societies* 11, no. 3 (1997): 560–574.
Wulf, Mieke, and Pertti Grönholm. "Generating Meaning Across Generations: The Role of Historians in the Codification of History in Soviet and Post-Soviet Estonia," *Journal of Baltic Studies* 41, no. 3 (2010): 351–382.
Wydra, Harald. *Communism and the Emergence of Democracy* (Cambridge, 2007).
Zerubavel, Eviatar. *Time Maps: Collective Memory and the Social Shape of the Past* (Chicago, 2003).

Index

A

Adenauer, Konrad, 33, 94, 211
Albania, 10, 149–63
Amersfoort, 123
Anaxagoras, 20
Anderson, Benedict, 2, 217–8
Antall, József, 29
Antifascism, *See* Fascism
Antonescu, Ion, 184
Archer, Margaret, 62–3, 66
Argentina, 4, 170, 173
Athenian democracy, 20–21
Asad, Talal, 161
Assmann, Jan, 20, 89, 99
Association of Concentration Camp Memorial Sites in the Federal Republic (of Germany), 196
Asturias Revolution, 33
Auschwitz, 77–8, 125, 132–4, 137, 167, 199, 210–1, 214
Austria, 7, 33, 71, 73, 78–80, 83, 82, 94–5, 115, 161, 169, 173, 194, 210, 212

B

Babi Yar, 210
Barroso, José Manuel, 2
Bauman, Zygmunt, 103–4, 108, 110, 112, 115–6
Beatrix, Queen, 130
Belarus/White Russia, 3, 214–5
Belgium, 124–5, 137, 212
Belzec, 78
Beneš, Edvard, 95
Ben-Gaviel, M.Y., 64
Ben-Gurion, David, 33
Bentham, Jeremy, 115
Berlin Declaration, 202
Bleiburg, and memory of, 169, 170–8
Bloch, Marc, 30–1
Blushi, Ben, 157
Bohley, Bärbel, 34
Böll, Heinrich, 8, 96–8
Bosnia (Herzegovina), 82, 98, 154, 157–9, 169, 174, 176
Bryld, Claus, 43, 87
Bourbon regime, 21
Briand, Aristide, 8, 94–5
Buchenwald, 125
Budak, Mile, 169, 173
Bush, George, 3, 201
Buton, Philippe, 137, 141

C

Caen, Mémorial pour la Paix, 9–10, 137, 139–43
Carillo, Santiago, 33
Çelebi, Evliya, 158, 164
Centre against Expulsions, 26, 189, 191, 201
Çetin, Hikmet, 157
Četniks (Serbian paramilitary), 167, 170
Chaban-Delmas, Jacques, 138–9, 143
Chamberlain, Neville, 18
Chelmno, 78
Chile, 4
China, 2, 4, 116, 201
Chirac, Jacques, 141–2
Churchill, Winston, 8, 96
Coetzee, J.M., 31
Cohen, Abner, 56–7, 59, 61, 66
Cold War, 3–5, 8–9, 63, 65, 96, 124–8, 180, 185, 195–6, 214
Colombia, 3
Columbus, Christopher, 84
Communism, 1, 11, 14, 24, 29, 33–5, 82, 93, 96–7, 110, 124–6, 128, 153, 160, 167–8, 172–3, 177, 180–92, 196–206, 209, 211, 214, 216
Connerton, Paul, 15, 20–21
Coudenhove-Kalergi, Count Richard, 8, 94–6
Croatia, 10–11, 26, 28, 40, 71, 81–2, 166–77, 184, 209, 214
Croce, Benedetto, 96
Cyprus, 3
Czechoslovakia/Czech Republic, 2–3, 9, 11, 29, 65, 95, 121–2, 128, 130–2, 181, 183, 188–9, 209, 214

D

Dačić, Ivica, 154
Dalai Lama, 141
Damasio, Antonio, 57, 59
Davies, Douglas J., 59
Declaration of Independence, 20
Delanty, Gerard, 216
Denmark, 6, 40–3, 46, 50–52, 71, 81–2, 161, 215
Dilthey, William, 57–8
Donja Gradina, *See* Jasenovac
Dostoevsky, Fyodor, 89, 93
Douglas, Mary, 59
Drakulic, Slavenka, 28
Durkheim, Emile, 88

E

Eagleburger, Lawrence, 157
Edelman, Murray, 56–7, 66
Eder, Klaus, 217
1848 Revolution, 21, 27, 95
Efendi, Vasa, 160
Elias, Norbert, 22, 32, 38, 218
Enzensberger, Hans-Magnus, 7–8, 97–8
Erdoğan, Recep Tayyip, 157
Eriksen, Anne, 43, 50
Estonia, 3, 26, 181–4, 209
European Central Bank, 218
European Charter of Human Rights, 2
European Market, Single, 112–3
European Union, 1–2, 4, 8, 14, 28, 67, 70, 97, 101–3, 111–8, 122, 129, 131–2, 134, 150–1, 154, 156, 158, 160–3, 174, 182, 184, 196, 199–206, 215–7
Eurozone, 8, 103, 112, 202
Évian Conference, 211

F

Fascism/Antifascism, 8, 10, 23–4, 26, 82, 90–1, 93, 96, 102–3, 100, 110, 112, 115–18, 126, 167–77, 180–7, 191
Field of the Blackbirds, and memory of, 10, 149–63
Finland, 161, 186, 214
Fischer, Joschka, 200, 203–4, 206
Fogu, Claudio, 83
Fortuyn, Pim, 131
Foucault, Michel, 68, 218
Foundation for Working-through the GDR Dictatorship, 188
France, 4, 9, 14, 21, 27, 32–5, 83, 91–5, 102, 108, 114–5, 121, 122–30, 130–1, 135–45, 162, 184–7, 191, 197, 201–2, 210, 212, 214
Francetic, Jure, 170, 173

Franco, Francisco, 3, 22, 24, 33, 169
François, Etienne, 84, 178
Frank, Anne, 210
Frankfurt School, 91
Franzinelli, Mimmo, 186
Freikorps (Germany), 33
French Revolution, 21, 91–92, 94, 102, 108, 115
Frugier, Raymond, 142–3
Frykman, Jonas, 122, 132–3

G

Gadamer, Hans-Georg, 18, 88
Garton Ash, Timothy, 25, 198, 202
Gasperi, Alcide de, 33
Gaulle, Charles de, 137–9, 141
Gauweiler, Peter, 203
Gazimestan, *See* Memorials
Georgia, 216
Germany, 3–8, 11–12, 15–18, 22–26, 31, 33–35, 40, 43–4, 46, 49–54, 56, 63–7, 70–85, 88–99, 110, 115–6, 121–34, 139–44, 162, 168, 175, 181–91, 193–4, 196–206, 209–19
Gide, André, 93
Gilbert, Mark, 111
Girault, Jean-Marie, 139–40, 143
Goethe, Johann Wolfgang von, 89
Gogh, Theo van, 131, 161
Goldhagen, Daniel, 186
Grass, Günter, 8, 96–8
Greece, 3, 8, 57, 92, 112, 124, 214, 217–8
Griffin, Roger, 109–10
Gross, Jan T., 79, 210
Groys, Boris, 184
Gysi, Gregor, 203
Guatemala, 4

H

Habermas, Jürgen, 2, 101, 219
Haffner, Sebastian, 17
Haider, Jörg, 210
Halbwachs, Maurice, 4, 19, 89
Harbsmeier, Michael, 129
Havel, Vaclav, 30, 130
Hebrang, Andrija, 174
Herling-Grudzinski, Gustaw, 34
Herriot, Edouard, 95
Hesse, Hermann, 8, 89, 92
Heydrich, Reinhard, 123
Hirsch, Marianne, 32
Historians' Dispute (West Germany), 199
Hitler, Adolf, 18, 23, 90, 95, 211
Hobsbawm, Eric, 107, 109

Hoffman, Eva, 31
Hoffmann, Kurt, *Karpfengasse,* 64-5
Hofmannsthal, Hugo von, 8, 89
Hohmann, Martin, 211
Holland, 9, 40, 71, 81, 120-34, 161, 187, 201, 209, 212
Holocaust, 3, 5, 11-12, 14, 16, 22, 25-6, 29, 31, 40, 52-3, 63, 65, 82, 85, 136, 140-1, 148, 166-72, 175-77, 180-7, 191, 196, 198, 200, 209-13, 218
Holocaust (TV series), 65-66
Holocaust Memorial (Berlin), *See* Memorials
Holocaust Task Force, 181-2
Hrebeljanovic, Lazar, 10, 149, 151-2, 155, 158
Hübinette, Tobias, 186
Hugo, Victor, 94, 138
Hungarian Revolution (1956), 27-8, 34, 180
Hungary, 3, 28-9, 33-4, 167, 177, 180-1, 183, 189, 194, 212-4

I

Ignatieff, Michael, 131
India, 2, 33, 98
Ireland, 8, 96, 221
Iron Curtain, 4, 28-9, 210
Israel, 33-4, 78, 200, 216
Italy, 6, 21-4, 32-4, 83, 110, 114-5, 124, 134, 161-2, 165, 186, 194, 209, 212, 215, 217

J

Jacobinism, 108-10, 114, 116, 118
Jadovno, and memory of, 176
Japan, 4, 16, 94, 116
Jasenovac, and memory of, 169-78
Jashari, Adem, 156
Jedwabne, 25, 210
Jefferson, Thomas, 58
Jews, 25, 26, 29-35, 64-5, 70, 76, 82, 121, 141, 162, 170, 174-8, 181-6, 192, 200, 210-3
Jinnah, Huhammad Ali, 33
Josipović, Ivo, 176
Judaism, 20
Judt, Tony, 15, 25-6
Jünger, Ernst, 93

K

Kaczynski, Jaroslaw, 181
Kaczynski, Lech, 3, 28, 181
Kadare, Ismail, 156
Karadžic, Radovan, 154, 157
Karadžic, Vuk, 152
Kasack, Hermann, 92

Käutner, Helmut, 63
Kansteiner, Wulf, 62-3, 66, 83, 88
Kant, Immanuel, 21, 95
Kastrioti, Gjergj, 156
Katyn massacre, 3, 28, 214
Kellogg-Briand Pact, 95
Kertzer, David, 57, 66
Keyserling, Eduard von, 93
Kielce Massacre, 182
Klaus, Vaclav, 2-3, 30, 130
Köhler, Horst, 203
Kohl, Helmut, 12, 140, 190, 197-201, 217
Kopiliq, Millosh, 150, 155-7
Koselleck, Reinhart, 15-16, 175
Kosor, Jadranka, 176
Kossert, Andreas, 191
Kosovo, 10, 117, 149-63
Kosovo, Battle of, *See* Field of the Blackbirds
Koštunica, Vojslav, 154
Kristallnacht, 216

L

Laclau, Ernesto, 45
Lafontaine, Oscar, 203
Lagrou, Pierre, 125, 137
Lapuelle, Robert, 142-3
Larsson, Stieg, 186
Latvia, 29, 181, 183, 187, 212
League for the Maintentance of German War Graves, 183
League of Expellees, 191, 193
League of Nations, 89-90, 95
Lebow, Richard Ned, 57, 66
Leggewie, Claus, 70-1, 210
Lenin, Vladmir, 36, 180
Lidice, and memory of, 9, 121-34
Lieux de mémoire, See memory
Lipke, Zanis, 182
Lithuania, 181, 183, 187, 212
Louis XVI, 21
Lowenthal, David, 117-8
Luther, Martin, 72-3, 84, 95
Lyotard, Jean-François, 98

M

Maidanek, 78
Maistre, Joseph de, 109
Malinowski, Bronislaw, 58-9
Mandelbrot, Benoit, 97
Mankell, Henning, 186
Mann, Heinrich, 8, 91-2, 94
Mann, Klaus, 8, 93-4
Mann, Thomas, 7-8, 18, 32, 89-93, 97
Mannheim, Karl, 15-17

Index

Markovits, Andrei, 56
Marxism, 96, 104
Masaryk, Tomáš, 95
Massis, Henri, 93
Matković, Hrvoje, 172
Mattéoli Report, 186
Mellado, Gutiérrez, 33
Memorial (Human Rights' organisation), 25, 81
Memorials, Memorial Sites and Museums
    Bronze Soldier Memorial (Tallinn), 181
    Central Memorial to the Holocaust of Jews (Bratislava), 182
    Gazimestan Memorial Tower (Kosovo), 10, 150–63
    Grutas Park Sculpture Garden (south of Vilnius), 181
    House of Terror (Budapest), 181
    Memorial for the Murdered Jews of Europe (Berlin), 36, 76–7, 186, 193, 200, 210
    Museum of the History of Polish Jews in Warsaw, 210
    Memorial pour la Paix in Caen, 9, 137, 141, 146
    Memorial to the Victims of Communism (Lodz), 181
    Memorial to the Victims of Communism (Trencin), 181
    Memorial to the Victims of Communism and of the Resistance (Sighet), 181
    Museum and Documentation Centre "Jews in Latvia" (Riga), 182
    Museum of Genocide Victims (Vilnius), 181
    Museum of Occupation (Riga), 181
    New Guardhouse (Berlin), 190
    Szobor Park/Memento Park (Budapest), 181
Memory
    Bonding, 19–20
    Collective, 3–7, 11–12, 15, 34, 47, 55–67, 88–89, 96, 99, 115–7, 122, 125, 136, 139, 141, 144, 148, 167, 182, 195, 197–202, 206, 209–19
    Communicative, 28
    Cultural, 6, 7, 12, 16, 20, 24–29, 71, 88–90, 96, 98–99, 101, 128
    Europeanisation of, 1, 5, 9, 11, 22, 24, 56, 67, 69, 128–31, 137, 139, 143–4, 167, 175, 177, 185, 213–9
    Family, 6, 30, 32, 39–53, 69–85, 104–7, 113, 118, 209
    Gendered, 5–6, 39–53, 210
    Generational, 3, 5–6, 11–53, 80, 83, 137
    Globalisation of, 5, 9, 11, 83, 122, 134, 137, 143, 175
    Lieux de mémoire, 28, 131–2, 137, 144, 169, 178
    National, 43–4, 102, 125–6, 130, 137
    Private, 43, 71
    Public, 71, 74, 186
    Regional, 131–4, 214
    Social, 16, 19, 21, 27
    Storage, 27
    Transnational, 9–10, 53, 67, 84–5, 132–3, 136–44, 215
Merelman, Richard, 56
Merkel, Angela, 3, 12, 195, 201–5, 217
Mesić, Stipe, 172–3, 176
Mezzogiorno, 21
Micknik, Adam, 34, 165
Mickiewicz, Adam, 27
Mikkelsen, Mads, 82
Miloš Obilic, Sultan, 150, 152, 155, 164
Miloševic, Slobodan, 151. 153–4, 157, 164
Mitterrand, François, 130
Mladic, Ratko, 154
Morocco, 161, 216
Mouffe, Chantal, 45
Moulin, Jean, 137–9, 145
Moulin, Jean, Centre National of Bordeaux, 9, 137–42
Munich Agreement (1938), 18
Mussolini, Benito, 23, 96
Murat, Sultan, 10, 149, 157–9, 161
Museums *See* Memorials
Musil, Robert, 92

N

Nage, Imre, 28
Naples, Kingdom of, 21
NATO, 51, 132, 150, 158, 196
Neuengamme, 120–1, 123, 126–7
Niethammer, Lutz, 88
Nietzsche, Friedrich, 19, 91, 93
Nikolic, Tomislav, 154
9/11 attack, 9, 29, 122, 125, 131, 161
1989, as turning point, 9, 25, 28, 30, 34–5, 121–31, 151, 167–8, 181, 197, 201, 212
Nora, Pierre, 113–4, 137, 145, 178
Normandy Landings, 132, 139–40, 147
Norway, 6, 40–3, 46, 49–50, 71, 81, 132, 208–9, 215

O

Obilić, Miloš, 150, 152, 155, 164
Occidentalism, 161–2
Oradour, and memory of, 9–10, 121–34, 137, 141–3, 147
Orientalism, 89, 150–1, 156, 160–1
Ortega y Gasset, José, 8, 15, 17–19, 24, 32, 34, 90, 94, 96
Ostpolitik, 188, 196
Ottoman Empire, 10, 149–63

P

Pakistan, 33
Palestine, 33–4, 221
Palmberger, Monika, 82
Pangalos, Theodoros, 3
Pan Europa movement, 8, 93–6
Partisans (communist guerillas, Yugoslavia), 167–75, 178
Pavelic, Ante, 169, 184
Pericles, 20
Pheidias, 20
Pinochet, Augusto, 3
Ploetz, Hans Friedrich von, 198
Poland, 3, 6–7, 11, 25–29, 34–5, 71, 73, 75, 77–85, 116, 121, 124–5, 132, 134, 162, 165, 167, 181–4, 188–9, 192, 194, 197, 210, 213–4
Poljakov, Leonid, 80–1
Pope,
    Benedict XVI, 162
    John Paul II, 162
    Pius XI, 95
Portugal, 215
Prague Spring (1968), 28, 34, 96, 180
Putin, Vladimir, 3, 201
Putten, and memory of, 9, 121–34

Q

Qosja, Rexhep, 157

R

Račan, Ivica, 172–3
Ravensbrück, 123
Reagan, Ronald, 58, 140
Resistance, 26, 28, 50, 52, 80–1, 125, 155–6, 168, 181, 190, 210, 218, 220
    Czech, 65
    Danish, 41, 44, 46–7, 82
    Dutch, 122–6
    French, 9–10, 27, 137–44, 184, 212
    German, 63–4, 213

Italian, 23
Polish, 27–28
Roma, 159, 165, 170, 175, 178, 182, 211
Romania, 167, 181–4, 188, 192
Roosevelt, Theodor, 58
Ross, Marc Howard, 56–7, 66
Rothschild, Baron Louis, 95
Rousseau, Jean-Jacques, 95, 138
Rousso, Henry, 139, 141
Rwanda, 4

S

Sachsenhausen, 125
Šakic, Dinko, 170–1
Šakic, Nada, 170
Sanader, Ido, 11, 167, 173–4, 176
Sarkozy, Nicolas, 144
Savić, Dragan, 174
Schacht, Hjalmar, 95
Schatzberg, Michael, 56
Scherbakova, Irina, 81
Schlögel, Karl, 69–70
Schneider, Peter, 8, 98–9
Schön, Bosse, 185
Scholl, Sophie, 213
Schröder, Gerhard, 12, 196–201
Schuman, Robert, 33
Sebald, W.G., 70
Seipel, Ignaz, 95
Šeks, Vladimir, 174
Serbia, 10, 26, 40, 71, 81–2, 149–63, 167–8, 174–8, 210
Slovakia, 3, 30, 161–2, 181–4, 189, 214
Snyder, Timothy, 210
Sobibor, 78
Solidarność, 28, 35, 181
Sophocles, 20
South Africa, 4, 31
South Korea, 4
Soviet Union/Russia, 2–3, 6, 11, 17, 25–6, 40, 80–81, 83, 86–7, 93, 96, 108, 111, 178, 181–9, 192, 196–7, 208, 214–5
Spain, 3, 6, 22, 24–5, 33, 90, 169, 186, 193, 209, 212, 215
Spanish Civil War, 3, 24, 148, 186, 212
Spengler, Oswald, 89, 93
Stalinism, 69, 180, 214
Stasi (East Germany), 187–8
Stauffenberg, Claus Graf von, 213
Stephen I, King, 189
Stresemann, Gustav, 95
Sudetenland, 2
Sweden, 41, 185–6, 211, 215
Switzerland, 70–1, 83, 95, 211, 215

T

Tadić, Boris, 154
Thatcher, Margaret, 197
Tiso, Jozef, 184
Tocqueville, Alexis de, 29–30
Tomac, Zdravko, 172
Treaties
    Lisbon, 1–2, 196, 202–4, 206
    Locarno, 95
    Maastricht, 129, 197, 204
    Rome, 2, 202, 216–7
    Versailles, 109–10
Treblinka, 78, 210
Tuđman, Franjo, 10–11, 167–9, 171–8
Turkey, 3, 10, 69, 150–1, 154–65, 216, 221
Turner, Victor, 35, 57–59

U

Ukraine, 3, 27, 30, 37, 124, 214
United Kingdom, 92, 128, 131, 197–8, 202, 204–5, 215–6
United States of America, 4, 20, 23–24, 27, 29, 58, 62, 94–96, 111, 131, 158, 218
Ustaša (Croatian paramilitary), 167–78

V

Vél'd'Hiv, and memory of, 142, 210
Vichy France, 137, 141, 185, 212
Vinci, Leonardo da, 84
Voltaire, 94, 138

W

Wagner, Richard, 92
Wehrmacht, 80, 122–3, 125, 128–9, 214
Wehrmacht Exhibition (German), 186, 211
Welzer, Harald, 83
Wajda, Andrzej, 28
Walser, Robert, 92
Warleigh, Alex, 110
War of Independence, 20–21
Warring, Anette, 43, 87
Warsaw Uprising (1944), 27
Watergate, 27
Weber, Eugen, 215
Wehler, Hans-Ulrich, 69–70
Wood, Nancy, 113
Workers' Uprising, East German, 34
World War 1, 17–8, 22–3, 32–3, 89–91, 94, 109
World War II, 1–2, 6–12, 16, 22–3, 26, 30, 32–4, 37, 40–4, 48–9, 53, 70–85, 96, 110, 115–6, 121–34, 137–44, 166–70, 175–77, 182, 185, 187, 189–92, 196–8, 201, 206, 209–18
Wright, Georg Henrik von Wright, 186

Y

Yad Vashem, memorial site, 174
Yalta Conference (1945), 29
Yugoslavia, 10, 26, 82, 124, 152–3, 158, 166–77, 188, 214

Z

Zec, Ivo, 174
Zionism, 33
Zola, Emile, 138
Zuckmayer, Carl, *Des Teufels General*, 63, 65
Zweig, Stefan, 92

www.ingramcontent.com/pod-product-compliance
Lightning Source LLC
Chambersburg PA
CBHW072150100526
44589CB00015B/2172